# Digital Mythology and the Internet's Monster

Also Available from Bloomsbury

*The Bloomsbury Reader in the Study of Myth*, edited by
Jonathan Miles-Watson and Vivian Asimos
*Martin Scorsese's Divine Comedy*, Catherine O'Brien
*Mysticism, Ritual and Religion in Drone Metal*, Owen Coggins
*The Sacred and the Cinema*, Sheila J. Nayar

# Digital Mythology and the Internet's Monster

## The Slender Man

Vivian Asimos

BLOOMSBURY ACADEMIC
LONDON • NEW YORK • OXFORD • NEW DELHI • SYDNEY

BLOOMSBURY ACADEMIC
Bloomsbury Publishing Plc
50 Bedford Square, London, WC1B 3DP, UK
1385 Broadway, New York, NY 10018, USA
29 Earlsfort Terrace, Dublin 2, Ireland

BLOOMSBURY, BLOOMSBURY ACADEMIC and the Diana logo are trademarks of
Bloomsbury Publishing Plc

First published in Great Britain 2021
Paperback edition published 2022

Copyright © Vivian Asimos, 2021

Vivian Asimos has asserted her right under the Copyright, Designs and
Patents Act, 1988, to be identified as Author of this work.

Cover design: Ben Anslow
Cover image: *The Slender-man* © Todd Squires / Shutterstock

All rights reserved. No part of this publication may be reproduced or transmitted
in any form or by any means, electronic or mechanical, including photocopying,
recording, or any information storage or retrieval system, without prior
permission in writing from the publishers.

Bloomsbury Publishing Plc does not have any control over, or responsibility for,
any third-party websites referred to or in this book. All internet addresses given in
this book were correct at the time of going to press. The author and publisher
regret any inconvenience caused if addresses have changed or sites have
ceased to exist, but can accept no responsibility for any such changes.

A catalogue record for this book is available from the British Library.

Library of Congress Control Number: 2020949135.

ISBN: HB: 978-1-3501-8144-1
PB: 978-1-3502-1093-6
ePDF: 978-1-3501-8145-8
eBook: 978-1-3501-8146-5

Typeset by Deanta Global Publishing Services, Chennai, India

To find out more about our authors and books visit www.bloomsbury.com
and sign up for our newsletters

# Contents

| | |
|---|---|
| List of figures | ix |
| List of diagrams | x |
| Introduction | 1 |
| 1 Mythology and digitizing Lévi-Strauss | 11 |
|    1.1 What is myth? | 12 |
|       1.1.1 Myth and popular culture | 14 |
|       1.1.2 Virtual storytelling | 17 |
|    1.2 Structuralism | 19 |
|       1.2.1 The Lévi-Straussian method | 20 |
|       1.2.2 Neo-structuralism | 22 |
|       1.2.3 Method | 24 |
|    1.3 Creepypasta and mythology | 25 |
| 2 Introducing the Slender Man | 29 |
|    2.1 Slender Man's history | 30 |
|    2.2 Slender Man as communal story | 32 |
|       2.3.1 Authenticity in inconsistency | 34 |
|       2.3.2 Authenticity in narrative | 36 |
|    2.3 Paedophilic connection | 38 |
|    2.4 Mythology and serious play | 41 |
|    2.5 The Slender Man as mythos | 43 |
|       2.5.1 Progression of the study of the mythos | 44 |
| 3 The origin of the Slender Man (Part 1) | 45 |
|    3.1 Victor Surge | 46 |
|       3.1.1 Initial post | 46 |
|       3.1.2 Steinman Woods and performance post | 48 |
|       3.1.3 Sensory codes | 49 |
|       3.1.4 Nature of violence | 51 |
|    3.2 Mr. 47 | 54 |
|       3.2.1 Those left behind | 54 |

|   |     | 3.2.2 Supernatural versus natural | 57 |
|---|---|---|---|
|   |     | 3.2.3 The Stirling City post | 59 |
|   | 3.3 | Conclusion | 61 |
| 4 | The origin of the Slender Man (Part 2) | | 65 |
|   | 4.1 | Aleph Null | 65 |
|   | 4.2 | Genesplicer | 67 |
|   | 4.3 | Shared themes in Something Awful | 69 |
|   |     | 4.3.1 In-character | 69 |
|   |     | 4.3.2 Facelessness | 71 |
|   |     | 4.3.3 Powerlessness | 73 |
|   | 4.3 | The structure | 75 |
|   | 4.4 | The uncategorizable Slender Man | 80 |
|   |     | 4.4.1 Playing with the monster | 81 |
|   | 4.5 | Conclusion | 82 |
| 5 | Marble Hornets | | 85 |
|   | 5.1 | The Marble Hornets' story | 87 |
|   | 5.2 | Mytheme breakdown | 89 |
|   |     | 5.2.1 Marble Hornets' characters | 89 |
|   |     | 5.2.2 Mytheme breakdown | 92 |
|   |     | 5.2.3 Locations in Marble Hornets | 94 |
|   | 5.3 | Marble Hornets' structure | 95 |
|   | 5.4 | The Slender Man's structure | 98 |
|   | 5.5 | Conclusion | 99 |
| 6 | Playing the Slender Man | | 103 |
|   | 6.1 | Screaming at webcams in the dark | 103 |
|   |     | 6.1.1 Video games and online narratives | 104 |
|   | 6.2 | Implicit myth | 106 |
|   | 6.3 | Introducing *Slender: The Arrival* | 109 |
|   | 6.4 | *Slender*'s explicit myth | 110 |
|   |     | 6.4.1. Locations | 111 |
|   | 6.5 | World building: implicit and explicit myth | 113 |
|   |     | 6.5.1 CR and Kate | 114 |
|   |     | 6.5.2 The flashbacks | 117 |
|   | 6.6 | *The Arrival* implicit myth | 118 |
|   |     | 6.6.1 Achievement Hunter playthrough | 119 |
|   |     | 6.6.2 Markiplier playthrough | 121 |

|   |       | 6.6.3 Scary Game Squad playthrough | 123 |
|---|-------|------------------------------------|-----|
|   |       | 6.6.4 Implicit myth structure | 124 |
|   | 6.7   | Conclusion | 126 |
| 7 | Loving the horror, romancing Slender | | 129 |
|   | 7.1   | Fanfiction | 129 |
|   | 7.2   | The Bride of Slender Man | 131 |
|   |       | 7.2.1 Transforming the Transformed | 132 |
|   | 7.3   | Slender Man erotica | 137 |
|   |       | 7.3.1 Sensory codes | 138 |
|   |       | 7.3.2 Locations | 139 |
|   |       | 7.3.3 Mythemes | 140 |
|   |       | 7.3.4 Slender's erotic structure | 143 |
|   | 7.4   | Conclusion | 144 |
| 8 | Laughing at the horror | | 147 |
|   | 8.1   | Parodying the Slender Man | 148 |
|   |       | 8.1.1 Trender Man | 149 |
|   |       | 8.1.2 Splendor Man | 152 |
|   |       | 8.1.3 Parodies and the Enderman family | 153 |
|   | 8.2   | Comedic fanfiction | 155 |
|   | 8.3   | The structure | 157 |
|   | 8.4   | Conclusion | 162 |
| 9 | A dog, a video game and a monster | | 163 |
|   | 9.1   | The Curious Case of Smile.jpg | 164 |
|   | 9.2   | The Rake | 167 |
|   | 9.3   | Ben Drowned | 170 |
|   | 9.4   | Creepypasta structure | 173 |
|   | 9.5   | Conclusion | 176 |
| 10 | The online hive mind's stories | | 179 |
|   | 10.1  | The internet plays Pokémon | 180 |
|   |       | 10.1.1 TPP mythemes and structure | 183 |
|   | 10.2  | The Great Space Butterfly | 187 |
|   |       | 10.2.1 Great Space Butterfly structure | 189 |
|   | 10.3  | Joint structure | 190 |
|   | 10.4  | Conclusion | 193 |

| | | |
|---|---|---|
| 11 | The Slender Man's culture | 197 |
| | 11.1 Digital culture and structuralism | 197 |
| | 11.2 The Slender Man: Mythos and community | 203 |
| | 11.3 Conclusion | 208 |
| 12 | Conclusion | 213 |
| Bibliography | | 221 |
| Index | | 239 |

# Figures

If any permissions have been inadvertently missed or it has not been possible to find parties, then we will move to rectify this at the earliest opportunity if notified.

| | | |
|---|---|---|
| 2.1 | Example of a 'binder full of women' meme | 33 |
| 3.1 | Victor Surge's initial post, 'Stirling City' | 47 |
| 3.2 | Victor Surge's prohibited image, or the 'performance post' | 50 |
| 4.1 | Two of genesplicer's images | 68 |
| 6.1 | Image of Note 7 from CR. Screenshot from own playthrough | 116 |
| 8.1 | One does not simply explain memes to someone | 150 |
| 8.2 | Trender Man meme example | 151 |
| 9.1 | Smile.jpg | 165 |
| 9.2 | Image of the Rake | 169 |
| 10.1 | Sample screenshot of *Pokémon Red* playthrough of Twitch Plays Pokémon | 181 |
| 10.2 | Egyptian tablet fan art of Twitch Plays Pokémon narrative | 186 |

# Diagrams

Created by the author

| | | |
|---|---|---:|
| 3.1 | Supernatural/natural scale | 53 |
| 3.2 | Character transitions | 56 |
| 4.1 | Current structural equation | 76 |
| 5.1 | Marble Hornets' structure with proxies | 97 |
| 5.2 | Structure found in Something Awful and Marble Hornets | 100 |
| 6.1 | Graph of ideal types regarding implicit and explicit myths in video games | 109 |
| 8.1 | Structural alterations | 160 |
| 9.1 | Full structure | 176 |
| 10.1 | Structure of Twitch Plays Pokémon based on Helix/Dome | 184 |
| 10.2 | Structure of the Great Space Butterfly | 189 |
| 10.3 | Joint communal narrative structure | 190 |
| 12.1 | Triadic structure with category labels | 214 |

# Introduction

The thin man fairy is a phenomenon seen in several cultures around the world. Known as Fear Dubh, or the Black Man, in Scotland, he haunts woodland areas, causing fear on the solitary footpaths which weave through the forests (Irisi 2009). In Germany, Der Großmann, the Thin Man, prowls the Black Forest, weaving tales of violence and mayhem in his wake. In these stories, he is known as a fairy, a tall one who appears almost like a man, and is known for making children disappear in the night. He even began to have stories in the United States, sometimes taking blame for missing children and mysterious fires. In 2009, users on the Something Awful forum began to accumulate narratives and images of the creature, bringing his presence into a much fuller light both to the online environment and to the users on it.

Or, at least, that is how the story goes.

In 2009 on the Something Awful forums, the story of the accumulation of tales from around the world began. Instead, these images and narratives were being created by the users themselves. They created old folktales their families would tell them, and photoshopped images to make sure he fit. They created newspaper articles, government documents and emails which discuss his presence. Through this process, they created an online mythology which quickly spread to a variety of different virtual locations.

Mythology's place in the anthropological study of religions seems to have not recovered since Lévi-Strauss was fashionable. It is still present, lingering in indexes, but rarely ever taking centre stage the way it has in the past. I believe the Slender Man is an interesting case study to demonstrate the role of mythology in the contemporary world. Whether anthropologists are studying it or not, mythology is still being created and told.

Looking for contemporary mythology brings us to contemporary culture. There are roughly six different definitions of popular culture, stretching from the culture which is not considered 'high' culture to that which is mass culture, to 'folk culture' (Storey 2018). What popular culture is, is all around us, in all areas of the world, and most likely directly affects the reader of this manuscript. It is an important element of the lives of students, friends, families and selves. Popular culture, then, is an important part of our material, economic and political culture (Fedorak 2009). Popular culture allows for shared experiences which then create a social solidarity. It is the key to 'norm generation, boundary maintenance, ritual development, innovation, and social change' (Kidd 2007, 86).

Therefore, academia needs to begin to take popular culture seriously. Paco Underhill believes that traditional gathering places are being replaced by places like coffee houses and, more importantly for our purposes here, in virtual communities (Underhill 2004). If we are to attempt to find contemporary expressions of ritual, mythic performance and the relationship of the social, then we must turn to popular culture.

The place of religion and popular culture in the world of religious studies has grown gradually throughout the years, with the addition of important academic journals such as the *Journal of Religion and Popular Culture*, as well as more specific journals such as *Journal of Religion, Media and Digital Culture*. But the discipline still has far to go. Often, scholars in the study of religion and popular culture are turning to these more specific journals due to the larger ones often not accepting popular culture studies as academically viable.

My own personal experience reflects this well. I often find myself occupying strange positions at conferences where I must begin my talk with a warning that my talk would be vastly different from even those I am on a panel with. When we are graced with our panel, and here I think specifically of the two video game panels at the 2017 European Association for the Study of Religion conference, we defend our place at an academic conference in our opening talks.

I hope this book will represent the possibilities of the study of religion and popular culture, and work towards academia taking the field more seriously. The research and methods are firmly anthropological, though I also reach into other areas of research when necessary such as folklore studies, media studies and monster theory. I focus the study around structural anthropology, anchoring the digital influence and other disciplinary theories around the Lévi-Straussian-inspired method. By using these more traditional methods, I hope to show that the field of religion and popular culture can be taken seriously.

Typically, studies in religion and popular culture are focused on one of three approaches: either looking at how religions use (or do not use) popular culture, how popular culture represents religion or how popular culture is religious. This particular study falls much more in the third category, though with some important distinctions. This approach typically appears, at first, to be more related to implicit religion. Implicit religion is about how religious-like experiences can be found outside of traditional religious circles (Bailey 1998). I find this more of an issue regarding the emic and the etic divide. I prefer to follow what my participants say – who would, at least in this instance, not compare their experiences of horror storytelling online to that of a religious experience. They would, however, compare it to a myth. Terminology regarding mythology is frequently found not only in this manuscript's case study, but in multiple areas of popular culture. References are made to a fiction's 'mythos' or 'lore', and they find nothing necessarily purely *religious* in the idea of myth.

Following this, I do not go so far as to equate my study with the realm of hyper-real religions, which use fictional worlds to create a new religion regularly practiced (Davidsen 2012; Possamai 2012; Cusack and Kosnáč 2017). While hyper-real religions are interesting and worthy of study, it is not the purpose here. I do not believe one has to put Jedi on a census record to feel *Star Wars* means something to them. I believe most of the people who strongly feel something for a popular culture narrative do not actually go so far into either the hyper-real or implicit religion categories.

This reveals a gap in the literature related to religion and popular culture. There is a neglected grey area in which meaning-making is occurring, but not to so strong an extent as that which is representative in hyper-real religions. In many ways, this will reveal much in the way the average person engages with popular culture.

These grey areas of engagement, and the Slender Man specifically, demonstrate how play can be much more than the frivolous. Users, creators and readers play with the narrative to push boundaries of beliefs and religious concepts. These, despite acts of play, are important to consider when looking at how popular culture can act as meaning-making avenues while retaining their fictional status.

When beginning the study of the Slender Man mythology, after introducing my research to various other academics at conferences and the like, I frequently was faced with the sudden question: 'Does anyone actually believe this stuff?' I admit it was a rather strange question to receive, particularly in religious studies circles. The question of 'actually' believing pushes the concept of belief to be essentially a yes or no answer. But belief, even outside of fictional considerations, is not a black or white concept. Belief itself can exist in grey areas. For example, if I were to ask my participants if they 'believed' in the Slender Man, the answer would be a firm and extremely laughable no. They do not think of him as physically existing anywhere. He is a fictional creation who remains wholly fictional. However, I can phrase the question differently. Does the Slender Man mean something to you? Does horror writing, or horror narratives, provide something important to your life? Suddenly the question is different. And if I ask if they 'believe' in the power of their writing or their narratives, they will probably now answer yes. Belief, here, is not a firm yes or no answer. Rather, creators are playing with their sense of belief in relation to the fictional – playing with the various boundaries of this grey area.

One example of this is in the theories associated with him. For example, many users began to expand on what was called the 'Tulpa Theory'. The idea is the Slender Man started out as a fully fictionalized narrative on the Something Awful forums, but as multiple people began to think of him, he became physically manifest as a Tulpa. Again, this theory is not used as a way of substantiating his existence, but more to continue the fear and trepidation for a creature whose origins are easily found and well documented. We revisit the Tulpa Theory again briefly in Chapter 2, but this helps to demonstrate how users test their own belief and frequently use religious literacy in order to do so. Suddenly, something fictional holds a possibility – one not 'believed' in the full sense of the yes or no understanding – but a *potentiality* which increases fear and increases the realms of thought and mind.

This grey area is seldom explored in religious studies, more generally speaking. The anthropology of religion and religious studies focuses more on the 'actual belief' which I am frequently questioned about. On top of this, the more popular culture-focused studies are typically also exploring more direct forms of belief, possibly to establish legitimacy to the study of popular culture.

This strange middle ground, and yet the one where most people engage, is the perfect location to bring the concept of mythology to the front. Mythology as a concept allows for this play with belief. Narrative telling emphasizes the individual creativity, and the ability for these individuals to push their own considerations of what is possible. The Tulpa Theory is a demonstration of the narrative push of theory, concept and belief. Narrative allows for individual creators to reveal their own cultural understandings, and to attempt to alter them if they wish to.

The Slender Man is perhaps the best demonstration of online mythology. Beginning in 2009, the narrative has spread to various different formats of narratives online and is an almost ubiquitously known character for multiple different subgroups on the internet, even to this day. Time moves differently online. Important and ubiquitous narratives come and go more rapidly than their offline counterparts. For a narrative to remain in such a place for almost a decade is a testament to the power of the narrative itself.

The Slender Man mythos is also fascinating in how it both began and spread. Both constitute a form of mass communal storytelling: individuals all contributed to the same narrative almost simultaneously, only using other narratives and communication as a guidance point. It spread in a very similar fashion – as individuals in other areas encounter him for the first time in different ways, even more varieties of myths begin to be told – from images to blog posts to web videos and even video games.

Previous studies of the Slender Man are small. These frequently focus on the 2014 Wisconsin stabbings, in which two twelve-year-old girls stabbed a third friend of theirs, and left her for dead in the name of the Slender Man. Most narratives take this event as a starting point for their study (Chess and Newsom 2015; Peck 2015). My own study will paint a very different picture of both the narrative and the community which tells these types of narratives online.

For many outside the community, the stabbing was their first introduction to the Slender Man, and what became reminiscent of a witch hunt began soon after. People who authored Slender Man narratives online were blamed for the stabbing. Many media outlets began to call the attack 'The Slender Man Stabbing'. One blogger wrote that 'there is something really sick and twisted about the people who put up websites like this' (Plattor 2014).

By centring the study of the Slender Man around the stabbings, academics are giving the same level of blame for this event on the community as the media outlets themselves. The result is a maintaining of guilt on the community, who, by all accounts, reject the action as being representative of them (The Angry Scholar 2014). When I first introduced myself as a scholar on a horror writing site, the community was hesitant to respond to me. When prompted to explain what I planned on doing and discussing, and the exact nature of my study was revealed, suddenly they opened up. I believe this hesitancy is based on the media, and sometimes the academic, approach of blame for the community.

By starting with that event, and centring the discussion about the community around it, we would already be starting with a misstep. The important questions around this narrative have nothing to do with attacks, but with the understanding on the deeper levels of the narrative. What is this narrative doing for the community that tells the story? And if we are searching for that answer, we should start with the community, and not the actions the community rejects completely. This research project will, therefore, not centre around the stabbings at all, but around the narrative itself and the users who created and told the story.

Beginning with the Slender Man narrative, there is a plethora of questions we could explore, but our study will focus on two specifically. The first is the question of what cultural group can claim the Slender Man?

By claim, I do not mean as an authorial type of ownership, nor in understanding of legal copyright claims. There have been many different horror narratives which have begun online, such as the Curious Case of the Smiling Dog, an image of an all-too human smile on a husky that is said to drive its viewers insane, or Jeff the Killer, a psychotic killer. But these different narratives have not spread in the same way as the Slender Man. This causes multiple inquiries as to where the culture in question, then, rests. Is the culture the whole of the online environment?

We do have the more obvious small elements and community groups who have produced Slender Man material, such as the forum groups like the Something Awful forum who first gave him birth, and the Slender Nation forum, which has become the new loci for Slender Man narrative telling. There are also individuals who have spread their narratives, such as the film makers who started the web series Marble Hornets, or the video game developers of both *Slender: The Eight Pages* and *Slender: The Arrival*. By starting with these more obvious locations, we can begin to test the boundaries of the different community groups and the scope that they may cover.

The second primary question is more directly related to the narrative itself: What is the mythos actually saying? This is an important question for the mythology, which will hopefully explore the deeper structural narrative of the mythology.

Both questions are usefully explored through structuralism, first established by Claude Lévi-Strauss. Structuralism has, in many respects, fallen out of fashion (Miles-Watson 2009a). However, I am an anthropologist who does not believe in going with trends and fashions, but rather with the method which best suits the questions I am attempting to answer. I believe structuralism is the best method to explore the answers to the two former questions. But this does not mean I necessarily need to use Lévi-Strauss's theories and methods unchanged; rather, I can follow a small group of neo-structuralists, anthropologists who still use Lévi-Strauss's methods but with alterations to the theory to make the most sense, both generally speaking and more specifically, to the case studies in question. This tradition is made up of structuralists starting with Edmund Leach (1969; 1972), reaching to scholars like Terence S. Turner (2017), and even to contemporary scholars like Seth Kunin (2003; 2004). None of these have yet brought structuralism to the digital world, which I intend to do with this study.

In fact, few studies of structuralism have attempted to bring the method to realms of popular culture. The closest of this was a study of a structuralist study of Western films by Will Wright (1975). This study, however, is over twenty-five years old at this point, and not focused on the digital environment. On top of that, Wright brings in Vladamir Propp's form of structuralism, which is quite different from that of Lévi-Strauss.

The importance of moving the structural method to the online sphere is twofold. The first moves to demonstrate that, despite often being considered as having fallen out of fashion, the structural method still holds relevance and can even be applied to an area as contemporary as the internet. The second is to attempt to discover something which is difficult to prove or substantiate regarding the online community. The structural method can demonstrate a similarity in world views which connect different online communities. This can point to some kind of cultural similarity, despite how it may shift from one group to another. While unable to point to anything definitive, the structural method can at least help us point to some kind of possibilities in regard to the question of digital culture.

The relationship of the digital, as well as a fuller discussion of both structuralism and neo-structuralism, will be explored in more detail in Chapter 1, 'Mythology and digitizing Lévi-Strauss'. In this chapter, we will also explore what I mean exactly by 'myth'. The combination of structuralism and the digital will be explored briefly, along with an explanation of the method which will be undertaken for the rest of the study.

Chapter 2, 'Introducing the Slender Man', gives us our first look at our primary case study of the Slender Man and his mythology. The mythology is sketched more broadly, along with some of the theoretical underpinnings of the mythos. The use of some religious literacy to explain the mythos, including the example of the Tulpa Theory as discussed earlier, will be explored and explained. This chapter is dedicated to a more general conversation on the Slender Man and his mythology.

The third chapter begins the analysis of the Slender Man. We start with the place the Slender Man narrative originated, on the Something Awful forum. We will be exploring several narratives by two of the users on the forum, Victor Surge and Mr. 47. User Victor Surge is most known for being the catalyst for the mythology, as it was his initial post which inspired so many after him, as well as the one who dubbed the monster 'The Slender Man'. Due to the importance of the Something Awful forum to the formation of the mythology, we will spend another chapter on what, essentially, the second half of the forum thread is. The fourth chapter will explore this through two primary narratives by two users, Aleph Null and genesplicer. By spreading the analysis through two chapters, we can show multiple places in the thread's life, from the first post by Victor Surge to one of the last posts by genesplicer.

Chapter 5 begins the spreading out from Something Awful. Beginning on the forum, user ce gars posted about a friend's abandoned film project which he was going through, but found some strange occurrences. He began to post small parts of this search on YouTube, and his audience grew far beyond the Something Awful forum users. In my own personal experience, Marble Hornets was one of the first encounters I had with the Slender Man narrative, even before I knew the name 'Slender Man'. Marble Hornets expanded the mythos by adding extra elements to the mythology, such as proxies, who are humans who work for the Slender Man, as well as expanding interest in the Slender Man and his mythology.

The sixth chapter considers structural theory and method, with its connection to the new medium of video games. Specifically, we will consider Lévi-Strauss's concept of implicit myth, and how it can be applied to video games to assist in the study of video games as a myth. We then pick up the analysis again with the study of Blue Isle Studio's *Slender: The Arrival*. The introduction of the Slender Man to the world of video games expands the audience and mythology once again. More importantly, the study of myth and video games is brought forward with the inclusion of Let's Players, people who record themselves playing video games and who upload this video online for others to watch. Let's Players are useful contributions as mythic performance, and a first-hand account of the thoughts and emotions experienced while playing a video game. *Slender: The Arrival* Let's Plays will, therefore, be included in the analysis as forms of personal mythic experience and individual mythic performances. These will be included in the analysis of the game itself.

Chapter 7 shifts track. In this chapter, we will see other forms of the Slender Man narrative when different community groups take hold of the narrative. The chapter, 'Loving the horror, romancing Slender' studies fanfiction narratives, typically those who focus on romance and erotic tales of the Slender Man. On a narrative level, this appears to be a strong departure from the horror narratives we have focused on up to this point. But deep structure should, theoretically, be unaffected by genre. Therefore, the question of what the narrative is actually saying should not be affected as much by this shift in genre. It is important as well to use this more romantic take as the narratives often centre more on women than our previous narratives have.

In another shift from the romantic tales, we then, in the eighth chapter, will shift focus to the humorous takes the Slender Man inhabits. The ubiquitous nature of the Slender Man narrative led to parodies of the original tale, including visual static images made into online memes, and videos which parody certain elements of the Slender Man jokes. These are frequently called 'happypasta', to compare to the term 'creepypasta', which is often used for horror narratives online.

Chapter 9 begins to push the fuller concept of community and cultural groups. This chapter takes a step back from specific case study narratives to fuller thoughts about more general subcultural groups online. The first, in the ninth chapter, is creepypasta, more generally speaking. To test this, we have three creepypasta narratives: the Curious Case of the Smiling Dog, Ben Drowned, and The Rake. These three arose at different time periods in the creepypasta community and span different types of narratives. While it seems obvious that the Slender Man started from creepypasta, it spread much faster and much wider than any other creepypasta narrative. This raises questions about the community more generally speaking in relation to the Slender Man, so testing the connection to a fuller creepypasta community is important to do.

As an extension from this, we will also test a broader digital culture connection. Chapter 10 tests the analysis found throughout the rest of the book to other narratives in different areas of the online world which were formed in a similar way. Other mass communal narratives are analysed and compared, specifically the two case studies of Twitch Plays Pokémon and the Great Space Butterfly. This chapter helps to establish connections the Slender Man has with other mass communal narratives in broader digital culture.

The last chapter, Chapter 11, returns to a more theoretical exploration. This chapter pulls back once again to study what has been found in all the previous chapters, in order to explore the question of digital culture, and where the Slender Man's culture can be found. This will take into consideration multiple anthropological theories of culture, and their connection to both what we found, structurally speaking, and what we know of the digital environment in its contemporary status. This will help us reveal the answer to our primary questions which guide this book.

Despite how the Slender Man mythology began in 2009, it is, in many ways, a more historical study. Many of the individual users are difficult to trace in order to find where they are now. The thread itself on Something Awful, which gave it birth, has long since closed. I could, theoretically, live on the Something Awful forums now, but the community may be comprised of vastly different people today. The following study, therefore, is a combination of historical mythological research, which does not include much participant observation, and contemporary fieldwork which does. I have 'lived' on contemporary horror narrative storytelling threads, most prominently the subreddit No Sleep.

Although different from the various threads my case studies are coming from, they help to paint a fuller picture of the way the community functions today, while giving a more historical glance to what we can see of the past. While 2009 may, especially for many academics, appear to be incredibly contemporary rather than historical, it must be noted that popular culture, and especially online digital culture, moves very quickly. Over a decade has passed since then, at the time of writing, and the appearance, actions and environment of the online world is vastly different than at 2009, with different jokes being told, different ways of communication being used and different users joining the world. Somewhere in the background of all this lingers a relic of this not so distant past, a looming figure of an all-too thin man wearing a suit.

# 1

# Mythology and digitizing Lévi-Strauss

When I was a child, my mother used to tell me a story of a Buddhist monk. The monk was walking through the woods when a rabbit jumped across his path. Soon after, a hunter ran by as well. The hunter stopped the monk and asked him if he had seen a rabbit pass by. 'Why do you need to know?' the monk asked. 'I am a hunter', the hunter explained, 'I need to hunt the rabbit so I may eat.' The monk was then faced with an ethical predicament: if he chose to tell the hunter where the rabbit went, he put the innocent life of the rabbit at risk. If he denied telling the hunter where the rabbit went, the hunter's life may be at risk. Both choices went against Buddhist precepts of causing no harm. And the story did not tell which way the monk chose – it ended at the choice being presented.

This may seem a strange way to begin a book about digital horror stories, with a short narrative of a Buddhist monk told to a child-version of myself. This narrative, however, is important to an understanding of myth which is used throughout this thesis. My mother's form of storytelling reflects the way most people tell stories. My mother was not concerned with whether or not the monk lived, nor was she concerned with which way this historic monk, if he did live, chose. She was more concerned with an underlying importance to the narrative. For her, the story was true, even if the characters never existed.

It may be a bit strange to start a thesis about mythology, and mythology online, with an older tale about a Buddhist monk. But a classic example may be the best to use as a way of leading into a discussion about stories in new media. Stories are a core element of the human experience, and this does not change between the nature of telling a Zen story to your child and horror narratives told visually online. At the base of this thesis is the theory that humans will always be humans; though the medium through which they act or create may change, they are still acting and creating. At times, scholars may forget that although they are sitting in front of a computer as they look at these narratives or watch web videos, there are people on the other side: commentating, creating and telling stories.

This chapter will review the theoretical and methodological elements which are the foundations for this study. What is myth in our understanding here? How is this reflected in the Slender Man mythos? What is structuralism, and what happens when we bring Lévi-Strauss into the digital world?

## 1.1 What is myth?

Some of the early anthropological understandings of myth came from Tylor and Frazer, who both gave definitions which understood myth as explanations of the world, a historic 'truth' which was similar to a science in how it explained phenomena in the surrounding world. Tylor understood myth as a rational explanation (Tylor 1871), while Frazer saw it as an explanation for the presence of a ritual (Frazer [1922] 1994). Similarly, Bascom famously distinguished between folklore, legend and myth through similar ideas. Myths are 'considered to be truthful accounts of what happened in the remote past', which is set in direct contrast to his concept of folklore as that which was regarded as 'fiction' (Bascom 1984, 9). These views of myth are also often substantialist in definition, involving specific features or content elements, most notably involvement of gods.

Earlier substantialist definitions are troubling as they cause the mythographer to choose which content elements are considered significant enough to be definable. These elements are often chosen from a more Western standpoint, as these were the more significant mythographers and anthropologists early on. The contextual elements should be looked at within their context.

Led by Bascom, these distinctions lay a foundation which has separated narratives into two distinct categories: the first fantastic or fictional, and the second truth or fact. For many of these scholars, the fundamental problem is the consistent belief in the paradigmatic opposition – and mutual exclusivity – of truth and fiction. If a community does not believe the narrative is historically accurate, it cannot also consider the narrative to be true. These inflexible categories are not accurate in how individuals engage with narratives. My mother's story of the Buddhist monk, for example, problematizes these issues. Despite my mother knowing the narrative as a work of fiction, she recognized other truths which justify the retelling of the narrative many times, and not only for herself but to her children. A narrative which provides meaning for an individual does not necessarily need to be tied to a more ostensive and non-fictional truth.

More functional definitions shift the focus from the content to the role myth plays. Famously, Malinowski's myth as a social charter (Malinowski 1948) demonstrates this more functional approach. Where the previous, more substantialist, definitions create a dichotomy between myth and history, functionalist definitions typically created a dichotomy between myth and science. In some ways, this is reminiscent of Tylor and Frazer's connection of myth as an explanation. Malinowski's assertion of myth as a social charter can sometimes be considered too literally. In these cases, the myth is seen as an exact blueprint rather than a metaphoric or symbolic one. In a similar way, Robert Segal understands myth's survival as through its link with science and fact (Segal 1996, 82). But science is not necessarily separate from myth, and in some ways we can see science as a myth. Bruce Lincoln, for example, sees myth as a form of ideology, and in doing so one can link academic work as a form of myth itself (Lincoln 1999).

The functionalist focus on what a myth is *doing* for a group of people is incredibly important to me and the study of this particular study. I believe there is a way to combine the functionalist essence to a structuralist method. Much of this kind of approach would solve some of the criticisms levelled against Lévi-Strauss and his structuralism. This is a particular approach not new to structuralism. Combinations of structuralism with functionalism have been done previously by Edmund Leach (Leach and Aycock 1983; Leach 1969; Leach 1972). More on how this looks will be studied in a later section. It serves to see how more structuralist ideas of myth see it as a pattern for organizing their reality.

As the term will be used here, myths are narratives, or similar cultural artefacts, which are used by a community or an individual in order to structure their understanding of themselves and the world around them. I am not the first to link this type of thought to myth, as it is similar to Seth Kunin (2003), who links his definition with a structural study of myth. Structuralism, although sometimes conceived of as being out of fashion, is most important to use here, in more ways than its linking to our definition.

The former definition is purposely void of substantial elements, such as depiction of supernatural entities, strict concepts of setting, or relations of mythic time or otherworldly locations. The purpose is to retain the attention on the function the myth plays for the community, rather than what it contains. It is the function, the deeper understanding of myth, which allows us to see myth in a more contemporary setting with contemporary narratives. Like my mother's Buddhist story, myth can be found anywhere inherent truth to an individual, and sometimes their children, can also be found.

In both connecting the way my mother tells a Zen story, as well as looking into popular culture more widely, we are discounting in many ways some scholars who see very little future for myth. Robert Segal, through the linking of science and myth, understands myth's death with the rise of science (Segal 1996). Most relevant to us is Lévi-Strauss's own assertion of myth's death. He claims that as myth spreads and shifts, it either becomes romance, or popular narratives, or legends which are worked into history (Lévi-Strauss 1983). However, the basis of Lévi-Strauss's thought is that all aspects of culture, from the myth to the houses, are based on the same underlying structure. This would mean that the historical legend and the popular romance narratives would have the same structure as the myth. Taken from this point of view, if there is no structural difference between popular culture, myth, legend and folklore, then they can be considered on the same level of understanding. Structurally speaking, I see no difference in these narratives. The importance is on the more functional role the story plays for the individual in order for it to count as a myth.

### 1.1.1 Myth and popular culture

I am not the first to see a correlation between mythology and popular culture. Some work is dedicated to the mythology in Tolkien's worlds (Chance 2004; Hiley 2004), the use and exploration of myth in live action role-playing games (Milspaw and Evans 2010), and even the relation of mythology's construction to the ability to sell toys and a television show (Laycock 2010). Some studies of online communication have led scholars to see a relation between digital and oral communication (Fernback 2003; Blank 2009; Blank 2012; Howard 2015).

What these studies explicitly show us is how myth operates, either linguistically or structurally, in these popular culture narratives. What they implicitly show us is how myth has not died, and it is far from dying anytime soon. Often, these narratives stop one or two steps shy of proclaiming myth's life, often discussing instead how these stories are *like* myth, or they *use* myth, but rarely that they *are* myth. Most often, when it is pushed to seeing these narratives *as* myth, it is pushed to the extreme of hyper-real religions, where the participants begin to engage with the narratives with a new form of fervour (Davidsen 2012; Cusack 2013). Both sides of this presentation – the narratives *like* myth, and the hyper-real myths – are important to study and realistically present in the world. These studies have laid the foundation for engagement with myth in popular culture, an important consideration to this study as it is necessary to take both a step forward (in the case of those *like* myth) and a step back (for the hyper-real case).

This study wants to look at these popular culture narratives *as* myth, but not to the same extreme extent as the hyper-real religion. It is not necessary to put Jediism on a census record in order for *Star Wars* to mean something significant to you. Our definition of myth calls for emotional investment in the narrative itself, seeing it as important not because it is *like* anything, but because it *is*, though with a differing knowledge of 'reality' and 'truth', different emotional and practical engagement, as their hyper-real counterparts.

This approach may recall elements of Bailey's implicit religion (Bailey 1998). That being said, I have some hesitation to fully place this study into the realm of implicit religion. Despite its positive intentions of attempting to define what has been related to spirituality, it often has the implication of attempting to demonstrate religion where participants may be hesitant to use the word. At its heart, it is an issue between the emic and the etic. Directly connecting implicit religion to forms of popular culture and the narrative of the Slender Man is not my intention. Comparisons between religion, popular culture and fandom is often over-exaggerated (Reysen 2006), and the comparisons revert the study from becoming about the strange and over-enthused Other. Early fan studies echoed this, understanding fans as 'fanatics', and overly stressed their connections to the element of popular culture. Connecting fans to implicit religion risks returning to the pathologization of fans (Duffett 2003; Duffett 2013, 149–50; Crome 2015). With that in mind, I choose to focus on the term 'myth' because it is a word used and chosen by the participants and the community without academic influence. Terms related to mythology are frequently used in popular culture more generally, including a world's 'mythos' or 'lore'. The fans and participants in my study are not crazed Others. The term 'mythology' is more useful in demonstrating a human connection to a narrative throughout many centuries; the term 'myth' demonstrates an emotional connection to the story.

And if we are looking for emotional investment to find myth, popular culture narratives are given mythic light. Emotional investment in popular culture is reiterated in both fan groups and fan studies. Cornel Sandvoss emphasizes this in his definition of fandom: 'the regular, emotionally involved consumption of a given popular narrative or text' (82005, 8). While fan studies once saw fandom as a strange subculture, or the misunderstood Other, contemporary fan studies only see fans as those who are emotionally engaged and invested in popular culture narratives (Gray, Sandvoss, Harrington 2007, 10). These fans, then, are clear indications of how contemporary audiences engage with contemporary narratives – with emotional connections and investments which have the potential to directly affect the audience on a deeper level. Popular culture narratives embody myth.

Often, popular culture audiences are described as passive, allowing the narratives to happen to them, but do little to act on the narrative itself. This is echoed more explicitly in discourse around digital popular culture. Massively popular videos or images are said to have gone 'viral' – a term denoting an idea of disease which passes over the audience, or something that happens to them without thought. But not everyone sees engagement with popular culture narratives as a passive experience. Michel de Certeau's view of readership, for example, is one in which readers 'poach' in their environment (2013, 174), which echoes Lévi-Strauss's concept of the *bricoleur* who draws from the surrounding events, grabbing at 'whatever is at hand' (Lévi-Strauss 1966, 17). Consumers, even online, are not passive, but actively engage with their surroundings and the narratives in their environment.

Engagement with popular culture is often related to 'fans', people who find a connection to the popular culture narrative itself. More detail regarding fans, and the fans' own narratives called fanfiction, will be studied in greater depth in Chapter 8. A connection between amateur writings and mythology has already been drawn, for instance Ika Willis has detailed the connections between mythology and fanfiction (Willis 2016). Here, we see how amateur writings can be considered on par with studies of more classic mythic texts.

Popular culture narratives come in many forms, as contemporary storytelling is often transmedia storytelling – a story which crosses many different media types and sources (Jenkins 2006). Growth in technological advances has led to a rise in different forms of narrative and narrative-based communication. Not only are there movies, novels and television shows, but the growth of video-sharing websites such as YouTube has led to a creation of web series. Online communication and the sharing of still or short animated images, called gifs, have led to a rise in the sharing of memes, spreadable media which is easily disseminated online (Wiggins and Bowers 2015, 7). Memes also have begun to get their own attention as important forms of cultural communication (Shifman 2014). Online storytelling through discussion boards and forums, such as reddit, also leads to contemporary forms of myth building and folklore (Fernbeck 2003; Blank 2009). Most information or separate segments of the narrative are spread into different sources and locations: web sources, film, television, etc. Online storytelling mimics this, locating narratives across multiple websites in a multitude of forms, including video games, images, written narratives and web videos to name a few. In order for an audience member to gather the whole story they must go to multiple different sources (Jenkins 2006).

## 1.1.2 Virtual storytelling

Previous explorations into myth, folklore and the virtual have not been favourable to the virtual environment. Fialkova and Yelenevskaya, for example, stated 'virtual communication, being the surrogate of the real, can only give an illusion of friendship, involvement, and belonging' (Fialkova and Yelenevskaya 2001, 87). What these authors fail to explain is how it is possible for one to measure an individual's sense and experience of belonging, an act which appears to be rather impossible. Linda Dégh gave an assessment of online communication which involved a heavy amount of negative stereotypes regarding those who actively use the virtual, and strong biases against online communication. She described participants in online discourse as 'loners' who are too shy to develop 'real human contacts'. Like Fialkova and Yelenevskaya, Dégh sees the virtual as essentially imaginary, pitted against the 'real' world, which is considered the only place in which 'real emotional bonds may develop' (Dégh 2001, 115). Statements such as these, which criticize the reality of the virtual and the emotional connection to the virtual, often reveal more about the biases of those constructing these arguments than on human online communication itself. Nowhere does Fialkova and Yelenevskaya, or Dégh, demonstrate how they assess a person's true level of commitment, other than their own conception that virtual communication cannot be as 'real' as the physical world.

These are by no means the only approaches which undoubtedly miss the point of virtual interaction and experiences. These scholars often ignore the fundamental fact that storytelling is performance based, and even when developed virtually it requires this involvement. No matter how the relationship between participants and the virtual environment may develop and change, the interaction and communication between peoples more generally will not disappear. Despite this communication occurring via computer screens and the internet, it still engages humans, acting and interacting in a very human venture. As Michael Kinsella writes, storytelling is 'fluid, dynamic, and a fundamentally *human* endeavor' (Kinsella 2011, 16 [emphasis in original]). The internet and the rise of the virtual has not dehumanized interaction; it has simply altered the means through which this communication occurs.

Kinsella determines legend-telling itself as a form of communicative technology, as 'they are both assemblages of cultural memories and knowledge, and processes that convey these memories and knowledge, we employ them to manage and transmit ideologies, behaviours, and experiences' (Kinsella 2011, 12). Similarly, Trevor Blank writes that the internet does not diminish the potency of folklore, but rather acts as a folkloric conduit (Blank 2009, 7). Blank continues, claiming the internet is a 'field' which cannot be separated from the more traditional folkloric field:

> While there are fundamental differences between the two – specifically that the former is virtual and the latter physical – they are bound by common themes. Both have folk groups, customs, lingo and dialects, neighborhoods, crimes, relationships, games, discussion groups, displays of emotion, banking, commerce, and various other forms of communication and education. (Blank 2009, 11)

Some work has been done to disprove the bias that online communication is 'unreal' as Fialkova, Yelenevskaya and Dégh believe. Several scholars have demonstrated that the internet leads to a more authentic demonstration of the user's 'true self' (Bargh, et al. 2002; Aresta et al. 2015).

The unfortunate consequence of the heavy bias against the virtual is that many scholars spend most of their time legitimizing human experiences, which leaves little time to study the virtual environment and virtual communication, and as such we have less research on this topic. The research that has been done connecting the online environment with folkloric research has been mostly focused on databases cataloguing ethnographically gathered folklore (Hansen 2009), or research on email-chains (Frank 2009; McNeill 2009), a phenomenon that has mostly died out. Storytelling centres online do not have to be as accidental as the email chain; many locations online are formed with the intent of storytelling, purposefully situating itself as a location for users to go for this type of interaction. My study takes storytelling centres such as these as the loci of storytelling online, with the specific example of creepypasta forums and sub-forums, and studying them with the internet as its own field.

Meme storytelling, for example, has developed as a form of mass communal storytelling online. 'Memes', a term originally taken from Richard Dawkins (2006), are defined by their spreadability and capacity for individual creativity (Wiggins and Bower 2015, 7). This means a meme is not a single video, a single image, or an individual online event, but is made up of a multitude. In order for someone to learn about a meme, they must search through many different forms and iterations, which will eventually give a grander view of the general concept. This defines a multitude of narratives found online and the way the narratives were shared. More information about memes is in the following chapter, involving examples and a more detailed discussion.

The narratives, web series, memes and forum threads, which make up this virtual communication, can be shared, and written, by people who connect to the narrative on a more fundamental level. Like my mother connecting to the Buddhist monk, the narrative does not necessarily have to have a historical truth to be relevant and important to an individual or community. Whether the monk truly lived or not is irrelevant to my mother – the importance was on the connection she had with the narrative's more fundamental level. The definition of myth which posits the attention on what the myth is doing for the individual and the community is obvious, and helps take into account the reasons why a particular meme or story is more popular than others – it speaks to a deeper relevance which the community may use, consciously or unconsciously, to understand their world.

## 1.2 Structuralism

The definition of myth we have chosen necessitates our attention to be on the more fundamental levels of myth. Our primary concern in this study is the Slender Man mythos, and the connection this narrative has on the community it shares. Due to this connection, and the definition of myth chosen, it makes sense to follow a more structural method. For structuralism, the importance of analysis is on getting to a deeper structural level of the myth. As Miles-Watson (2009a) points out, it has been 'fashionable' to see structuralism as not on trend. However, those who follow Lévi-Strauss currently have taken criticisms against him and the structural method seriously, and current structuralists, or neo-structuralists, have shifted some of these into a form of structuralism which does not lose its core notion.

The method, for me, should follow from the questions being asked of the study and the field in which the questions arise. We begin this study with two primary questions: What is the Slender Man narrative saying for the community who tells it? And what community is it? I find structuralism as a method useful for answering these questions for several reasons. The first is that if we are to determine what the narrative is saying beyond the narrative level, then structuralism appears to be the most suited for the endeavour. The second reason is that discovering the specific cultural group who tells the Slender Man's story, and to test where the Slender Man's culture truly is, seems to be good for structuralism as well. According to Lévi-Strauss, the structure reflects the cultural thought. Revealing the boundaries of where this structure appears can help in pointing out where the culture exists.

Beyond our main two questions, structuralism also seems to be most suited to the narrative of the Slender Man. The Slender Man arose as a mass communal narrative, the mythos building based on individual creators telling their versions of the Slender Man. According to Lévi-Strauss, every version of a myth is the myth, and there is no 'true' version the mythographer needs to discover (Lévi-Strauss 1963b). This fits with the community's understanding of their own narratives. And based on his theory, each one of these narratives would have the same structure. For these three primary reasons, structuralism seems the best method for our present study.

### 1.2.1 The Lévi-Straussian method

Structural anthropology has its origins in the works of Claude Lévi-Strauss. Lévi-Strauss gained inspiration from linguist Saussure, and utilized his understanding of language in his analysis of myth. For Lévi-Strauss, myth is language itself, and is an essential part of human speech and communication. As such, its meaning does not reside in its style or syntax but rather in the story itself. His method follows the finding of small constituent units which make up a myth, which he calls mythemes. Likes a phoneme in linguistics, mythemes are the smallest element of a myth that cannot be broken down any further. Each mytheme functions, at any given time, as a given subject, causing a relation between the subject and the mytheme. The point is not to isolate mythemes, but rather to find these bundles of relations (Lévi-Strauss 1963b, 210–11).

The point of structuralist analysis is to elucidate the deepest level of structural thought, which Lévi-Strauss understood as biologically derived. This is a contentious point, which many neo-structuralists alter; this will be discussed in the next section. Essentially, he recognized any particular myth as having various structural levels. While he did not explicitly describe these, he did implicitly allude to their presence (Lévi-Strauss 1969, 12). These have been described in fuller detail by others (Kunin 2004; Miles-Watson 2009a), which end up being fragmented as such[1]:

$$\underline{N \text{ level} = \text{cultural/context specific}}$$
$$S^3 = \text{cultural specific}$$
$$S^2 = \text{culture group specific}$$
$$S^1 = \text{universal}$$

---

[1] This detail, and the following explanation of each step, is primarily reliant on Kunin (2004) and Miles-Watson (2009b).

The $S^1$ level is considered by Lévi-Strauss to be universal and biologically derived. This level of structure is not detailed structure but is rather the potential for structure. It provides the foundation for the development of many different structural possibilities. $S^1$ is more present for the potential for structure, rather than structure itself. Lévi-Strauss developed here what he called the canonical formula of myth, an idea of the formula that fits for every context as a biologically derived structural formula. This concept has been contentious, even for neo-structuralists, and has been frequently reworked (Mosko 1991; Kunin 1998; Miles-Watson 2009b).

The $S^2$ level begins to be shaped by culture or cultural group. While it does not provide any specific content, the potential shown in the $S^1$ level has become solidified into significant categories and relations between these categories, written out in a pseudo-equation. Relations can be categorized into three ideal types: a positive relation, which has a high overlap between the categories; a neutral relation, which has different degrees of exchange or overlap; and a negative relation, in which there is no possible overlap or exchange between the two categories. For example, a reading for this structural level would be $A(+)B$ for a positive relation, $A(-)B$ for a negative, or $A(n)B$ for a neutral.

The $S^3$ category is the least abstract of the underlying structural levels, and becomes more culturally specific. This level uses mythological elements or mythemes which are appropriate and available within their own context. These mythemes are categories into the relationships of the $S^2$ level, and relate to one another in these relations. These categories are more generic, less specific and less developed relations.

The N level, or the narrative level, is the most surface level of the myth. This is the most culture and context specific. The narrative level refers to the format of the story itself, and can relate directly to various cultural practices. Being the utmost level, these elements have been shaped by all the other underlying structural levels, and thus is a coherent myth, ritual or practice. Any transformations on this narrative level are not considered significant because it does not reflect structural change. Being the most connected to cultural context, the N level is the most prone to transformations in this content, though, again, this often does not reflect a change in structure. These transformations reflect a conscious process, and are done through the agency of the storytellers. Issues here will be addressed in a subsequent section.

The former descriptions are based on Lévi-Strauss's understanding. The earlier explanation is not new to this study, but a useful way to understand the structuralist method. Neo-structuralism, however, uses Lévi-Strauss as a foundation, and while not deviating from his more primary thoughts, has taken into serious consideration his critiques. The two main critiques we will be assessing and also taking into consideration is the claim that he does not truly take into account a true ethnographic or 'lived' experience of the myth, and also his examination of the cognitive and unconscious elements of structural thought (Andreski 1972; Merleau-Ponty 1974; Douglas 1999).

### 1.2.2 Neo-structuralism

While this section is meant to demonstrate the ways in which neo-structuralists have added to or altered the original Lévi-Straussian method to fit a more contemporary anthropological approach which more accurately paints the picture of the community the myth rests in, it is beyond the scope of this section to provide a full defence of structuralism from its critiques. In reality, this would be another book by itself. Rather, I choose here to provide a full explanation of some of the core challenges, and the alterations to this met by neo-structuralists, which will have an effect on our study of the digital community and the Slender Man narratives.

One of the primary concerns levelled against Lévi-Strauss is his lack of attention to the social elements and ethnographic reality of the myths he studies (Merleau-Ponty 1974; Douglas 1999). Many structuralists after him have proven how the method can be used in conjunction with a focus on the social realities the myths are told within (Hugh-Jones 1979; Kunin 2009; Miles-Watson 2015; Turner 2017). The more pressing issue for our purposes here is his reliance on the cognitive and unconscious elements of structure.

One of the primary departures of neo-structuralism from traditional Lévi-Strauss is the focus on structure happening in the brain to structure happening in the mind. The essential result is to give less attention to biological elements, and more to social and cultural influences. Structure can be affected by the interactions between an individual and their environment, both social and otherwise (Miles-Watson 2009b, 22). This would lead to structure being more entrenched in social interactions and relations, especially relating to how the individual perceives the environment surrounding them. Structure, therefore, is not found in universally biologically held categories, but one which the community in question holds.

The language surrounding the term 'structure', as is used by Lévi-Strauss, keeps the word rooted in notions of rigidity and immutability. This is most exemplified by the former discussion in which Lévi-Strauss sees a connection of structure with the biological human brain. By using such a rigid notion of structure, the concept of an individual's agency is lost, and the efficacy of human action in general can be questioned, as it appears to be ineffective in the face of such an overwhelming idea as 'structure' (Sewell 1992, 2). The neo-structuralist removal of the biological brain to the mind is the first step in also making a change away from the strict restriction of personal agency. Transformations in structure do happen, and the strict conception of the human brain and a lack of concept of agency seem to negate any of the possibilities of transformation. The shifting to look at the surrounding social reality of the myth as well brings in the more functionalist approaches to the study of myth, marrying it to a structuralist approach.

An emphasis of this agency is reflected in some neo-structuralist approaches. The shift comes from understanding, as we have stated earlier, that structure can arise from the interaction with the surrounding environment, both social and otherwise. Seth Kunin even suggests that structure is both reflected in social practice and transformed by it (Kunin 2004, 22–5). By emphasizing the agency of human actants and storytellers, the process of transformation is no longer a problem. The actions of the human can be undertaken in order to both unconsciously and consciously emphasize and de-emphasize certain aspects of the present structure, which in turn aids transformation, in a process Seth Kunin calls *jonglerie* (Kunin 2004, 23; Kunin 2009).

The process of emphasis and de-emphasis of the structure, leading to long-term change, recalls Bourdieu's concept of the *habitus*. Social engagements both shape, and are shaped by, structure. Bourdieu's *habitus*, including practices and institutions of a community, is also influenced by these practices and institutions (Bourdieu 1990, 53). Bourdieu moved the understanding of structure from the brain to the mind before the current neo-structuralists did. Miles-Watson (2009a) connected *habitus* to Palsson's *enskilment*, or a form of learning which 'emphasizes immersion in the practical world, being caught up in the incessant flow of everyday life' (Pálsson 1994). Thus, Kunin's *jonglerie* demonstrates how structure can be constructed through the way in which we perceive the environment we are surrounded by. As Miles-Watson puts it, 'the Structural Anthropologist is learning to see the world from a unique perspective' (Miles-Watson 2009a, 74).

Lévi-Strauss did have a preference for discussing elements of culture other than myths in some form of analysis, including music and visual art (Lévi-Strauss 1997). His analysis has been brought to Crypto-Jews in America (Kunin 2009), the narratives in India's Shimla Hills (Miles-Watson 2015) and even to

American Western films (Wright 1975). Lévi-Strauss has yet to be digitized, and brought into the online sphere. This monograph seeks to answer the question of what happens when we bring him online.

### 1.2.3 Method

The structural method in its approach to a narrative, or similar cultural artefact, is to metaphorically replicate an archaeological excavation on a narrative. Starting at the N level, the purpose is to find key elements and begin working downwards to more abstract levels of the underlying structure. The key elements, or mythemes, are found by narratively significant roles and relations, either through action or inaction (for example noise or silence) and can often be representative in the key character or theme. The extraction of one mytheme can often lead to others through its relations. Once the mythemes are determined, their relation to other mythemes are established, which can be either simplistic or complex.

This method inevitably involves a process of experiments. After extracting one set of equations and relations, one can apply them to another myth in the mythic complex and find it partial and fragmentary. Another set of experiments is then enacted, each myth chosen from an aspect of spiralling out. So here, we will start our study with Slender Man – a complex of myths which begin with the Something Awful forums – and begin the spiralling out to other Slender Man narratives, taking on different forms and narratives. As we reach the end of the Slender Man spiral, we continue the spiralling outwards to other forms of creepypasta, and other mass communal narratives. Each step outwards involves another set of experiments.

My analysis may, at times, read just as experimental as the method itself, with findings maybe seeming contradictory until we take it back to the previous myths to compare and adjust. This is inevitable, and the readings may be kept in order to demonstrate the experimental nature of this form of study, with the conclusory end points gearing towards a firm and harmonious structural foundation which is finally rid of all partial, fragmentary or contradicting elements.

What can be elucidated in the former methodological explanation and the earlier sections of more theory-related content is that structuralism tends to be considered as similar to textual analysis. The narrative is relegated in some way as a text and analysed as such as well. However, the point of the study is not to determine the text as a text, but rather to assess what the narrative is doing for the community it is present in. This calls for a textual analysis to be done for a functional purpose. In order to accommodate this, there has to be several changes to the traditional approach, most of which are accounted for in neo-structural alterations, primarily that of giving social actors cultural and social agency. This difference in the question which is being asked of the structural method – what the narrative is actually doing for the community it is shared within – is preferable for several reasons. The first is that myths have continued, and have not died, as several theorists have assumed they would. Not only have they continued, but old myths are reworked and new myths created. This continued and renewed presence in the form of newly created myths shows that there is a need for what myth brings. The society and community in which new myths are created can be studied and talked to in order to discover the intent and purpose of these narratives. Therefore, myths are not explanations for a world without scientific reasoning, which at the time was equated with 'rational' thought, but serve some other function for the community it is shared in. Our goal is to figure out what this function is. But we also do not assume the function is the same for every community universally. Thus, we will focus on the online storytelling community, beginning with creepypasta and seeing how far this structure will stretch.

Following the move of neo-structuralists to also incorporate lived experience or fieldwork into structural analysis, fieldwork components will also be incorporated into this analysis. It is necessary to get both the narratives of the Slender Man shared and the narratives of the people within the community creating, enjoying and sharing those narratives. Thus, I did online fieldwork, gathering narratives from the community and 'living' in the spaces these narrators also dwell in. The goal of the ethnography is to provide a social backdrop in which the myths arise and continue to thrive. The nature of the fieldwork itself was mostly a lived experience with participant observation. Most of the conversations had with participants were simple conversations while in the field rather than any formal interviews. The purpose is less to gather formal interviews for a more direct type of study in that regard, but more to provide context to the background of the narratives.

## 1.3 Creepypasta and mythology

The Slender Man mythos was built from creepypasta. 'Creepypasta' as a term came from the old term of 'copypasta' or 'copy paste'. Early sharing online necessitated the sharer to copy the text and paste it somewhere else. The narratives which would be copied and pasted were called 'copypasta' as a quick, and admittedly silly, version of copy and paste. The horror version of these were called 'creepypasta'.

This form of mass storytelling lost all connections to ideas of authorship – there was no single author, the community became the author. The goal in creating a narrative was to have it shared and added to openly without connection to the original author. This is just exemplary of the way mass communal storytelling works online. Internet memes are often defined by their ability to be shared, mimicked and 'remixed' by a large number of people (Wiggins and Bowers 2015, 7). Memes are not demonstrated by one video or image, or ones that have gone 'viral', but rather by many of them.

There are a few questions this book attempts to answer. The first is the simplest: Why is the Slender Man narrative so popular? Narratives are shared and connected to for a reason, an underlying connection the community relates to on both a deep and narrative level. The employment of the structuralist method pushes a secondary question: What is the cultural group this narrative belongs to? Lévi-Strauss often found connection to similar linguistic groups, though I sometimes feel he drifts from this too far, at times comparing his studies in the Americas to mythology in Japan (Lévi-Strauss 1973b).

Neo-structuralists have done successful work in much smaller realms of study (Hugh-Jones 1979; Kunin 2009; Miles-Watson 2012). The issue with moving these elements to the online environment shifts the question of where the boundary marks may lie. The question of whether or not a 'digital culture' exists is a question which, sometimes implicitly, floats in the air without a large amount of discussion on answering it. Perhaps structuralism may allow us to answer this question.

The result will be to learn how to view the world in a way which echoes those who tell the Slender Man mythos. The new view will paint a different picture of not only online horror storytelling, but the online storytelling community as a whole. By demonstrating how these narratives work as myth, we as anthropologists and scholars will be seeing the material in a similar way to how the community already sees these stories. Members of the community have already discussed openly how they see the Slender Man narratives as a form of urban legend and myth (Nashie 0 2009; Moto42 2009; Slender Nation Podcast 2011). Folklorists working in the online environment have already understood the virtual as being able to communicate in similar ways to more oral folklore (Fernback 2003; Blank 2009; McNeill 2009; Blank 2012). But more than this, we can also shift our understanding slightly of myth – see how the concept works outside of the confines of Greek mythology, or other older myths we often think of when the word 'myth' is initially spoken. Now, we will think of the Slender Man, looming ominously in the background of photographs. And we can understand the online environment as capable of producing these myths – of crafting and sharing and thinking in unique and mythic ways. They build their community around the narratives they tell.

The following chapter will give a more detailed look at mass communal storytelling, internet memes and the Slender Man specifically. In order to give a full analysis of the Slender Man narrative, we first must make a more formal introduction to the monster himself.

2

# Introducing the Slender Man

*But there is no person – not the people making photoshops, not his original creator, and not the guys making the Marble Hornets videos – who is solely in charge of this story anymore. He's growing organically from our combined feedback and contributions. He's the larger organism and we are his cells. We're simultaneously in control and not in control. For all intents and purposes, the Slender Man is a living entity.*

(rinski 2009)

In 2009, the internet gave birth to a monster: a horror which embodies a fear of the unknown, which twists the familiar into something utterly unfamiliar, and is so subtle and well hidden in the back of photographs that the audience begins to see him even in photos he is not in. But he is not just a monster who lives online, nor is he meant to exist only in the realms of fiction where the audience suspends disbelief. His origins online are well founded which no one attempts to hide. The Slender Man exists as a living entity, as rinski writes in the quote provided, growing and thriving on the contributions which first gave him life.

Although beginning on the forums of the comedy website Something Awful, the Slender Man's mythos has since spread to many online arenas, and is now only historically linked to Something Awful. The Slender Man appears in many places online and in popular culture at large: featured as memes, both scary and humorous (Trendorman (knowyourmeme n.d.), see Chapter 8); the subject of several web video series (Marble Hornets (2009–14), see Chapter 5); involved in several blogs ('Just Another Fool' 2009–10); and the subject of horror video games (Parsec Productions 2012; Blue Isle Studios 2015; see Chapter 6). There is even a movie recently released.

The Slender Man appears, at a distance, as an unusually tall man, with very few discernible features, if any at all, and appears to wear a black suit. As you approach closer, however, things start to change. His size is more extraordinary than just tall (Mr. 47 2009). His suit appears to be almost like a second skin

(Chaos Hippy 2009). His proportions are regarded as being more than just slightly unnatural (Victor Surge 2009d). He sometimes is portrayed with growing appendages from his back, appearing branch-like (Victor Surge 2009c), or insect-like (genesplicer 2009), and even sometimes like tentacles (Victor Surge 2009b). His face sometimes has no facial features at all (Marble Hornets 2009–14), other times the features are present but oddly proportioned (Victor Surge 2009d), while at other times he has just glowing white eyes (cloudy 2009).

He typically makes children disappear (Victor Surge 2009a; Mr. 47 2009), often without any depictions of violence. The violence, when displayed, is saved for adults (Victor Surge 2009c). But his modus operandi shifts as much as his appearance. In some, especially the early narratives on Something Awful, he attacks adult victims by impaling them on tree branches (Victor Surge 2009c), while in others, or sometimes alongside other actions, his victims are disembowelled (NicolBolas 2009). And even some have the adults simply disappear (Victor Surge 2009a).

What is clear from the many 'sometimes', 'or', and 'other times' in this description is that very little is firmly set as canonical when it comes to the Slender Man narratives. Much of this is due to the need to retain authority for every author's rendition, a necessity to keep communal creation and re-creation, active and thus the mythos kept alive. It is through this communal interaction with the story that the Slender Man continues to grow, as rinski writes in the quote provided. He grows from their combined feedback and contributions.

## 2.1 Slender Man's history

Something Awful forum user Gerogerigege created a discussion thread for creating paranormal images. They claimed creating paranormal images had been a hobby of theirs and invited the Something Awful community to 'make a shit load' (Gerogerigege 2009). For the first two or three pages of the thread, the posts were varied; images and discussions arose on how best to make a photo realistic enough to fool the paranormal-believing community, but vague enough to blend with photos in similar circles.

On the third page, the flow of discussion began to change. User Victor Surge posted two of his photoshopped images, accompanied by short captions. His photos depicted a strange humanoid creature with too-long-of-limbs and an eerie feel who lingered behind children – a creature he dubbed 'The Slender Man' (Victor Surge 2009a). Very quickly, Victor Surge's images caused a shift in conversation.

Other users, inspired by Victor Surge, began to post their own take on the Slender Man, and soon the forum thread – once dedicated to creating paranormal images in general – became like a digital campfire for users to swap harrowing tales and eerie images of the Slender Man. The tales took many forms – some retained the initial purpose of the thread by presenting their tales in the form of photoshopped images (Victor Surge 2009a; Gyver Mac 2009a). Others wrote their narratives. The written narratives took two forms: personal tales in which users detailed a horrific encounter with the Slender Man (Irisi 2009); more frequently, however, narratives took the form of pseudo-documents (Aleph Null 2009a) and fake reports from fictional academic texts (Prior Marcus 2009), copies of classified emails and accounts (BooDoug187 2009), reprints of newspaper articles (Mr. 47 2009), and other formats which writers utilized as formats of 'proof'.

About halfway through the lifespan of the forum thread, one user named ce gars began to post videos of the Slender Man, this time in the form of a web series. His web series, called Marble Hornets, took a *Blair Witch*-style documentary-esque approach; the user ce gars was uploading segments of a friend's unfinished film project which came to a mysterious stop (ce gars 2009). The series became immensely popular outside of the original audience of the Something Awful forum. Simultaneously, other storytelling forms around the Slender Man began to find a foothold online. Blogs such as 'Just Another Fool' began. Entire websites of forums started to provide a location for the Slender Man narratives to exist, with one, Slender Nation, even supporting its own podcast.

An indie video game developed entirely by only one developer called *Slender: The Eight Pages* (2012) appeared. It is a short game in which the player has to collect eight pages scrawled with strange writing, mimicking a similar style in writing to the victims in Marble Hornets. It found quite a large amount of success, mostly due to the rise in popularity of Let's Plays – a form of online video in which players record themselves and their gameplay and upload this for others to watch. Several years later, Blue Isle Studios created another video game entitled *Slender: The Arrival* (2015) which enjoyed even greater success.

The mythology of the Slender Man perhaps best embodies the way stories are now told, particularly online, through transmedia storytelling. Transmedia storytelling relates to how narratives are often spread across many different media sources (Jenkins 2006). The Slender Man's narrative is spread across the internet in many different formats: digitally manipulated photos, pseudo-documents, personal narratives, video games, web videos and so forth. In order for an audience member to gather the whole story, they must go to multiple sources of information (ibid.).

The Slender Man is perhaps one of the most popular creepypastas, especially in regard to its recognition by those outside the creepypasta community. 'Creepypasta' as a term refers to horror stories found and authored online. Along with the creepypastas Jeff the Killer and smile.jpg, the Slender Man is one of the most prominent creepypastas, and is often the only one those outside the creepypasta community can recognize. Its prolific nature is somewhat due to its transmedia nature – its presence across many different formats and websites. However, it is difficult to tell if the popularity is due to its transmedia form, or whether its transmedia form is a side-effect of its popularity.

The Slender Man is an icon of creepypasta and horror in the digital age. His history is filled with communal re-creation and transformation. As Something Awful forum user rinski said, quoted at the beginning of this chapter, the Slender Man has meticulously and, as if planned and controlled, spun out of control of the audience who gave him life. Each subsequent story both spread the narrative to new grounds and rooted its presence in the online field, refusing ownership and allowing many to own him all at once.

## 2.2 Slender Man as communal story

The Slender Man exists due to mass communal storytelling. The Slender Man's story does not exist in only one image or one story, but in a large network of narratives created by many people. Mass communal storytelling of this sort is not new or unique to the Slender Man, and is, in fact, frequently found in the history of various online phenomena. Internet memes are often defined by their ability to be shared, mimicked and 'remixed' by many people (Wiggins and Bowers 2015, 7). Memes are not demonstrated by one video or image, but by many of them. In this regard, the Slender Man can be defined as an internet meme, despite how a common thought of online memes are that they are humorous (Shifman 2014). Like the Something Awful forum's thread on paranormal images, mass communal storytelling often arises from one specific event or post, which then spins into a much larger phenomenon.

Twitch Plays Pokémon is one example. In 2014, an anonymous programmer hooked up an emulator of *Pokémon Red* to the video game streaming platform twitch.tv. The emulator was programmed in such a way as to allow the viewers in the chat to input commands to the game. If a viewer typed A, the game would register a player pushing the A button. The purpose was a 'social experiment', to see what would happen if several hundred players all attempted to play the same game at the same time. Twitch Plays Pokémon got their several hundred players, but also got several thousand more. By the time it ended, Twitch Plays Pokémon's playthrough of *Pokémon Red* had over one million people participating, and over thirty-six million total views (Chase 2014). So many participants led to inevitable chaos, and the many factions of the community went to separate forums to plan out strategies for the best approach for success. Some of these strategies utilized elements of the game in an attempt to calm the chaos, which led to patterns in the turmoil. These patterns were soon written out by emulating a mythology. Users wrote and drew memes which praised the benevolent Helix fossil, or in praise of the Pokémon pidgeotto named Bird Jesus, who saved their collective team. Twitch Plays Pokémon will be described in greater length in Chapter 10.

Memes also sometimes draw on political or other popular culture events. Kanye Interrupts, inspired by when Kanye West interrupted Taylor Swift at the Video Music Awards, had a collection of images in which Kanye was interrupting various moments in history, such as Martin Luther King, Jr. A screenshot from the viral video 'Gangnam Style' was cited with the words 'My binder full of women exploded', a reference to US presidential nominee Mitch Romney caught mentioning his binder of specific female job applicants (see Figure 2.1).

Online storytelling frequently follows this pattern. The nature of the online medium allows for the incredibly fast dissemination of information, and equally a fast dissemination of individually made content. The purpose

**Figure 2.1** Example of a 'binder full of women' meme (Watercutter 2012).

of memes, which all the former examples demonstrate, is for individually made content to contribute to a wider communal cultural narrative (Shifman 2014; Milner 2016; Nissenbaum and Shifman 2017). This type of participatory storytelling is not new, as several scholars before this have pointed out. The communication showed here mimics that of oral folklore, for example (Blank 2009; Foley 2012).

The process of making memes relies on a primary other event, whether this be a viral video or an image, a social event in popular culture, a political event, or some other well-known occurrence. Twitch Plays Pokémon was the initial catalyst for the mythological memes which followed; political events led to the 'binder full of women' meme. Meme-makers drawing on images, words, videos and structures – of which they, and their inevitable audience, are aware of – echoes Lévi-Strauss's concept of *bricolage*. Like the mythmaker of Lévi-Strauss, the meme-maker uses 'whatever is at hand' (Lévi-Strauss 1966, 17). This is not unheard of in regard to the creation and dissemination of popular culture. Michel de Certeau wrote of readers as not being passive, but as active engagers. The audience is actively 'poaching' (1984, 174), and he determinedly points out that even though the consumer may be participating in consumption, this does not mean consumers are passive or at the mercy of larger corporations (ibid., 166). Memes demonstrate how meme-makers are involved in *bricolage*, poaching elements from popular culture and the things they consume in an active way to disseminate individually created content quicker in order to spread communal ideals.

The strong emotional statement voiced by rinski, quoted at the beginning of this chapter, demonstrates the power of mass communal storytelling, and the ways users feel connected to, not just the community but the subject of the story itself. Despite how wonderful this may sound, mass communal storytelling also comes with issues of authenticity. The ways in which these questions were answered is integral to the formation of the Slender Man story into a mythos.

### 2.3.1 Authenticity in inconsistency

As the Something Awful forum began to spin tales of the Slender Man, one obvious issue began to spring up. With each recreation and retelling of the Slender Man, his form, actions and hunting style sometimes shifted depending on the author. Some began to speculate on whether or not to determine if there was some form of 'canon' – a collection of rules governing the Slender Man's appearance or actions the authors must adhere to in order for their narratives to be considered an authentic Slender Man narrative. The mere idea of this was met with grim response, and often posted 'in character' – meaning users wrote from the standpoint of belief and researchers rather than authors. The dismissal of this idea flowed in favour of authorial creativity.

One of the outcomes of the communal flow of authorial creativity over canonical determinations was that the authentic and true Slender Man became defined by his inconsistent nature. By allowing each writer or artist's view of the Slender Man to stand as authoritative and accurate, the Slender Man himself shifted in understanding to one that was constantly changing. User cloudy described the Slender Man in a short narrative as having 'several consistent identifying markers, with other traits changing or "transforming" from image to image' (cloudy 2009). Chaos Hippy wrote: 'You don't understand. You don't understand! He's not transforming or coming out of his shell. What we see is changing as we're exposed to something we should never see' (Chaos Hippy 2009). Perhaps most succinctly clarified, the supernatural view of the ever-changing Slender Man was summed up shortly by TheRiffie, who commented that the 'Slender Man is beyond our comprehension' (TheRiffie 2009).

The supernatural state of the Slender Man, viewed accurately due to his changing nature, may have originally arose mostly as an excuse to allow more narratives to creatively flow from the group. The result, however, located the Slender Man in an area of supernatural, typically reserved for divinity. The unknowable Slender Man was viewed, essentially, with something akin to apophatic theology – the belief in the inadequacy of any human conception of the divine (Louth 2012).

For many, the questions of who the Slender Man is, and how and why he acts, being left unanswered is where Slender's horror truly lays. Snucks's earlier description of the Slender Man as 'some alien piper' who was taking children for 'some unknowable purpose' (snucks 2009) is an example of how the fear of the unknowable manifests in their consideration. This consideration of the Slender Man is not one who can be fought, has no weakness and cannot be known. His force as an online monster, therefore, only grows with the use of this unknowable strand.

The fear of the unknowable is similar to older horror narratives, particularly of H. P Lovecraft. Lovecraft's monsters in his Cthulhu Mythos are comprised of older beings which humans have no capacity to comprehend. The Ancient Ones, as they are called, are unknowable. Lovecraft called this type of horror 'cosmic fear' – an instinctual feeling similar in both origin and feeling to a religious feeling (Lovecraft 1973). As Lovecraft writes:

> The one test of the really weird is simply this – whether or not there be excited in the reader a profound sense of dread, and of contact with unknown spheres and powers; a subtle attitude of awed listening, as if for the beating of black wings or the scratching of outside shapes and entities on the known universe's utmost rim. (Lovecraft 1973, 16)

Horrific cosmic fear and its connection to religious feelings and emotions has been connected to Rudolf Otto's *Idea of the Holy* (Carrol 1990), in which he described a religious experience as that which can inspire fear and awe. For Otto, religion has a non-rational element, which he called the *numen*, and a religious experience can bring about a tremendous fear in the subject. Experience of the religious is the *mysterium, tremendum et fascinaus*, that which inspires fear, and awe – that which was wholly other and mysterious, in a way which lay beyond the sphere of our normal usual consideration (Otto 1923).

The inspiration of 'cosmic fear' has not left horror after Lovecraft, but has laid the foundation of horror storytelling, and its historical traces can be found in the horror genre (see for example King 1987). Lovecraft's 'cosmic fear' puts the reader in a fearful interaction with the *numen*. As storytelling continued on the Something Awful forums in 2009 – and even far after – the connection of the Slender Man with his wholly other, wholly mysterious and unknowable nature puts readers and storytellers into a position of retelling the horror involved in 'cosmic fear', playing on ideas of religion which can be awe-inspiring in a fully terrible way.

Either consciously or unconsciously, the users on the Something Awful forum employed negative theological terms and understanding in order to describe their online monster. The authors and artists on the Something Awful forum poached from religious literacy, building on concepts such as negative theology in conjunction with Lovecraft's 'cosmic fear' to build a stronger framework for the foundational aspects of the Slender Man.

### 2.3.2 Authenticity in narrative

The participants on the Something Awful forum, as well as the other authors and contributors to the Slender Man mythos in his life post-forum, all contributed due to a shared interest in horror stories. The original thread call-to-action involved a contribution to paranormal photographs, and even after the shift for the forum thread to be about the Slender Man specifically, the stories and photographs were creepy, scary and firmly in the horror genre.

The issue became twofold for the participants on the forum. How does the concept of the Slender Man as a horror figure spread when the origin is so easily found? And more importantly, how does the horror stay scary when the participants are directly contributing to the concept? How does something you actively create continue to scare you?

The solution came about halfway through the forum thread's life. Something Awful forum user soakie first broached the idea of a Tulpa, leading to what is commonly referred to in Slender Man lore as 'the Tulpa Theory', where the Slender Man has become manifest as a Tulpa, or thought form. The idea of a Tulpa, as used here, has its roots in Tibetan Buddhism; however, this link is only tangential at best as there is little evidence to solidly demonstrate this link. The only connections formed come from more Western esoteric movements, most specifically that of Theosophy (Mikles and Laycock 2015). Similar to the Theosophical concept of affirmations, the power of thought allowed for actual manifestations to occur. For affirmations, this happens in an actualization of repeated phrases (i.e. 'today will be a good day'). For thought-forms, this can be a physical manifestation of a being thought about at length.

The first recorded Tulpa was from Alexandra David-Néel, who claimed to learn this from Buddhists she was living with while in Tibet (David-Néel 1936). Others followed David-Néel's record of thought-forms in Tibet and referenced them as their primary source of information on the topic (e.g. Evans-Wentz 1960). Further details of thought-forms, the more Western name to Tulpas, is found in Annie Besant's book *Thought-Forms* (1925), which details the more Theosophical take further. David-Néel and others also detailed how some Tulpas or thought-forms can grow too powerful for the creator to actually control, and become loose in the world.

If Tulpas gain their strength and form from the power of thought, it becomes easy to see how the Slender Man can become an even more horrific creature when shaped through the lens of the Tulpa Theory. The stories of the Slender Man may have started out just as fun stories, according to this theory, but soon became the reason for Slender Man's physical manifestation in the world. He may not have existed before, but he exists now. The ultimate power of many people all contributing and thinking about the same idea at the same time is given full reign. Like rinksi's quote at the beginning of this chapter, the fear is not only in the figure of the stories but also in the contribution. They are contributing to a larger idea – a figure which is growing and manifesting as the contributions continue.

It is important to keep in mind, however, that this theory is not quite as 'real' for the Something Awful participants as it was for the Theosophical thinkers who brought the idea to the West. The Tulpa Theory was utilized in order to continue the fear, though it was done in an act of play. The users who called upon the Tulpa Theory did not fully 'believe' in the Slender Man's physical manifestation. This complicated notion of the use of these theories and concepts in a playful manner is examined further in the following section. The use of the Tulpa concept, and negative theology from the previous section, is not used to solidify the Slender Man's existence firmly. The authors would all firmly state that they do not believe the Slender Man to truly exist – the fun is in playing with the idea that he just might be.

## 2.3  Paedophilic connection

The static image of the Slender Man, as a tall man wearing a suit, raises questions regarding Slender Man's connection with paedophilia. The image he immediately resembles is an adult male in a business suit, and his seeming fascination with children, as many storytellers describe, may recall contemporary fears of paedophilia.

Through my research, I did not encounter any story or depiction of the Slender Man which directly connects him with paedophilia. Rather, his human male appearance is only a front, and when the audience gets a closer look, they truly see how alien he is. In many ways, he resembles a fairy of more traditional folklore, especially when connected to the supernatural elements he embodies.

The fairy connection is made early on the Something Awful forum. User Thoreau-Up first affiliated the Slender Man to German folklore: 'They called him "Der Großmann", the tall man. He was a fairy who lived in the Black Forest. Bad children who crept into the woods at night would be chased by the slender man [sic], and he wouldn't leave them alone until he caught them, or the child told the parents what he or she had done' (Thoreau-Up 2009). In response, user Shai-Hulud corrected: 'Actually, he is called "Der grosse Mann". At least in the storys [sic] my grandma used to tell me about him. I still live in the Black Forest and i [sic] still hate to go outside at night' (2009). User snucks later described the Slender Man as 'some alien piper', (2009) in reference to the Pied Piper.

The link to fairy lore does not stray far from the more traditional stories involving child-stealing. Many fairy tales and folklore refer to fairies stealing children. Following a more comparativist method, the Aarne-Thompson Motif-Index lists several entries regarding supernatural creatures taking children, including F320 'Fairies carry people away to fairyland', F321 'Fairy steals child from cradle', F420.5.2.4 'Water-spirits steal children and leave changeling' and G442 'Child-stealing demon', to name just a few (Thompson 1955).

Alongside fairies, the Slender Man also has connections to UFO and alien sightings, especially in appearance. The vision of the Slender Man as a tall, all-too-thin man wearing a suit is incredibly similar to the Men in Black narratives of UFO viewers and abductees. In these narratives, those who saw aliens or who reported – or even did not report – abductions were soon visited by strange men in suits, often with bodies which were just slightly inhuman (Redfern 2011). These men would strongly discourage the individual to not share their narrative, or to not pursue investigation into the matter (Robertson 2016). The Men in Black narrative demonstrates some sort of illustration of fear associated with tall men wearing suits that goes far beyond an issue of paedophilia. Similarly to the Slender Man as well, the Men in Black are also often theorized as being Tulpas (Kissel, Parks and Zebrowski 2018).

Paedophilia is ultimately a human issue: the fear is of a human taking advantage of a more vulnerable human. When the Slender Man's incredibly inhuman nature becomes more revealed in his narratives, any paedophilic connection is stripped from him as his humanity is simultaneously stripped from him. In many ways, this leads to a greater fear, because, to use snucks's description, the fact that the children are taken for 'some unknowable purpose' (snucks 2009) leaves us more confused as to how to protect ourselves, and children, against the strange figure.

The way the narratives are constructed often echoes folkloric approaches. This fabricated folklore is frequently linked with a form of pseudo-folklore called fakelore. As the field of folklore studies grew, so did a growing trepidation of what Robert Dorson called fakelore. According to Dorson, folklore was the traditional and authentic spread of narratives from the 'folk' while fakelore was not. Fakelore was almost entirely fabricated, with no connection to an older tradition. Dorson's vitriol was found in stories from the United States, most particularly Paul Bunyan (Dorson 1976; Dundes 1985). The attack on fakelore only grew. The search to find and study only authentic folklore was an important consideration for folklorists, and the spread of fakelore was something that folklorists would by all costs avoid (Dorson 1976).

At its heart, the concern regarding fakelore was twofold. The first was the seemingly tenuous position of folkloric studies as an academic discipline. To be seen giving authentic credence to a narrative not regarded as authentic would be difficult to sustain. But more important for Dorson and others was the effect of fakelore as an untrue representation of the type of stories the 'folk' both want to share and need to share (Fox 1980).

The 'folk' in 'folklore' was initially described by Joseph Jacobs as peasants, and especially the illiterate (Jacobs 1893). Andrew Lang also saw the folk as from the lower class, poorly educated and lacking 'progress' (Lang 1884, 11). This dichotomy between the literate elite and the peasant 'folk' continued for some time even in more anthropological approaches to the study of folklore, for example Robert Redfield who placed the urban in direct contrast with the peasant folk (Redfield 1960). Folklorists began to shift their understanding of the folk to a more comprehensive – and less pejorative – view in the late twentieth century. Alan Dundes, for example, defined the folk as 'any group of people whatsoever who share at least one common factor' (Dundes 1980).

Perhaps the least insulting is the consideration of 'folk' as a group of peoples within a grander culture. Folkloric narratives are considered as those which rose from the everyday 'folk' up to the grander narrative. These were seen as often uprooting the traditional cultural and social systems which were often what kept these peoples as oppressed in these systems. Folklore was therefore an outlet to express displeasure with the greater system. Fakelore, on the other hand, was from the other direction, originating from the greater institutions and pressing downward. These enforce the systems rather than uprooting them (Fox 1980).

By its purest definition, the Slender Man is fakelore. It is spread around the internet in much the same way folklore is (Blank 2009; Chess and Newsom 2015), but it is never seen as 'real'; it is not believed, and its origins are very easily traced. The narrative is entirely fabricated, and yet spread as if the same level of folklore as other online legends with less obvious claims of fabrication, such as the Black-Eyed Kids (Harvestwind 2001; Bethel 2013). However, I argue this does not mean the narratives are not 'authentic'. While the focus here has been slightly more on folklore than myth, there are similar issues of questioning 'authentic' expressions of myth, even though the narrative itself is still coming from the people themselves, echoing the same thoughts.

The concept of the divide between folklore and fakelore stems from a greater concern of listening to the voice of the lower classes or commonly oppressed, who have no voice in greater society. But the spread of the internet gives these groups a voice. The Slender Man was not created by a larger institution, ticking boxes off on what a typical hero or monster must be, and then unleashing this gradually to the public. The Slender Man was created quickly by a group of people, of everyday people, who spend their nights posting on forums and digitally manipulating images for fun. The story of the Slender Man, then, is a representation of the people.

Despite many large institutional names as centres for online engagement, such as Google or Facebook, these larger corporations are at the whim of the flock of online communication and movement. Smaller, more homegrown, sites may be the next port of call, which will then grow into their own larger force, until the flow of users shift somewhere else.

Therefore, online communication and storytelling must be considered along different understandings than the dichotomy of folklore and fakelore, or, in other words, historically established authentic narratives and newly created narratives. In many ways, the realization that this narrative is fiction is not important, as is the consideration of what fakelore is in the eyes of Dorson (Dundes 1985). For William Fox, the distinction is not what is considered fiction and what is considered folklore, but in what is being told by the 'folk' (Fox 1980), which the Slender Man undoubtedly is. The Slender Man, then, is folkloric fakelore, a fictional narrative both created and spread online by the internet's 'folk'. Alan Dundes has also pointed out how fakelore can, through its exchange and spread, become folklore (Dundes 1985). The Slender Man represents the way fakelore can become folklore through its spread and the way in which the narratives are told. This is especially relevant in how the Slender Man narrative has arisen from the internet's 'folk'.

## 2.4 Mythology and serious play

As mentioned previously, there is a disconnect in acknowledging the 'realness' of the Slender Man. Despite the conversations engaging with religious literacy as detailed prior, if one were to directly ask the community if the Slender Man is real, they would respond with an emphatic no. However, if you were to phrase the question differently – asking instead if the Slender Man means something for instance – you would get several answers in the affirmative. Despite the use of religious literacy, and often in a sincere way, the purpose is entirely playful.

The importance of play was first broached to the academic world with Johan Huizinga's *Homo Ludens* ([1938] 1980), which first connected play as an essential part of culture, including ritual. Despite the promising nature of his work,

Huizinga's relationship between play and ritual, and in taking both seriously, did not dramatically shift the nature the conversations had on the subject (Raj and Dempsey 2010). Huizinga's approach helped to illustrate the concept of a 'magic circle' of play (1938, 10), which has since been picked up as an important aspect of game studies (e.g. Salen and Zimmerman 2004). However, often the nature of Huizinga's concept is lost. His initial comment about play being set apart also alluded to a porous boundary. As he put it: 'But the feeling of being "apart together" in an exceptional situation, of sharing something important, of mutually withdrawing from the rest of the world and rejecting the usual norms, retains its magic beyond the duration of the individual game' (1938, 12). There is clear crossover between the worlds of play and non-play.

The term 'serious play' is sometimes found in aspects of anthropology and anthropology of religion (Luhrmann 1989; Ortner 1999) The need for play to be seen as 'serious' is in contrast to the popular concept of play as being something childish and almost, therefore, not worth studying. When anthropology has turned to studying play, it is in contrast to other play and detailed as more adult, like sports or gambling (Hamayon 2016). Play's direct contrast to work forces play to be regarded as less important. As time has shifted, play is beginning to be considered more important, but it is surprising that anthropology did not initially lead the way. Initial understandings followed much of what Roger Caillois thought of play, as 'an occasion of pure waste' (1962, 5).

The term 'serious play', like Geertz's 'deep play' (1973), is made as a distinction to make play seem more relevant for scholarly debate. However, it is often used in such a way that makes whatever form of play at the heart of the study an example of serious play, thereby different than the normal unserious and thus unimportant play. But play can be important in and of itself, and all play is both serious and not serious simultaneously. The Slender Man, and horror storytelling online, represents this. The participants involved in discussing and creating are knowledgeable of the story-element, and through which can play with concepts, ideas and emotions in a way that is deeply impactful, while still remaining playful. The usage of religious literacy is an example of this.

Serious play can also happen on a deeper level with online storytelling due to Taussig's concept of memetic excess (1993). Like memes in general, as discussed in the first section of this chapter, the Slender Man was created through a process of *bricolage*, as participants drew on concepts they knew around them to incorporate into the narrative at hand. The religious terminology utilized is an example of this. *Bricolage*, and de Certeau's 'poaching', demonstrates the active participation of the audience, authors and artists which gave rise to memes in general and the Slender Man specifically. Working alongside *bricolage* in an active way would be Michel de Certeau's concept of the active participant – the reader is not passive but actively 'poaching' (de Certeau [1984] 2013). The usage often drawn on, or poached, are those found in the offline world. As stories replicate the offline material in their storytelling, the memetic connection between the two worlds begins to fade, as one replicates the other and vice versa.

The separation between the two conceived of as different worlds begins to break down as the two worlds replicate and interact with one another, and this is where memetic excess occurs (Taussig 1993). It is within the grey area between these two worlds that the Slender Man thrives. It is within this lack-of-boundary where the community plays. It is in the boundaries between the digital and the non-digital, the non-religious and religious and fiction and reality that the Slender Man lives and haunts. This memetic excess brings the story of the Slender Man to a field of contemporary mythology, the engagement with religious literacy creating an extensive and intricate mythos.

## 2.5 The Slender Man as mythos

The memetic excess of serious play, and its reliance on *bricolage*, helps to create an aspect of collectivism. The collective experience helps to make the internet feel more like a place (Milner 2016, 33). The collectivism which assists in the emotive spread of memes is remanence of oral and folk cultures (Kuipers 2002; Blank 2009; Foley 2012). The collectivism, therefore, can have the same emotive experience, creating a mythos.

Memetic excess and the engagement with serious play forms the foundation of the Slender Man mythos, which causes us to reassess the first appearance of the Slender Man. Like his narratives, he first appears one way but on second look appears completely different and more alien. The authenticity issues the community faced were solved via religious literacy, but it also demonstrates that while the Slender Man is just a story, it is also more than a simple story. The Slender Man is a virtual monster, lingering menacingly on computer screens, hiding behind digital photographs and haunting online social spaces. But the active engagement with him, from the side of the participants, blurs the lines of virtual and concrete in both types of narratives, use of photographs and government documents, and religious literacy explanations.

This paints the quote from rinski at the beginning of this chapter in a slightly different light. 'He's growing organically from our combined feedback. . . . For all intents and purposes, the Slender Man is a living entity' (rinski 2009). For all intents and purposes, the Slender Man *is* a living entity, while he also remains entirely fictional. His existence focuses on the collectivity of the community's engagement with him, given birth through the memetic excess which complicates his existence. While he is entirely fictional, his life is given through the real social engagements, real issues and real communal engagement he embodies.

In this we can see the connection the Slender Man has with our definition of myth, provided in Chapter 1. Myth is a narrative, or something similar to a narrative which an individual or community uses to structure their understanding of themselves and the world around them (Chapter 1; see also Kunin 2003). The Slender Man demonstrates the way the audience is playing with serious communal engagements with social issues. He reveals the way the community structures their own understanding. And it is this structure we seek to uncover more substantially in this book.

### 2.5.1 Progression of the study of the mythos

A structuralist analysis starts at an arbitrary starting point – the key myth – and then spirals out from there. We stop when we face a boundary point. These boundaries are much more complicated when we move this to the digital sphere. Linguistic or geographical boundaries are not nearly so obvious on the internet. At what cultural or subcultural boundary does our structure exist? As we bring Lévi-Strauss into the digital sphere, these questions become increasingly important to ask. Now that we have established how the Slender Man mythos can be seen as mythology more theoretically, we now need to see what the deeper structure is that this mythos is drawing up.

The Slender Man mythology is not made up of just one narrative. Nor is the ending point for this group of myths as obvious as just the end of the Slender Man collection. Is it with the subcultural group of creepypasta? Or even wider in digital communal narratives, more generally? Our arbitrary starting point will be the Something Awful forum, simply as it is also the starting point for the Slender Man mythology. From here, we will spiral outwards to other Something Awful forum narratives, and other Slender Man myths.

# 3

# The origin of the Slender Man (Part 1)

In 2009 on the Something Awful forums, user Gerogerigege began a discussion thread for creating paranormal images. The idea was to alter photos to replicate photos of paranormal phenomenon such as ghosts. Victor Surge's posts on the Something Awful forum, beginning on the third page of the thread, caused the conversation to shift from paranormal images in general to specifically the Slender Man – an unnaturally tall humanoid figure who sometimes is less than humanoid and appears to be wearing a suit. In referencing particular users from the Something Awful forum, I will be using the usernames given and posted on Something Awful including Victor Surge. The reason for this is due to many of these narratives and images having been reposted on various other sites, sometimes connected with the username provided. By citing their username, I aim to retain individual authorial recognition where possible, despite often having no connection to their offline name. Victor Surge is a major exception as between the time of his posting on Something Awful and the writing of this study; their offline name has become known. During the lifespan of the forum thread, however, Victor Surge never personally made his name known, therefore I will only use the name provided on the forum thread, and cite the usernames provided there.

This chapter will analyse the thematic nature and structure of stories which exist at the beginning of the Something Awful forum thread. The first will be focusing on Victor Surge, presenting three of his posts which formed the foundation of the Slender Man mythos. Several days after Victor Surge, user Mr. 47 posted a narrative which had the appearance of a newspaper article. As this only forms the first half of the Something Awful forum thread which gave life to the Slender Man, the second half, providing case studies of both Aleph Null and genesplicer, will be studied in the following chapter. The structure of the narrative will be actively played with throughout, at times providing examples and ideas, and at times questioning the previous presentations.

## 3.1 Victor Surge

Within the first couple pages of the Something Awful forum thread, 'Create Paranormal Photos', user Victor Surge posted a handful of times, each reiterating the paranormal creature he created and dubbed 'the Slender Man'. These images of a tall humanoid figure appearing to wear a suit captured the attention of the thread. His creation of multiple images was the result of other users who wished to see more. Afterwards, many others took up the effort and created their own stories and images inspired by Victor Surge. Regardless of what he meant when first posting on the thread, Victor Surge laid the foundation for the creation of a new online mythology. We will be exploring a couple of his early posts, as well as how these images and stories formed a structural basis for the narratives which followed.

### 3.1.1 Initial post

The third page of the forum for creating paranormal photos included a post by user Victor Surge. He presented two edited photos, both depicting children with a looming figure in the background – a strange character who vaguely resembled a man in a suit. Each had a small caption accompanying it.

The first image, of which I am calling 'photographer unknown', carried a short but strange caption: '"we didn't want to go, we didn't want to kill them, but its persistent silence and outstretched arms horrified and comforted us at the same time . . ." 1983, photographer unknown, presumed dead.' Directly underneath this, and in the same post, a second image, Figure 3.1, and of which I will call 'Stirling City' for ease of reference, had the caption:

> One of two recovered photographs from the Stirling City Library blaze. Notable for being taken the day which fourteen children vanished and for what is referred to as 'The Slender Man'. Deformities cited as film defects by officials. Fire at library occurred one week later. Actual photograph confiscated as evidence. 1986, photographer: Mary Thomas, missing since June 13th, 1986. (Victor Surge 2009a)

These two images inspired the Something Awful forum to create more images and stories involving this supernatural creature dubbed 'The Slender Man'. Something about Victor Surge's images and narratives, and the many others which followed his initial post, captured the attention of both the Something Awful forum and the wider online community.

*The Origin of the Slender Man (Part 1)* 47

**Figure 3.1** Victor Surge's initial post, 'Stirling City' (Victor Surge 2009a).

Before examining the other posts made by Victor Surge, it may be useful to see what is structurally happening to the images and captions presented here first. As these were the first narratives and images, and are often cited as the beginning of the mythos, analysing this initial myth is important.

Lévi-Strauss's most notable works tend to focus on more textual narratives, such as the myths from the Bororo or Ge mythology (1963b; 1969; 1973b; 1973c). Lévi-Strauss, however, did not solely deal with these types of narratives. He also studied masks (1982), as well as seeing his structuralism as able to be applied to music and art (1997). He also constructed a dichotomy between the explicit myth, the textual myths he typically focuses on, and implicit myth, which is seen as aspects of a ritual. Implicit myth is fragmentary, while more textual mythology is seen as complete (1981, 669; see also Chapter 6). This implicit mythology is also seen as a form of structural analysis in a study of shamanic ritual (1963a), demonstrating how myth can be seen and applied in non-textual or literary ways. The study of more unconventional approaches to structuralism has continued past Lévi-Strauss as well, including a study of Western films

(Wright 1975). Essentially, the application of structuralism to images like Victor Surge's is not new with this study, though it is new to bring Lévi-Strauss to the digital arena.

| Children | Slender Man | Present |
|---|---|---|
| Taken | Deformities | Normal |
| Missing | | |

Anything more detailed would require more narratives to add to the mythos. In the beginning of Slender Man mythos building, Victor Surge posted more narratives. One of which was longer and more detailed, which I'll call 'Steinman Woods', and was immediately accompanied by a 'performance post'.

### 3.1.2 Steinman Woods and performance post

In contrast to the short captions of 'photographer unknown' and 'Stirling City', 'Steinman Woods' is a significantly longer narrative consisting of two images and two different, but connected, narratives. The images conceal the Slender Man somewhere in the forest background, surrounded by fog. The audience member is left searching for the anomaly in the image. The accompanying captions are written as a report: the first tells of two hunters who were attacked by the Slender Man; and in the second an investigation team stumbles onto a grisly scene of many dead bodies impaled on tree branches, whose deaths are attributed to the Slender Man. The second narrative ends with a comment from the Something Awful user, claiming he is unaware of what anything he found means. He is having trouble sleeping but is feeling slightly calmed by knowing his friend is coming over soon (Victor Surge 2009c). A second post, 'performance post' from this point onwards, immediately follows: a picture depicts one person going upstairs, and an eerie inhuman humanoid figure reaching for the camera lens with too long fingers (see Figure 3.2). The caption reads: 'My friend is herejus camein barely made up stairs got pictur locked door but it s right there inthe hall dont look at its pictures it doesnt want to be known about dont loo [sic]' (Victor Surge 2009d).

Here, no children are directly talked about, but violence is. The first two posts, which heavily feature children, are also void of any direct reference to violence, while here the violence is described in intense detail with children absent from the narrative. The violence detailed in the narrative of the two hunters involves complete dissection and disembowelment, and the second has bodies impaled on trees. Despite the stark difference in narrative between the 'Steinman Woods' posts and the initial posts, they do possess similarities in their sensory codes and the nature of violence presented.

### 3.1.3 Sensory codes

When reading Victor Surge's posts, sensory codes – images and phrases which refer to and recall the senses – are prominent. Victor Surge tells much of his story through images, which require sensory codes of the audience. The narratives accompanying these images are noticeably short, especially when compared to the longer narratives in the wider creepypasta community, due to their intention as captions or small excerpts from reports. In these posts, there are three types of sensory codes: (1) prohibited senses, (2) sounds and (3) obscured senses.

Prohibited senses directly affect the relationship between post and audience. The images which first accompanied the narratives prohibited sight, as the Slender Man is obscured and hidden in the background of photos. The audience member actively searches for him, in what one user described as 'the worst game of Where's Waldo' (VR Native American 2009). The one image which does not is the image in the 'performance post'. The image itself has the Slender Man incredibly close to the lens and reaching out to the camera. His face and form take up most of the image (see Figure 3.2). This image is accompanied, however, with a warning to not look at the image: 'dont look at its pictures it doesnt want to be known about don't loo [sic]' (Victor Surge 2009d). In the one image where the Slender Man is easily viewed, we are strictly told we should not be looking.

Sound is the only sense not obscured in any way. In the account of 'Steinman Woods', sounds accompany the Slender Man's attack. After the fog increases, the hunters hear 'a constant murmuring sound accompanied by a low hum', and the attack itself comes after hearing a 'low children's laugh, like a giggle'. The unobscured sound is thus linked to the Slender Man specifically.

Obscured senses, or senses which are either hidden or in lack, are referenced in all of Victor Surge's aforementioned posts. The constant silence – a lack of sound – is mentioned in the initial post ('. . . but its persistent silence . . .'), and it directly refers to the experience of the taken children, where the quote is assumed to be from. In 'Steinman Woods', the two hunters experience increasing fog, which obscures the sight. The 'Stirling City' caption cites the deformities of the Slender Man as 'film defects by officials', which causes the reader to question the veracity of what the eye sees – is the truth hidden by the claim of film defects, or is the eye truly tricked by the damaged film? The film defects are

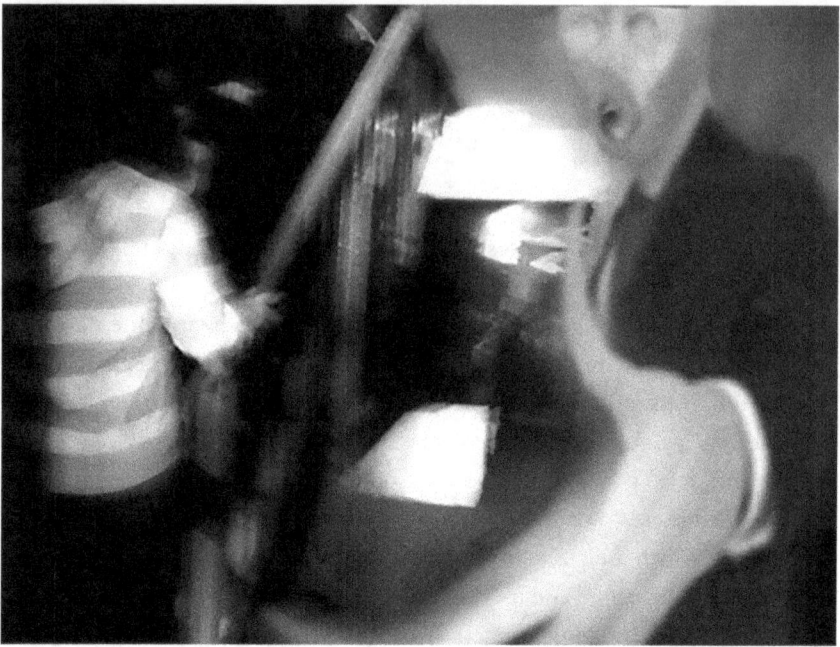

**Figure 3.2** Victor Surge's prohibited image, or the 'performance post' (Victor Surge 2009d).

simultaneously questioned and known to be a false reasoning by the audience member/reader narratively speaking, as the audience is in the locale of horror storytelling and has become aware of the inhumanity of the Slender Man simply due to this locale.

The prohibited senses are often tied to the non-supernatural explanations associated with those uninvolved or ignorant of the Slender Man's presence. The defects attributed to the photos, specifically in the Stirling City image, are addressed logically. The immediate reaction to seeing a semi-humanoid figure with strange tentacle-like appendages outside of the digital campfire setting is to assume film defects and not film accuracy. By prohibiting the full view of the Slender Man, or the unfamiliar, we remain within the category of those who are unaffected by his presence. More often, the sensory codes are not mentioned at all or the attention is on their lack, such as the silence mentioned in Victor Surge's 'photographer unknown'. When the sensory codes are purely existent, for example in sound, it is often associated with the Slender Man. The insertion of sound is correlated to the insertion of a foreign and unfamiliar element – the Slender Man is the 'noisy' interference in our familiar quiet lives.

The images of the Slender Man hidden in the background forces the audience member to seek for the unfamiliar in the familiar. The digitally manipulated photos cause the viewer to pursue the Slender Man's image, forcing the audience away from the familiar in search of the unfamiliar or supernatural. When the unfamiliar does not have to be sought for, as it is in Victor Surge's 'performance post', the audience is forbidden from looking at the supernatural itself. The audience is thus separated from both the familiar and the unfamiliar, relegated to a strange middle ground between the two: estranged from their familiar environment and not allowed to be involved with the unfamiliar.

The Slender Man mythos is a clear example of how audience participation in the narrative typically operates in creepypasta. The audience interacts directly with the text through the communal creation of the narratives and the role-playing which occurs in the context of the digital campfire setting. The digital campfire provides a locale in which the audience can play with belief, a game which exists in the act of users engaged with role-playing. Users engaged with 'in-character' communication on the Something Awful thread – the audience members and storytellers correspond with each other as if they believed in the truth of the narratives they were telling. If the narratives were styled as reports, the poster would feign 'searching' for the information (GyverMac 2009b). This form of in-character communication is found frequently on creepypasta forums and websites and mimics the 'as if' form of storytelling found around the digital campfire. The audience, through this, can affect both the format of narrative storytellers present and the content of these stories. In-character communication fuels the form of 'belief' characters within the narrative take. The interactivity of this brand of storytelling brings the audience into the narrative – the audience has multiple simultaneous roles as audience member, storyteller and even a role in the narrative as well. For the narratives styled as images or reports, the readers themselves become characters simply through the act of reading.

### 3.1.4 Nature of violence

The progression of Victor Surge's posts also has a progression of violence. The first two posts simply allude to violence, with no specifics of any kind. The most detailed is the quote from, presumably, one of the children: 'we didn't want to go, we didn't want to kill them.' The progression culminates in 'Steinman Woods' where the visceral nature of the attacks become more known and can be figuratively *seen* by the audience. The strongest display of violence is on the twenty-two bodies impaled on tree branches. The violence in 'Steinman Woods' is no longer assumed or alluded to, but is terribly apparent, creating a greater sense of dread in the performance post when the Slender Man is present in the poster's home.

In 'Steinman Woods' we see an unknown victim, separate from the twenty-two other bodies, who has been dissected precisely. His organs are found still in his ribcage in a clear bag. This rather gruesome description of a victim of the Slender Man also recalls images of how science often treats the nature it uses to understand the world. Human beings typically use nature, and understandings of nature, to interpret the world around us. By doing this, we are inherently placing ourselves in a separate category from nature. Nature is something which is *used* to understand the world – and in relegating it as such we instinctively separate ourselves from it. Animals are dissected, their organs bagged and categorized. The adult male victim has become like nature through his precise disembowelling. In a similar way, the twenty-two bodies impaled on trees are also forcibly returned to the category of nature: the tree branch is not just present to drape the bodies over, but goes through the body, becoming attached and integral to the bodies. However, the presence of the Slender Man, and its odd inhumanity and inherent incomprehensibility, places it automatically in the realm of the supernatural.

The use of impalement as a method of violence is an example of how the Slender Man is depicted as a separate Other. In most art, impaling became a symbol of not only cruelty but absolute otherness (Madar 2015, 185). This is most exemplified in Vlad the Impaler, the inspiration for the vampiric monster Dracula. His cruel actions also helped the perception of him as something supernaturally Other, leading to his depiction as a monster. The Slender Man's role as supernatural in such a strong and violent way keeps human beings from also existing within the category of the supernatural. Thus, humans exist in a separate category, somewhere between the stages of the natural and the supernatural. The attack thus leaves the human victims no longer in a middle ground between the natural and the supernatural but has forcibly returned them to the category of the 'natural'.

Despite all humans existing in this middle category, they are not all treated equally. Rather, the middle category exists on a scale ranging between the two more stable categories of the 'natural' and the 'supernatural', and arranged hierarchically. A small glimpse of this can be found in Victor Surge's posts.

The first category on the scale would be children. In Victor Surge's posts, we find children are taken more often, or become missing. This is primarily evident in the initial post, with narratives/images 'photographer unknown' and

'Stirling City'. The initial posts, primarily 'photographer unknown', focus on the victimization of children. There is no insinuation of violence enacted on the children themselves, they simply leave or disappear. There is insinuation, however, of violence enacted *by* the children, primarily with the written caption: 'we didn't want to go, we didn't want to kill them'. The manipulation implied here is vastly different than other Slender Man victims, which could demonstrate a close relationship to the supernatural. This connection to the supernatural is also evident in 'Steinman Woods'. The attack on the two hunters was directly preceded by a 'low children's laugh, like a giggle'. Slender Man is presumably using the sound effect of children, whether knowingly or not, which helps to designate a relationship between the supernatural Slender Man and the children. This relationship places children on the scale closer to the supernatural.

Comparatively, adult males appear to be placed on the opposite end of the spectrum, closer to the nature category. As mentioned previously, the unknown male victim which the two hunters encounter is dissected precisely, with his organs in clear bags. He is treated as science does nature. This reverses the traditional role, making him the natural subject with the supernatural having the scientific endeavour. This reversal of roles relegates the unknown male victim closer to nature on the scale. Similarly, the various twenty-two victims, which also include adult male victims, have been impaled on tree branches, involving a forceful return to nature.

The placement of adult females on the scale is less clear. The twenty-two impaled victims, which helped to locate the place of adult males near the natural category, also involved females. Hence, it would make sense to place adult females in a similar location on the scale as adult males. However, adult females are also treated similarly to children in the initial post: both children and adult females are missing. Thus, the exact placement of adult females on the scale is questionable. Tentatively adult females can be categorically placed in between adult males and children.

This scale would be detailed as provided in Diagram 3.1.

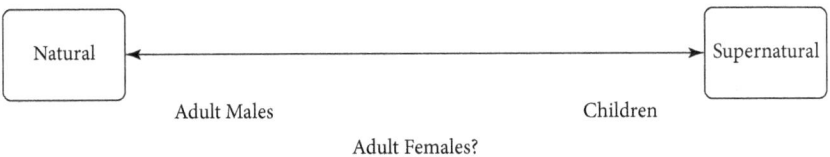

**Diagram 3.1** Supernatural/natural scale.

In Diagram 3.1, we can more clearly see humans in their mediatory category. Their arbitrary hierarchy detailed in the diagram determines the possible course in which their mediation is remedied – a remedy which only occurs through the intervention of a supernatural figure: the Slender Man. The Slender Man's various forms of taking determine which side of the scale the mediatory human is in – the violent death brings the mediatory category to nature, while mysterious taking brings the victim to the supernatural. The victim, however, is never in control of their own transition and mediations. They are powerless to their own situation and are left to wait for an outside figure to mediate on their behalf and force the transition on to them.

Lévi-Strauss's understanding of myth is tied to how myth moves from establishing an awareness of oppositions and progresses towards their resolution (Lévi-Strauss 1963b). While the progression towards resolution in character transitions may appear to have no resolution at all – as the movement forwards is essentially death – a negative resolution can still be a resolution. This is not without its grounding. Lévi-Strauss found a similar resolution in his essay 'The Story of Asdiwal' where the hero Asdiwal dies as a rock on the mountain, which neutralizes his place as mediator (Lévi-Strauss 1973c). The mediatory category progressing towards a subjectively identified 'negative' resolution could reflect the community's view of mediatory categories, and thus should not be dismissed.

## 3.2  Mr. 47

Five days after Victor Surge's original Slender Man post, Something Awful forum user 'Mr. 47' posted a narrative mimicking a newspaper article about a missing child in Stirling City, as a reference to Victor Surge's post. The narrative centres on the police investigation into the disappearance of eight-year-old Katrina Elkins. The report informs the reader there are few leads in the case, as the only witness was the victim's ten-year-old sister, Alice, who speaks of a tall thin man who would come to the girls' bedroom window at night. On the night of her sister's disappearance, the man also beckoned for Alice to join, but she was scared and pretended to be asleep. The police disregard her account due to the irrationality of a man being able to tap on a second-story window (Mr. 47 2009).

### 3.2.1  Those left behind

In Mr. 47's narrative, there are three character types, categorized by their relationship to the Slender Man. The first are *those left untouched*, represented by the narrator/

reporter of the article, the investigators and the parents of the two young girls. These characters have not heard of the Slender Man and have not experienced him.

The second are *those left behind* and is exemplified by the witness Alice. She stands somewhat outside of the first group due to her experience with the Slender Man. The reporter describes her testimony as the result of an 'overactive imagination' and the police dismiss it as just a 'dream'. She is, accordingly, one step removed from *those untouched* – she can no longer situate herself within the 'typical' society due to her experience of the Slender Man. She is seen as disingenuous, not given a proper place to speak, and is barred from being fully represented in society.

The third is missing from society and the narrative entirely. Both Katrina, who was taken, and the family's cat have been removed. The family's cat is only discussed at the end of the narrative, reported only as a passing disregard: 'Police believe that there is no link between the disappearance, and the vicious killing of the Elkin's cat by disembowelling in April.' Both removed characters are representative of the two ways one can be taken: either an often-violent death (as the cat) or simply disappeared (as Katrina). *Those taken*, like *those left behind*, are removed from the typical society, but their removal is complete. *Those taken* are no longer present to contend with their lost place in society.

The middle stage of being *left behind* places the characters in a strange middle ground in which they are removed from society while still being both present and alive. The character thus finds themselves in a state of anxiety at being in the middle of two more stable stages. The anxiety is epitomized in their relationship with *those untouched*. Those *untouched* strip authority from the voice of *those left behind*, leaving them without social representation despite still being present members of the society.

The characters in Mr. 47's newspaper narrative are portrayed in the context of transitions. Each stage corresponds to the former progression of character types. When the character first encounters the Slender Man, the character begins their transition to the stage of *those left behind*. In this stage, the characters are still present members of the society, but are considered non-active members by those still *untouched*. In many cases, the accounts of these characters are discounted. The characters are not seen as fully participating in society, and yet these characters are still inherently present. Alice, although both alive and present in society, is disregarded and not given representation in society. Her testimony is ignored as a dream.

The last stage of the transition is for the character to be taken, whether violently or just through disappearance, Katrina and the cat, respectively.

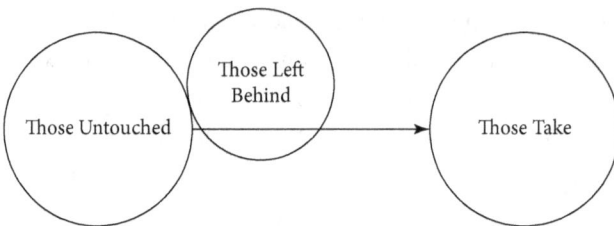

**Diagram 3.2** Character transitions.

Both removals conclude the characters' transition outside of society, albeit in two very different modes. The difference in removal types will be examined in Section 3.2.2. Character progression in transitions is solely a one-way evolution – once moving to the stage of those left behind, the character cannot return to being untouched. The category of untouched is reserved for those who have no knowledge or experience with the Slender Man. An experience had, or knowledge gained, cannot be given up. After Alice saw the Slender Man and heard him tapping at her window, she could not return to a time before this occurred. The final stage of being taken is seen as necessary to conclude the social movement (Diagram 3.2).

Diagram 3.2 is not meant to sketch out a structural diagram or equation at this point. Rather, the point of the diagram is to see the movement which is occurring between the categories or groups we have found up to now. This is to assist us in seeing all the aspects of the structure which need to be considered for when we are to attempt to draw a more complete structure.

For the characters within the narrative, the true horror is being stuck in this mediatory position. The anxiety of being an alive and active member of a society in which you are disregarded and estranged is a disturbing position to find oneself. In these cases, as well, it is impossible for a character to be able to return to their previous status of 'untouched', rendering the only redemption or resolution possible as being fully removed from society at the completion of the transition, and theoretically reclaim a sense of relief. However, all transitions are controlled by a secondary and supernatural figure – the Slender Man. This leaves *those left behind* with no agency in their own transitions, making it fully possible to remain trapped in the mediatory category.

The anxiety felt at this stage is demonstrated in Mr. 47's post. Many of Alice's quotes regarding the abduction are provided – her witness account gives an exact description of her sister's disappearance and the culprit. She recounts the nights leading up to her sister's disappearance, detailing the Slender Man coming to her bedroom window to 'tap on the glass, "make faces" and watch the girls'. She even tells the reporter and investigators the things he would say:

> He scared me. He told us to not tell Mom and Dad, or we'd be in trouble. He told us that he was our friend, and that he would give us anything we wanted, but we had to keep his secret. His smile was scary ... and his voice. He said nice things but he sounded mean. (Mr. 47 2009)

Despite the level of detail given by Alice as a witness, the headline of the newspaper report is still 'Police Have Few Leads in Missing Girl Case'. The reader feels a frustration with the account not being given its complete attention, a frustration which spreads to the anxiety of the position Alice's character rests in. Despite over half of the report being dedicated to Alice's testimony, she is described only as a 'possible' witness and was written off as 'unable to provide many details to investigators'. These descriptors heighten the frustration and anxiety related to the status of being *left behind*.

As mentioned previously, the characters who reside in this anxiety-ridden middle ground are unable to transition backwards, only forwards. The only relief which can be sought is in being taken. In Mr. 47's small narrative, two characters have already been removed, though the ways in which they were removed are vastly different – one through a violent death, the other quietly. This leaves a question of why such an opposition between the two forms of removal exists. I believe it would be a misstep to assume these two forms of departure are created equal. The extent of the differences in removal and character needs to be uncovered, specifically in relation to the actions undertaken by the character of the Slender Man.

### 3.2.2 Supernatural versus natural

Both the appearance and actions of the Slender Man label him as something unnatural and supernatural. Appearing at first glance as only a tall well-dressed man, further attention reveals his proportions as more than slightly off and his height more than just extraordinary. In Mr. 47's narrative, the overwhelming height is emphasized; the Slender Man would tap on the girls' bedroom window and talk to them, despite their window being on the 'second story, with no support beneath it'. Other narratives and images on Something Awful depict the Slender Man with extra appendages which can appear or disappear from his back. These are tentacle-like appendages, though some users describe them as firmer and more branch-like. The oddness of his appendages is also mentioned in Mr. 47's narrative: the arm used to indicate to Alice to join him and her sister was described as a 'snaky arm', emphasizing the fluid inhuman movements of his limbs. Even though he is often seen by witnesses or survivors of attacks, the Slender Man can disappear and re-appear seemingly at random. He is able to make his victims disappear in a similar way. Katrina, the child taken in Mr. 47's post, was taken through this kind of disappearance ('It's like she disappeared into thin air').

Placing the Slender Man in the category of the supernatural allows us to see the difference which exists between him and the family's disembowelled cat. The cat is an animal, a member of the natural category. The Something Awful forum and other major centres of online storytelling, which will be considered in this manuscript, are primarily English-speaking locations, which means they are typically dominated by countries in which English is the prevalent language, that is, the United States, the United Kingdom and Australia. These countries are also typically considered 'Western' in consideration. The details therefore seen here are primarily focused on these typical ways of thinking. When encountering the supernatural Slender Man, the cat did not just disappear, but died. The death itself is negative in description – it was not just a death, but a dissection and violent, vicious death. Thus, we see how the supernatural has a cruel and negative affect on the natural: the natural cannot physically survive an encounter with the supernatural.

Slender Man: the cat :: supernatural: natural

However, the cat is not just some wild animal either. The cat is a household pet – one close to family and home. The relationship of the cat to ourselves relates directly to how characters and readers understand the supernatural element of the Slender Man. Our explanations and understandings of the world are tied to ideas of the natural. The cat as pet provides a sense of home and familiarity to the natural. The natural in this case has been domesticated and made familiar to both family and society. The cat's death, thus, correlates to the incomprehensibility of the supernatural – the familiar natural cannot stand up to the calculated violence of the unfamiliar supernatural.

The cat is not the only character to be taken, however. Alice did not witness the cat's disembowelment, but she witnessed the disappearance of her sister. Her sister was not left dead in the narrative – the girl simply disappeared 'into thin air'. Despite being in the same category of taken as the cat, the girl is removed in a completely different manner, and one which cannot be simply labelled as on par with the violent nature of the cat's death.

As mentioned in regard to Victor Surge's posts, human beings, particularly those in the society of *those untouched*, use nature and understandings of nature to interpret the world around us. All of this inherently separates us categorically from nature. Nature is demoted beneath humans as something to be controlled. However, with the category of the supernatural given with the extreme example of the Slender Man, we cannot say we are supernatural either. We are left to stand somewhere between these two categories: separated from nature but not so far removed from nature as to be considered something other-than nature, or supernatural. We have somewhat unconsciously placed ourselves, once again, in a mediatory category.

In this narrative, children are not destroyed or killed at the hands of the unfamiliar; rather, they are taken by it. Unlike the natural, which dies violently, Katrina is physically taken by the supernatural. This is not to be confused with surviving or withstanding the encounter; she is still at the mercy of the supernatural but is able to stand against it better than her natural counterpart. If we imagine the mediatory category of humans as a scale which stretches between the natural and the supernatural, as we did when looking at Victor Surge's posts, we can place human children as being on the end of the mediatory scale closer to the supernatural. Her disappearance exemplifies her inability to survive or withstand the encounter, but her lack of violent death assumes a similarity or nearness to the supernatural. Her affinity with the supernatural is also exemplified by *how* she disappears. She is not taken in a way most found in cases of human-based kidnapping – she 'disappeared into thin air', a quality more associated with the supernatural Slender Man than with either nature or the created secondary category of human. Additionally, the quality is directly associated with her, and not with any outside force. The child category seems to have a similar affinity with the supernatural as seen in Section 3.1.

### 3.2.3 The Stirling City post

Some folklorists have begun to turn their attention to online narrative transmissions (Fernback 2003; Howard 2008; Blank 2009; Blank 2012; Howard 2015; Peck 2015). The virtual 'field' of the internet cannot be appraised as completely different from the more physical field folklorists are used to. As Trevor Blank describes, both these fields 'have folk groups, customs, slang and dialects, neighbourhoods, crimes, relationships, games, discussion groups, displays of emotion, bankers, commerce and various other forms of communication and education' (2009). While virtuality does present a different way of interacting with others than face-to-face communication, the computer screen is still capable of providing a locus where folklore, urban legends and myths are communicated widely online due to an essential feeling of 'being there' found among participants on online forums (Fernback 2003, 31) such as Something Awful (see Chapter 1).

Despite the similarities between more traditional modes of storytelling and the online environment, the difference of the virtual medium allows for new formats for narratives. The posters on the Something Awful forum mimic styles popularized on other fakelore (manufactured folkloric narratives, presented as if real) websites such as SCP Foundation (Secure, Contain, Protect), a website stylized to appear as an international government paranormal containment facility. Something Awful forum posters often utilized this document-style writing, some as censored government documents, others finding information regarding artists, including German woodcuts. Mr. 47's post was stylized as a newspaper report and used the quoting feature of forum posting as an added step of separating the author from the material. A fuller discussion of fakelore, folklore and its connection to the Slender Man can be found in Chapter 2.

The function of the style the narrative appears in also has a relation to the content of the narrative. The newspaper article is titled 'Police Have Few Leads in Missing Girl Case', and the uncertainty surrounding the crime is present throughout the article:

> A spokesman for the Stirling City Police Department admitted this week that there were no promising leads in the case of eight-year-old Katrina Elkins, who went missing from her home Thursday night.
>
> 'It's like she disappeared into thin air', said neighbour and family friend, Marybeth Carlisle. (Mr. 47 2009)

The narrative of the newspaper article is filled with uncertainty, from both the characters being interviewed within the article (apart from Alice who is quite certain of what happened) and the events being reported on. The uncertainty often surrounds the supernatural elements involved in the kidnapping, such as how the girl just 'disappeared', and the only lead is a story told by a ten-year-old girl of a perpetrator who could not rationally exist. The lead was dismissed as 'a dream' due to the bedroom window being on the second story with no support, and no one could be so unnaturally tall.

In contrast, the narrative's format implies a level of certainty. Often, the documents and reports the narrative mimics are used by people as avenues of truth and proof. The posters on Something Awful play directly with this contrast in posts where they remain 'in-character': claiming to be doing research into the Slender Man, they produce this information, even sometimes citing academic books which do not exist, as forms of essential 'proof' and certainty in the existence of the supernatural.

In-character communication is frequently found through creepypasta and other horror storytelling online. The subreddit r/nosleep, for instance, has a rule which states that 'everything is true here even if it isn't' (reddit n.d). Creepypasta is based on an aspect of believability. For the Slender Man, part of this believability is in the format these narratives take. These narrative formats of proof also lead to in-character communication, which is essentially retaining the illusion of the formats as proof and reality. This emphasis of believability is discussed in much greater detail, especially in comparison between creepypasta and other forms of horror storytelling, in Chapter 11.

The certainty of the narrative's form and the uncertainty of its content, while a fundamental contrast, also work in a symbiotic duality. While the uncertainty of the event and the unbelievable information provided counteracts the certainty in the article, the certainty of the article format also works to give a level of credence and believability to the supernatural.

The articles and documents often used as forms of proof and certainty are employed to question our relation to the familiar. A newspaper is familiar – it is a knowledgeable tool which has been around to disseminate information for generations. In contrast, the content of the narrative is uncertain and unfamiliar, especially with its description of the supernatural. The supernatural introduces elements of both uncertainty and unfamiliarity which directly contradict the informational and familiar aspects of the newspaper article. The familiarity of the style is faded in contrast to the unfamiliar aspect of the Slender Man, as his presence centres the article. In a similar manner to how the supernatural affects the natural, the supernatural unfamiliar also affects the familiar. By destroying the familiar and the natural, the supernatural causes what is commonly associated with the Slender Man: horror at being estranged from what is familiar and known. The reader of Mr. 47's article is thus placed in the same position as Alice, categorized as *those left behind* and estranged from their familiar place in society.

## 3.3 Conclusion

In Victor Surge's posts, the level of 'different' and what is missing can be summed up in the following relations:

Children/Missing :: Slender Man/Deformities :: Not-missing/Normal

The missing children are only connected to the normal present members of society through the deformed Slender Man. Slender Man's presence is both present, yet too different and sometimes missing (ability to disappear). His deformities are cited by 'officials' as being film defects, so although they are present they are considered not present. Slender Man therefore bridges the two links between what is present and what is missing, forcibly moving children specifically from one category to the other.

His mediation here is reflective of the senses in Victor Surge's posts. The missing children relate to the obscured or missing senses, and the prohibited senses are primarily directed to the present and normal society. The only sense directly present, sound, is directly associated with Slender Man and his attacks:

Obscured : Children :: Sound : Slender Man :: Prohibition : Normal Society

Again, the directly present sound mediates between the senses which are there, but restricted, and those hidden completely.

We are beginning to see how the formula works. Those who are taken by the Slender Man are opposed to those who are still present in society, and their transition from one category to the next is determined through their interaction with the Slender Man himself. He sits between categories.

We also see this in the more detailed diagram of *untouched*, *left behind*, and *taken* in Mr. 47's analysis. Put differently, the *untouched* is equated to the 'normal' society with the prohibited senses, and the *taken* are those missing with senses obscured. The piece left is the mediator between the two categories, *those left behind*. These are those directly affected by the Slender Man.

However, this structure still has some unanswered questions. In Mr. 47's narrative, the *untouched*, or those of 'normal' society, also are those who believe they have knowledge, are certain and have social status. They're able to remain this way due to the prohibited senses which restrict their viewing and understanding of the supernatural. Once viewed, as *those left behind* have, the illusion is broken. The sounds are heard, the certainty of the world is suddenly lost. The loss of certainty and emotional social knowledge is lost the minute supernatural knowledge is gained. The anxiety of this position is only obtained when the one in this position is taken and leaves the society entirely. When missing, their position is obscured once more like the obscured senses. The process of this transition is summed up in the provided table, where the second column is acting as a mediator.

| Untouched | Left behind | Taken |
|---|---|---|
| Normal | Deformed | |
| Present | Slender Man | Missing |

The issue I am presently questioning is the free association with *those left behind* and the Slender Man. In the relation of senses and missing/present society, the Slender Man is a mediator. The *left behind* category is also a mediator in its own position. While either end is combined similarly, the process of which *left behind* has reached this status is through knowledge of the Slender Man. The Slender Man himself is left unaccounted in this, unless we combine him in the mediatory category of *those left behind*.

What is necessary to solve this question is to move on to other Slender Man narratives and to return when appropriate to assess our current analysis. The following chapter will take into consideration the second half of the Something Awful forum, represented in two narratives by Something Awful users Aleph Null and genesplicer.

# 4

# The origin of the Slender Man (Part 2)

Victor Surge's posts eventually led to the spread of the Slender Man narratives in multiple places online, though it first spread far throughout the forum thread. The Something Awful forum experienced a shift in understanding very early in its life. After Victor Surge's images and captions took off, the thread once dedicated to sharing tips on photo editing was now dedicated to sharing narratives of the Slender Man. Posts which shared information on the process of creating their manipulated photos hid the technical information in reveal-able censor bars to keep from spoiling suspension of disbelief for the audience.

In the previous chapter, we saw the mythemes falling into three categories: *untouched*, *those left behind* and *those taken*. But there were still some lingering questions. The association of those left behind with the Slender Man does not quite work, as their position of *left behind* is based on knowledge or relationship with the Slender Man. The role of the triadic nature in general is also currently in question, as structuralist anthropological analysis, based on Lévi-Straussian thought, is based on oppositions, which is dyadic. The first two narratives of the last chapter are both from around the first half of the Something Awful forum thread, thus it seems appropriate to give a look at the second half of the Something Awful forum thread. Both Aleph Null's 'Observations' and genesplicer's 'Concord', as they will be called for ease from now onwards, continue to give us information on the beginning elements of the structure of the Slender Man mythos.

## 4.1 Aleph Null

Something Awful forum user Aleph Null posted his own contribution to the Slender Man mythos on the twenty-first page of the forum thread, about halfway through its life. His story was presented as a book section he found, called *The Observations*, by a mysterious author calling himself 'Nathaniel V'.

The user described the book as 'a grimoire of sorts' and posted a segment which discussed the idea of the Transformed – what happens when a human peers into 'impossible' places. The user puts several phrases in bold that reminded him of the Slender Man, though the writing never directly references him, instead focusing on strange observations and the fearsome idea of a Transformed man. For ease of reference from now on, Aleph Null's narrative will be called 'The Observations'.

The excerpt starts by reiterating a point which was supposed to have been made earlier in the text, referring to 'the Outside and the Things that swarm around our fragile existence, paying us little mind'. He says if someone, 'a fool', were to attempt to seek out more information on the Outside he would ultimately lose his sanity, and maybe even his life. We need to focus, however, on those who survive this and become Transformed. 'Such a Transformed man would exist among us but no longer of us. His appearance may be human or merely human-like, but his thought forms are unintelligible.' He described multiple disconcerting images, such as 'the tall man with shadowed face who bumps into you at market', 'the liquid darkness that pools itself in dim corners and gives itself weight' and a 'reflection in the mirror that lags behind or the movement seen on one side but not the other'. The wise magician is advised to 'avoid such a Transformed man' due to 'all logic, honour, and fairness' (Aleph Null 2009b) not existing with the Transformed.

We can begin to see a separation of elements which begin to fall similarly to what we saw with the structuralist analysis of the first half of the Something Awful forum thread. In the previous chapter, we sketched out three separate categories: Untouched/Normal/Present; Left Behind/Slender Man/Deformed; and Taken/Missing.

Similarly, we can see that which is associated with This World, our world, in Aleph Null as following into a similar section to the Untouched category. Here, the 'logic, honour and fairness' which is lacking elsewhere is shown to be present in the Untouched or This World. This is set in stark contrast to the Outside – a world which is not only something in which This World cannot fathom or else we may lose our sanity or die. The Outside also consists of 'the Things that swarm around our fragile existence, paying us little mind', implying that the Outside does not often directly interact with This World; it pays us little mind.

But where does this leave the Transformed? The Transformed are those who were once in This World but have become changed by an interaction with the Outside, which does not happen often. Many elements of the Outside have passed onto the Transformed, but they also remain at least appearing to be of This World: 'His appearance may be human or merely human-like, but his thought forms are unintelligible.' After a description of strange occurrences, the uncertainty of the Transformed as human is expressed:

> The tall man with shadowed face who bumps into you at market, the laughing child who points at you when you pass, the whispering woman who sparks your interest but disappears before you even catch her name.
>
> But these are human, yes? Perhaps. (Aleph Null 2009b)

The Transformed are thus both of This World and the Outside. As mentioned in the previous chapter, I feel somewhat hesitant to be placing the Slender Man into the same category as the *left behind*. If we remove him for now, we can see how Aleph Null's 'the Observations' details three primary modes:

| Untouched | Left behind | Taken |
|---|---|---|
| Normal | Deformed | Missing |
| The World | Transformed | The Outside |

A shift from This World to the Outside would require a dance with the Transformed. The Transformed are both of This World and the Outside, just as those left behind are both the society of those Untouched and Taken. Once of the Outside, once removed, the subject cannot move backward to return to the Transformed.

To better test this, we should add one more narrative from the Something Awful forums, one near the end of the thread's life cycle. To do this, we will shift to Something Awful forum user genesplicer's narrative 'Concord'.

## 4.2 Genesplicer

Something Awful forum user genesplicer's narrative, here referred to as 'Concord', was posted four months after Victor Surge's original posts and appeared near the end of the lifespan of the forum thread. His narrative takes the form of a psychologist's report on a dozen children following the disappearance of a classmate during a fieldtrip in the Appalachian Mountains. The report gives a short summary of the kidnapping event but concentrates on the students who witnessed the event. These students provide an account of the Slender Man, but the reports are disregarded outright. A series of images are then presented which are recorded as drawings by the children depicting who they saw take the missing child – all of which depict the Slender Man. A conclusion to the report reiterates the rejection of the eyewitness reports, and presents a view against the images of the students presented previously (genesplicer 2009).

Like Mr. 47's narrative with Alice, the children who witnessed a crime are heavily disregarded and ignored. We begin to see a reiteration of the *untouched/left behind/taken* categories which we first saw with Mr. 47. The report, for instance, claimed 'the students misinterpreted the appearance of the assailant' because of how he appeared 'nonhuman' (genesplicer 2009). The discarding of the children's narratives was bolstered by how these images all looked somewhat different from one another (see Figure 4.1).

This goes back to our constantly changing concept of the Slender Man (Chapter 2). The idea was originally brought about by how individual creators had their own take on the Slender Man. The Slender Man then became defined by an ever-changing nature, set this way due to the human mind not being able to comprehend the supernatural (Louth 2012). This led to the Slender Man having a Lovecraftian feel, especially recalling his concept of 'cosmic fear' which calls up both horrific and religious experiences (Lovecraft 1973).

The *untouched* are once again those who are narrating, on the N level, as it is their voice guiding the narrative. The reporting style insinuates a form of certainty, proof and knowledge which has come to define the *untouched* category. The writing here focuses as well on ideas of data and factors. The *taken* is the reference to the abducted child.

The *left behind* are where the other children reside. The obscured vision, through the relative descriptors of it being night, the details being confused and the presence of rain helps to instil a sense of uncertainty to what was seen. This uncertainty and presence of questions extends to the people existing in this category – they are misinterpreting the things they saw, an element of 'creative

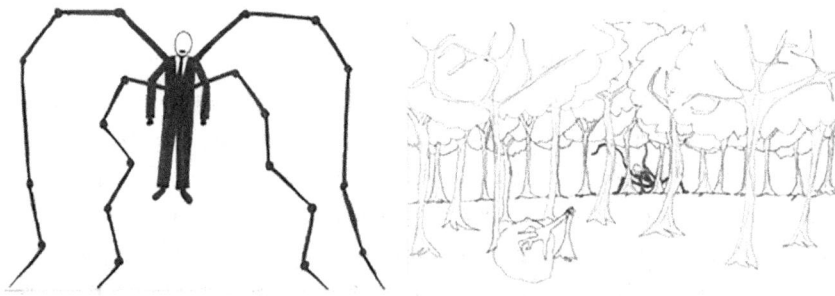

**Figure 4.1** Two of genesplicer's images (genesplicer 2009).

thinking' and the effect of hearing ghost stories. The odd depictions of the man who took the child is brought up to 'mass hysteria' and that the children are 'deeply traumatized' (genesplicer 2009).

Again, we see a reiteration of the three main categories as shown earlier in Diagram 3.1. If we are to take this as the beginnings of the underlying structure, there are some more specific ideas we can pair down to, as well as elements, such as the triadic nature, which are important to discuss. Before configuring a more detailed structure, we should first review shared themes, and previously discussed elements, which will all share the same structure.

## 4.3 Shared themes in Something Awful

Although the stories on the Something Awful forum are all written by different people who have seldom met each other in a physical sense, there are many shared thematical elements in the narratives on the Something Awful forum. This section will compile the themes found in both the narratives of Aleph Null and genesplicer, as looked at in this chapter, but will also combine these with the previous chapter's look at the early Something Awful forum narratives. There are some primary main themes carried forward through all these narratives: writing 'in-character', being faceless and being powerless.

### 4.3.1 In-character

One of the commonalities of the narratives on the Something Awful forum is the separation of character types into the three categories of *those untouched*, *those left behind* and *those taken*. The transformation which exists between these categories is what centres much of the discussion and narrative fear. While there is a fear in being *taken*, particularly in the more violent manner, there is a greater and more overwhelming fear which resides with the audience – the audience is in the precarious and dangerous position of knowing what should remain unknown as it is unfamiliar. This knowledge pushes the audience itself into the *left behind* category.

Many of the discussions and narrative presentations on the Something Awful forum thread stick to 'in-character' presentation – users assert the truth and veracity of the narratives they share without ceding their position as the author. For those whose narratives simulate reports, posters claim they had 'found' the reports and are sharing this find with the online community (for examples see

LeechCode5 2009 and TrenchMaul 2009). Some post what I call 'performance posts', in which they write entirely in character. One example of this can be found in the performance post of Victor Surge (2009d; see Chapter 3), while others discuss reading the stories on the forum thread while hearing Slender Man's characteristic tapping at their window (KatWithHands 2009; An observer 2009; Verloc 2009). In many instances, when users post information directly out-of-character, they mark it as a 'spoiler' – the words are covered by a black censor bar, and the writing is only revealed if the reader wishes it to be (Aleph Null 2009a; BooDoug187 2009).

Posting 'in-character' is not unique to the Something Awful forum. Discussions about and involving narratives in comment sections or threads are frequently held in-character on many creepypasta websites. During my time on the forums, many participants voiced how in-character discourse provides interactivity – the audience and author interact on the same level, and the audience has an impact on the narrative's telling. One participant told me that commenting in-character 'keeps the story alive'. Another explained how in-character comments tend to reinforce 'one of the somewhat unique traits of creepypasta' and cause the narrative to feel 'more real than novels or movies because of interactivity and being posted on message boards/places you could realistically believe someone might post their personal horror story'.

The interactivity occurring here encourages transformation of the text, whether by act of author or audience member (Cover 2006). The storytelling remains communal, despite individual creators arising. The interactivity and audience transformation in the Something Awful forums led to the Slender Man transforming from one single narrative to a detailed mythos. The narrative development of the Tulpa Theory, which is derived from Theosophy (Mikles and Laycock 2015), and the concept of the Slender Man as ever changing due to the inability for the human mind to truly comprehend the supernatural (Louth 2012), grew as a way of revealing and giving importance to this interactivity and agency (Chapter 2). In fact, this agency often typifies creepypasta, through the interactivity, in-character communication and the letting go of authors (Chapter 11).

'In-character' communication highlights, in an interactive way, the force the community holds above the individual. While the author may hold some creative licence, the authority of authorship is often non-existent due to this in-character communication – the ultimate authority is given to the community as opposed to the individual. Even the original creator of the Slender Man, Victor Surge, never stepped in to correct or claim the Slender Man narrative as his own (Slender Nation Podcast, 2011). The Slender Man in this sense was always communal property. This is not unique to the Slender Man, but he is a representation of the way this works for online mass communal storytelling. Other mass communal narratives will be studied in relation to the Slender Man in Chapter 10. The formation and spread of online memes, for instance, are based on similar principles and ideas (Chapter 2).

While this has impacted how the story is told and controlled, it also reveals a lack of control the storytellers have over their own narratives. The minute a story is posted, or an image shared, the narrative is no longer related to author, but is ultimately the property of the community. The individual creates with little ownership. The connection is to the community as opposed to the individual – to the development of mythos above authorship. In this case, the individual reflects the two primary mythemes found in the narratives themselves: facelessness and powerlessness. This lack of authorial connection defines the creepypasta community's engagement with narratives (Chapter 11).

## 4.3.2 Facelessness

According to Lévi-Strauss, a myth, made up of all its variants, can be divided into small fragments called mythemes. These are irreducible and unchanging essential elements of a myth (Lévi-Strauss 1963b). One of the mythemes found in the Slender Man mythology, seen thus far, is facelessness.

The first obvious connection is how the Slender Man is typically depicted as lacking a face. The faceless monster is known to have a strange fascination with an audience, echoing the cosmic fear of Lovecraft by invoking both fear and respect (Lovecraft 1973). The depiction of the faceless man is found frequently in surrealist art, where it symbolizes the human condition (Bohn 1991). This interpretation is similar to what is found with the Slender Man because his facelessness is also put onto the audience.

One of the common threads found in the narratives studied earlier is the categorization of characters into the three groups of *those untouched, those left behind* and *those taken*. The characters in the narratives are often in transition from the first category to the third. In the preceding chapter's analysis of Mr. 47's narrative (Chapter 3), I depicted this transition in Diagram 3.1, in which characters move in only one direction, from being *untouched* to being *taken*.

There is much anxiety accompanying the position of *those left behind*. Many of the narratives involve characters inhabiting this category. As discussed in both Mr. 47 (Chapter 3) and genesplicer's sections, the audience also occupies this position. The act of communal storytelling influences the audience's direct experience of the narratives, as they become intimately aware of the Slender Man narrative through both the reading and participation of the narratives. By partaking in the communal act of storytelling, they have placed themselves into the category of *those left behind*.

This category is also often associated with anxiety. While a transition is needed – and happens – for many of the characters, the ability to move between these three categories does not rest with the character themselves, but rather with the outside force of the Slender Man. The movement from *untouched* to *left behind* is based on experience of the Slender Man, and one must be taken by him in some way (violent or disappearance) to transition to the third category. All transitional agency is given to this secondary and supernatural figure – the Slender Man. This relegates those *left behind* without any agency in their own transitions, rendering it entirely possible to be stuck in the mediatory category.

The anxiety of this position is present in many of the narratives. In Mr. 47's account, this is experienced in how Alice's detailed witness account is disregarded (Mr. 47 2009; Chapter 3). In genesplicer's narrative, twelve children similar to Alice are also having their testimonies ignored. Other narratives on the forum denote this category by depicting characters as either insane or acting 'creatively' – either way they are silenced in any official record. Some storytellers wrote their narratives to resemble official reports. User BooDoug187, for example, wrote reports from an international government organization titled Optic Nerve, whose purpose was to kill the Slender Man, and later reduced to just observe and study him (BooDoug187 2009). Each one was drafted like an email to different members, with names redacted. The redaction feature was found in many of the report-style writings. For BooDoug187 it was names, while others used the redaction to filter out other information as well, resulting in these official reports which claimed a truth to Slender Man encounters as silenced and layered in secrecy. The redactions were carried out by utilizing the 'spoiler' feature on posts. By marking something as a potential spoiler, which some readers may not want disclosed, the text would appear in a censored black box. The writing would be revealed by either highlighting the box or hoovering the mouse over the box. For the narratives which used the redacting feature for censored writing, the words under the censored box are just asterisks when scrolled over. From reading through with the censored black boxes, as they were presented on the forum itself, the post resembled a censored government document.

*Those left behind* are stripped of their voice, an act which forces silence upon these characters in a similar way to the reports which have names and information redacted. All voice and representation are stripped from these characters. When laid against adults, these characters are often considered insane, while if they are children they are simply ignored. Despite not being removed or taken by the Slender Man, these characters are still in some way removed from the society of the *untouched*. Their mediatory category renders them socially faceless.

Even in narratives which would alleviate the anxiety of being disbelieved, silence is still intensely present. The facelessness is social – in the character's separation and lack of representation in the society of the *untouched* and is also present in the format of the narratives. The narratives themselves are silenced, pushing the feeling of facelessness onto the audience through the act of reading or participating in the storytelling. Chaos Hippy, for example, wrote in a discussion on the Slender Man about the social facelessness of knowledge, which plays on the awareness of the reader. The reader in this instance is no longer an idle passive audience member, but actively involved in the storytelling process:

> The more you see him, the more you know, and the more you're doomed. . . .
> And I'll never be able to tell, not in words that can be understood. I can hear him. I can always hear him, every day. Far, far away, but getting closer with each scratching step. Only a matter of time until he comes back, and I learn everything. (2009)

The knowledge and information which are silenced by force on the characters and by censorship in the narrative formats become the greatest enemy for the readers. Knowing is the fear, but what this knowledge is has also been forcibly silenced.

As mentioned earlier, the communal act of creation which defines the Slender Man mythos, and often creepypasta in general, grants authorship to the community as opposed to the individual. Communal authority over a text is not new – Ben-Amos wrote of the desire for folklorists to attribute authority somewhere, often giving this to the entire community when a singular author could not be found (Ben-Amos 1983). The primary difference here is how the digital community and narrative coexist: in non-digital communities, stories arise from pre-established communities; here, communities arise around the narrative itself. Regardless, the authorial authority bypasses the individual and is given instead to the community, leaving the authorial individual faceless as well.

### 4.3.3 Powerlessness

The characters either transitioning, or awaiting transition, between the categories of *untouched*, *left behind* and *taken* have no agency over their own progression.

This agency is instead given over to the secondary and supernatural character of the Slender Man. The characters are powerless in their own social movement. The facelessness inherent in their social categorical position is not a result of their own doing, but due to the actions of another.

Lévi-Strauss understood myth in its ability to move from establishing an awareness of oppositional binaries to their resolution (Lévi-Strauss 1963b). The complication in the mythology of the Slender Man is that all characters, aside from the Slender Man, are without power over their own resolution. The resolution does occur, however, but only in a move towards death. This negative relationship is resolution in Lévi-Strauss's concept of a resolution but differs from other more positive resolutions due to the inherent powerlessness the characters have in their own transitions.

The powerlessness of the characters is also extended to the audience in a similar way to how the audience was impacted by the facelessness mytheme. The visual narratives, encapsulated by digitally manipulated images, have a sense of control instilled in them. This control is kept away from the audience, who is forced to view only what has been presented to them. A well-made image will leave little evidence of the manipulation, even to a well-trained viewer. But powerlessness also extends to the audience in the form of the actual narrative. The Tulpa Theory demonstrates this quite well. The concept arose as a way of allowing the narrative to exist as an urban legend despite its origins being known. Tulpas are a Theosophical concept (Mikles and Laycock 2015), where the power of thought leads to a physical manifestation of that thought (Besant and Leadbetter 1925). Here, the power of everyone's thoughts and contributions has led to the once-fictional Slender Man to now be in physical existence (see Chapter 2). The Tulpa Theory reflects the lack of authorial control the contributors working on the Slender Man mythos truly have.

The characters usually most affected by the Slender Man in the narrative presented are those typically most powerless in society. In order to understand this better, let us first be reminded of the natural/supernatural dichotomy and the hierarchical human mediatory category first depicted in the section on Victor Surge (Diagram 3.1).

The hierarchy of human society in this middle category of the natural/supernatural oppositional framework also mimics a social hierarchy: children are the most powerless, and adult males are the most powerful. Racial dynamics are not well exemplified in these narratives, as many of the narratives do not mention race. Accordingly, I will be focusing on social hierarchies based on age and identified gender. The intervention of the Slender Man progresses the loss of this mediatory category – the victim of the Slender Man attack is moved from this human mediatory category to one of the more stable categories. The differences in how this progression takes place is reflected in the differences in the hierarchies within this mediatory category which relates directly to power relations. The typically more powerful members of the mediatory society are transitioned to the nature category through forceful and violent death, while the more vulnerable and thus powerless members of society are treated to the supernatural category by being taken through seemingly magical disappearance. The mentally infirmed, or at least those regarded as such by the *untouched*, can be added to the child or adult female category. Many of the victims are regarded as the most socially powerless: the mentally infirmed, children and, sometimes, women.

Mr. 47's narrative describes Katrina's kidnapping as not being forced – Katrina is portrayed as complicit in her sister's account (Mr. 47 2009; Chapter 3). Another narrative by Hog Inspector describes the finding of many bodies which were victims of the Slender Man, all without marks of abrasion (Hog Inspector 2009). These narratives insinuate a certain level of control levied on the victims. The victims are so powerless to the control of the Slender Man that they do not need retraining before the violence – the Slender Man is too powerful for them and thus does not even need typical restraints as they are overly powerless to even warrant fighting back as a possibility.

## 4.3 The structure

Most of the mythemes present in the Something Awful forum narratives were that which separated the Slender Man as something supernatural rather than a more human type of monster: his height, his facelessness or inhuman features, the appendages and so forth. Much of this is discussed in the sensory codes; sounds were associated with the Slender Man, though he mostly was obscured. Those who catch glances of the supernatural obscured are often those who fall into the category of the *Transformed*. Sight specifically is connected to normal society.

We can begin by taking the three categories as depicted in Diagram 3.1 by pairing them down into three main categories. The first, associated with This World and the *untouched*, we should continue to call the 'Untouched'. This will help to distinguish it from the idea of the physical touch and change which occurs in the following categories. The category of *taken*, missing and the Outside should from now on be called the 'Removed'. Most of the focus of this category is on those abducted or killed, and thus allow us to focus more on ideas of social removal. The last category – the *left behind*, deformed and transformed – we should from now on call it the 'Transformed'. Using the descriptor from Aleph Null's narrative, we can see how *left behind* characters in the other sections were emotionally and socially Transformed through their experience. The focus on these categories is thus more socially determined: those present in society, those Transformed away from society and those completely removed from society.

Rewritten to allow these new categorical names, the movement taken and the triadic nature of the categories, the structure begins to look more like the following diagram (Diagram 4.1).

The movement is only in one direction, moving from Untouched, to Transformed to Removed. Once removed, you cannot become Transformed, nor once Transformed become Untouched. A more detailed discussion of this and how the relations occur between each category will be revealed in a later section. The triadic nature depicted is a variant on the more traditional Lévi-Strauss approach which normally only sees binaries in opposition (1963b; 1969) – the third mediatory category here, for Lévi-Strauss, would only be within the overlap of the two more strict binary categories.

However, the triadic model is not completely unheard of in structuralism. Georges Dumézil used a triadic model for his analysis of Norse mythology (Dumézil 1977), and Rodney Needham sketched out a variety of more complex structuralist possibilities including a triadic model (Needham 1979). Most importantly for our purposes is Seth Kunin's use of a triadic structure regarding Mormonism (Kunin 2003).

Like Needham, Kunin sees the structural levels as being more 'plastic' and capable of not only dyadic models of opposition, but triadic and even more

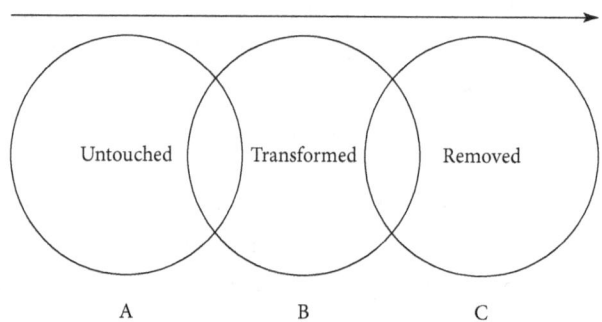

**Diagram 4.1** Current structural equation.

complex (Kunin 2003, 109). Kunin's structural model for Mormonism is representative of the system of citizenship in the United States, the country in which Mormonism was founded. At first, the individual is a complete foreigner. But the process is not as simple as going from foreigner to citizen, as there is a middle stage in which the individual has a green card – is no longer foreign, but not quite a citizen. The process of becoming Mormon is similar. From outsider, the individual can become transformed through a process of not only accepting the faith but also a rewriting of genealogies, until finally the individual becomes a full member (Kunin 2003). Like our structure, Kunin's movement is also a one-way progression. It is much easier to become a member then to give up membership. The connection Kunin found to the United States is important. Most of the groups involved in Slender Man, including the Something Awful forum, are on English-speaking websites, resulting in a higher proportion of users from the United States.

Before dedicating ourselves to the triadic structure, we should first consider what a triadic structure actually means. By making the Transformed their own category, rather than an overlap between two dyadic categories, what emphasis are we gaining, and what may we be losing?

The primary consequence of the triadic formula is an extension of the mediatory category – from no longer simple overlap to its own full category. The effect of making the Transformed its own category is important specifically to the study of the Slender Man mythos in one very important way: the narratives themselves put great emphasis on this category. The mediatory stage, of being removed from society – yet not as completely removed as the category of the Removed – leaves the characters who find themselves in this state in a great deal of anxiety and loss. Like the Untouched, the Transformed are still present – still technically part of the society. They participate and are present, just like the Untouched, and yet are altered. Frequently, the Untouched do not regard the Transformed as fully present, nor do they see them as fully present. They are one step Removed from normal society. They are missing knowledge, but not full knowledge, so they have the knowledge like the Untouched, but are beginning to miss it like the Removed. The Transformed, as considered almost human in Aleph Null's text, and the children in both Mr. 47's and genesplicer's narratives are disregarded and demeaned as being too insane or too childish to have their testimonies count for the present society. The Transformed as a separate category, therefore, put stress on the importance of this location, as a mediatory category between the two more stable categories.

Put another way, the middle stage, which is typically a temporary liminal stage, can become permanent. As a prolonged example, let us consider the typical dyadic structure, with mediatory overlap, as a categorical representation of a ritual. One begins in the first category – say the uninitiated society. After the ritual, they will become part of a different segment of the society, one which is apart and initiated. The ritual which leads to this change is a liminal point, where one is in both categories simultaneously. In this case, extending this mediatory position to be its own separate category (thereby making a triad) seems unnecessary. However, let us consider what would happen if it were possible to be lost in the ritual – to be stuck forever in the ritual. Now, the initiate cannot move outside of this middle position in either direction: they are forever in the liminal stage of both, and yet not fully of either. This is what is occurring in the structure found here. The liminal mediatory position is one which is extended, hauntingly providing the possibility that the initiate, or the character, or the audience member, even, may never leave.

Much of the analysis of this structure, as well as that leading to the structure found here, have mediatory categories: departmentalizing of characters, actions and audience members in a section between two more stable oppositional groups. Most of the characters in the narratives are in the process of their transition from *those untouched* to *those left behind* or are already placed in the *left behind* mediatory category. The audience also frequently finds themselves in this category. In addition, most humans are placed in a human middle category between the natural and the supernatural.

Lévi-Strauss's analysis of myth often incorporates the oppositional framework and the categories which do not quite fit in the binary system, and the progression of the myth also comes with a progression towards a resolution (Lévi-Strauss 1963b). Mediatory categories present a mythic problem: an anomaly, which, however dealt with, demonstrates how the community in question treats such anomalies. For example, the Christian view of Jesus is a character who is in a mediatory category between divinity and humanity and is regarded favourably. Despite his positive regard, the anomaly still needs to progress by the end of the myth to a resolution, and the end of Jesus's mythic story is a death and a movement to fall more firmly in the divinity category. A less subjectively positive resolution is not abnormal. Lévi-Strauss examined one such resolution which required death for resolution in his essay 'The Story of Asdiwal' where the hero Asdiwal dies as a rock on the mountain (Lévi-Strauss 1973c).

Taking only one narrative into consideration, for example the Mr. 47 newspaper article, there appears to be very little resolution between the binary categories. Alice, our *left behind* character, has no anxiety or resolution solving her mediatory status. However, when we extend to the full Slender Man mythos, we are able to see the resolution take form. The horror of the singular narrative is caused by the heavy attention on the mediatory category and the negative understanding presented about this category. All characters in this mediatory category are stripped of social representation and power, and a high level of anxiety is associated with this category due to this social facelessness and lack of power.

When it comes to the relationship categories have with one another, especially in the way of mediation, there are three types of relation which could occur. The first is a positive relationship, often represented by a (+) in structural equations. In a positive relationship, there is movement between the two categories, where something or someone can move from one category to the other. The second kind is a negative relationship, represented by a (-) in equations. Negative relationships do not allow overlap or movement between the categories. There is no ability for movement or transition between the categories. The third type is neutral (n) where there is only some movement and overlap.

The progression in our present model, as is for Kunin's Mormon triadic model, is that the social movement through the three categories is only a one-way progression. The Untouched move to the Transformed, which in turn are the Removed. Those Removed do not return to being Transformed, nor do the Transformed ever truly return to being Untouched. Essentially this means the Untouched has a positive relationship with the Transformed, and the Transformed has a positive relationship with the Removed. However, the Removed has a negative relationship with the Transformed, and the Transformed with the Untouched. The positive relationships are only in one direction. The movement, however, is performed entirely from an outside source, the Slender Man. The Slender Man belongs to none of the mentioned categories, and his position outside of this context will be explored in Section 4.4. His function here, more importantly, is to be the one who moves and defines one's placement in these sociological categories. Due to this, if one is moved from Untouched to Transformed, suddenly finding themselves in a category dictated by its relationship to madness, childishness and a treatment of general disbelief, there is no way for them to return to the Untouched. Theoretically, and in none of the stories described, is it possible for them to also move themselves to the Taken category. Suicide, which could be a solution to the anxiety problem of the Transformed, is not explored in the stories analysed so far. Thus, it is fully possible for a character to find themselves forever trapped in the Transformed category. The Transformed category is an extended position, the middle stage, a mediatory position, between the Untouched and the Removed. Mediators are typically a troubling position to be in, and this is felt by those in this category. And due to the movement being controlled by an outside force, it is possible for those in this category to feel as if they cannot progress. Due to the strong and lasting effects of this category, it seems necessary to consider the Transformed as a category of their own.

The creation of a middle position in our triad, and thereby making it a triad, is one with heavy consequence. It takes what is typically considered the normative mediator and extends it to be something more than a categorical position in which one can move away, but also can remain stuck within.

## 4.4 The uncategorizable Slender Man

As can be seen from the aforementioned categories of Untouched, Transformed and Removed, the Slender Man fits into none of these categories. He is not Untouched, he is not a Transformed member of the Untouched society, and while is not a member of the Untouched society or of the Transformed, he is also not Removed. The categories are also determined almost fully by him and his interactions with these characters. The movement from Untouched to Transformed happens upon interaction of some sort with him, and the Removed are removed from society by him as well. While he is not a direct member of any category, he is directly responsible for these categories.

In Jeffrey Cohen's work, which set out the main dimensions of the interdisciplinary field of monster theory, he determined one of the theories in which monsters function as a determination of 'categorical crisis' (Cohen 1996, 6). Even though anthropology has made few strides to join the interdisciplinarity of monster theory (Musharbash and Presterudstuen 2014), structuralism can demonstrate this type of monster well, as it functions on the understanding of categories and finding elements which do not fit. Mary Douglas, for example, found that in Israeli food laws, the pig sat outside the structural categories, and was thus seen as monstrous (Douglas 2001). The pig, according to Douglas, is considered monstrous by its inability to fit fully into a category. By this understanding, we can see the monstrous nature of the Slender Man, highlighted not only by his monstrous actions but also his fearsome inability to fit into the categorical understandings of the social constructions formulated. His fearsome nature, therefore, comes not only from a lack of agency on behalf of those who forcibly move to various categories but also from his inability to be fully understood in categorical notions. He sits outside these categories and demonstrates a crisis in them.

In this sense, he could be a form of mediator, but one who sits in none of the categories rather than in all of them. Although he sits in none of the categories, his nature and power have established the categories themselves and therefore it could be argued that he sits within them all. It is a lack of relationship with him which defines the Untouched, interaction with him which defines the Transformed, and it is his actions which take the Removed.

The horror element of the narrative alludes to a more negative view of the mediator. He is one to be feared, and the movement induced is not wanted. Typically in structuralism, a mediator is either regarded as an abomination (such as the Israeli pig) or deified (as the Christian Jesus). The Slender Man is a complicated mediator, where the horror element regards the mediating element as a negative abomination, but one which is also in some ways deified. One cannot get rid of the Slender Man, he is unable to be killed or defeated, but he is also regarded as powerfully supernatural. Although the narrative level (N) is often disregarded in structuralism, I think the N level here, which is in the genre of horror, helps to demonstrate that the mediating here is a deified abomination. Although regarded as powerfully supernatural, he is not to be worshipped or praised, but feared.

### 4.4.1 Playing with the monster

The use of 'in-character' communication is the way in which users engage with the Slender Man narrative. The conversation is truly as a character, not a genuine expression of how they believe. If one were to directly ask the community if the Slender Man is 'real', they would firmly state the negative. However, the phrasing could be given slightly differently – is the Slender Man communally important? The answer would be more likely a yes here. The extent, and the why, of its importance is what this manuscript seeks to discover. But it is important here to see the playing of the monster as an important element of the storytelling process.

The concept of 'serious play' in relation to the Slender Man has been discussed already in Chapter 2 regarding the various religious literacies used in relation to the Slender Man's description and treatment (Chapter 2). Play, which is both serious and non-serious simultaneously regardless of circumstance, is at work with the Slender Man. Its form is playful – it mimics formats of physical world documents and elements. The narration is playful – it is given in-character, with narrators performing their story like true storytellers.

Mythic performance is still present, just in more textual or visual forms. These forms are part of the myth. As discussed in Chapter 1 regarding theory and method, the definition of myth for our purposes here is a narrative, or similar cultural artefact, which is used by a community or an individual in order to structure their understanding of themselves and the world around them. The forms the narratives take for the Slender Man is important in revealing these structures. These forms are chosen for a reason.

As discussed in Section 4.4, the Slender Man, as far as we know so far, is not directly in the structural formation. He impacts the structure, and he guides the structure, but does not have a direct place within it. There are elements which are the cogs driving the structure (Miles-Watson 2009b) while not fully being within the structure. The monsters who do not fit the structural equations can demonstrate to us a great understanding of the fundamental mechanics of the structure we are looking at. Even though the storytellers on the Something Awful forum are telling their stories playfully, the narratives still reveal fundamental information regarding their social understandings, cultures, and what they see as fearful and monstrous.

## 4.5 Conclusion

The stories on the Something Awful forum were, here, separated into two different chapters in order to give them fuller attention, as they do make up the bulk of the beginning narratives. These are often the ones new storytellers turn to when they begin to form their own narratives, which is why it is important to spend two chapters on the exploration of these narratives.

Through the last two chapters, we have sorted through mythemes and narrative elements in order to attempt to garner a glimpse of the structure underneath. The first chapter on Something Awful was a first attempt, but this second chapter gave us a better grasp. The structure we have determined is a triadic structure, with a prolonged mediatory category which sits in between the two more stable structural categories of those in normal society, dubbed the Untouched, and those completely gone, or the Removed. Most of these categories reveal society's connection to itself. The Untouched have marginalized the Transformed, pushing them away from what is considered normal society.

But the Something Awful forums are not the only place where the Slender Man narratives are being told and shared. These narrative levels may change, especially in genre or format, but the question is whether the structure also shifts, and if it does why it may. As the narrative grew, even simultaneously with the growth of the narratives on the Something Awful forum, they began to appear in other places on the online environment. Something Awful user ce gars posted on the forum regarding finding the Slender Man on a student film project a friend of his had. The next chapter looks at the videos he began to upload on YouTube, called Marble Hornets.

# 5

# Marble Hornets

At the Something Awful forum's height of Slender Man creation, re-creation and sharing, a user by the name of ce gars wrote a post explaining how he had received some video tapes of a friend's student film project which had been abandoned with no explanation. He began to post video entries of his search through the various tapes and his investigation into what had happened to his friend. The user worked through YouTube, posting links to the videos on the forum thread. The student film, called Marbled Hornets, was the name of the YouTube channel, and he began to upload sections he 'found' from these strange films (ce gars 2009).

Marble Hornets mimics the mockumentary style made popular by movies like *The Blair Witch Project*. The set-up begins with Jay, our initial Something Awful forum poster, commentating in basic white text on a black screen. The footage consists of scenes from the student film, as well as other tapes, all supposedly found in the mess of tapes obtained from his friend. The tapes were said to be jumbled, and so they appear out of chronological sequence, and were somehow combined with random other tapes of his friend, Alex, filming himself doing mundane tasks. As strange things begin to also happen to Jay, he begins filming himself too.

Marble Hornets demonstrates in a visual sense the elements of playing with believability the narratives on Something Awful presented. The images and captions from Victor Surge's approaches, for example, are presented as if they were images discovered (Victor Surge 2009a, 2009b, 2009c; see Chapter 3). Mr. 47's newspaper article is styled and written to emulate the way newspapers are read (Mr. 47 2009; see Chapter 3). The pseudo-documentary style of Marble Hornets echoes the way 'found footage' videos may be presented. Playing with the 'as if' presentation, the creators of Marble Hornets are playing with notions of reality in a similar way to the Something Awful forums. This type of presentation is connected to the debate between the difference of folklore and fakelore, as the narrative construction often echoes folklore, both in the way the narratives are created and spread (Blank 2009; Blank 2012; Howard 2015), but also in the themes and elements the narrative draws on (see Chapter 2). The narrative of believability is typically a facet of creepypasta (see Chapters 2, 4, 9 and 11).

The narrative jumps around in time: sometimes presenting old tapes in a lack of strict time sequence, sometimes the 'real time' filming of Jay and his trials. When there was a gap in video uploads for the channel, there was a gap in time for the story. For example, when the channel was without uploads for several months, the next video to be uploaded explained what had occurred in the narrative during that gap in time (Entry 27).[1]

The narrative is, thus, confusing, out of sequence and very much tied to the format the narrative is presented in. The YouTube upload sequence is made a part of the narrative – the Twitter exchanges and discussions on the Something Awful forum and elsewhere help to paint a fuller image of the narrative as well. All posts made were in-character, meaning the Twitter and exchanges made outside of the YouTube context remained within the character of Jay, and presented as if the actions undertaken in the film were real. The believability of the narrative is extended, so it includes not only the way the narrative is presented and told but also in the transmedia (Jenkins 2006) aspect of the narrative. Characters in the narrative even sometimes refer to the YouTube channel. In a video entry of an argument between an actor in the film (Tim) and Jay, for instance, Tim is made angry by having done an online search for 'Marble Hornets' and finding the YouTube channel the audience is currently watching (Entry 59).

The jumps in time, jumps in footage source and, as is found later in the series, jumps in narrator, all serve to confuse the viewer. The timeline is messy at best, and there are often gaps of knowledge. The constant presence of 'the Operator', the Marble Hornets' name for the Slender Man, who appears in the distorted films yet only occasionally referenced by the characters, all confuse and distance the viewer. The viewer wants to scream out and explain, but there is little one can do. The ability to interact with the characters on all formats helps to immerse the viewer in a way which was almost impossible before online communication. The ability for a narrative to exist all around a viewer, in many different formats and contexts, is unique to the virtual communication and storytelling, deemed by Jenkins as transmedia storytelling (Jenkins 2006).

---

[1] Due to the large number of entries, the citations will simply refer to the title of the video, which is often simply the entry number. The full playlist, of all entries, is Marble Hornets 2009–14.

The viewer, the audience member, is confused and separated. The process of viewing the narrative, and the ability to interact on all fronts, makes them a character themselves. In-character communication allows for the audience to directly take part, and in doing so become part of the narrative themselves. Their confusion leads to an element of lost knowledge, their anonymous nature similar to the masked figures in the narrative. The audience, through their interaction with the narrative, are *Transformed* themselves.

## 5.1 The Marble Hornets' story

As mentioned previously, the channel was set up in reference to the act of sifting through old film tapes, so the order of events witnessed by the audience member is non-chronological to the actual series of events. Due to this, it is somewhat difficult to relay a shorthand summary of the events of Marble Hornets. What follows is my attempt to lay down a summary of the myth as experienced by the audience.

The story follows Jay, the Something Awful forum user ce gars, who is compiling the videos and documentary he finds. He is searching for answers to why his friend Alex dropped the film project and moved away. There are two actors in the film: Tim and Brian. The first video entries show Alex sneaking around his house late at night and seeing a strange figure (Entry 1; Entry 6), driving out in search of something (Entry 2) and filming himself in a form of self-surveillance (Entry 3). Many of the clips are random, without much context, and includes visual tears, or when the video splits randomly with a line down the middle, and audio distortions. Often these video and audio distortions are later associated with the Slender Man's presence related to obscure senses for Chapter 3 (discussed more in Section 5.2). Soon, Jay begins to do more direct investigation and seeks out some of the previous actors to ask them questions, under the guise of attempting to finish the film (Entry 15). He seeks out abandoned houses, which were once where some of the actors lived (Entry 16).

Jay now begins to lose small bits of memory, and so begins to film himself in a similar way to Alex's strange videos. A masked man (called Masky by the community, and so will be here as well) breaks into the house but does nothing to harm or steal from Jay (Entry 19). The masked nature of these characters brings up a connection to the facelessness mytheme discussed in Chapter 4 and will be explored further. Jay continues to go through the Marble Hornets film and finds old footage of some of the actors behaving weird and coughing frequently (Entry 20). Searching in a strange location outside, Jay finds another of Alex's tapes which has a confession in which Alex says he remembers nothing and that everyone is 'gone' (Entry 22) and he is going to burn his tapes. Jay experiences strangeness in his own home, where doors sometimes open and he walks through them but does not end up on the other side of the door. He has no memory of leaving and going anywhere, and he vows to find Alex (Entry 24; Entry 26).

Seven months pass without any upload. As mentioned previously, when the video series continues, Jay comments he has no memory of the last seven months (Entry 27), waking up in a hotel in an area he does not recognize. He meets a woman in the same hotel named Jessica, who causes audio and visual disruptions when she appears on camera. She admits to having the same strange occurrences as Jay but then disappears. Jay is attacked by Masky when he finally opens the safe in his room.

At this point, the entries begin to go back in time to fill in the missing seven months. In these, Masky is revealed to be Tim (Entry 35), one of the actors, who Alex (apparently having reunited with Jay at some point) quite violently attacks. This reveals a sudden level of violence which until now has been only hinted at or quietly demonstrated. Another hooded figure (called Hoody from now on) seems to be following Jay around. Jay finds footage from a chest camera Alex was wearing, which shows Jay and Alex returning to a house Alex and his girlfriend Amy had previously escaped from. The Slender Man appears again, which brings Alex to a debilitating coughing fit (Entry 43).

Jay sneaks into Alex's house to steal something, but is stopped by the Slender Man. He manages to flee but grabs a spare key to Alex's house on the way out (Entry 46). Jay begins to stalk Alex. Footage from the filming of the movie Marble Hornets captures Alex and Brian, the other actor, in an abandoned building. The Slender Man appears here, causing Alex to disappear somewhere, leaving Brian alone in the building to find Tim in a corner coughing (Entry 51). Alex later leads Jay and Jessica into the woods where he attempts to shoot them, but they get away due to Masky.

The series now shifts to take place in 'real' time, where Jay finds Tim again, who reveals he knows nothing and remembers nothing. He blames Jay for bringing it all back to him, as he found out about the YouTube channel (Entry 59). Jay also receives from Hoody information on Tim's past and present mental health issues.

Jay and Tim continue their investigation together, and discover Alex's burnt and buried tapes. Footage reveals when Jay first requested the tapes from Alex, which led to the creation of the channel, Alex attacks him. Jay says he has no memory of this occurring (Entry 71). When Jay finds out Tim has been hiding a tape from him, he attacks him and steals it. This reveals Masky and Hoody stealing Jessica from the hotel. Tim ties up Jay and leaves him, but Hoody gives Jay a knife to free himself.

They all end up at the old university's grounds and encounter Alex with the Slender Man. Jay dies in the altercation (Entry 80). Tim takes over the filming now. Tim chases Hoody through the university, but they are teleported from setting to setting, including many of the old locations they had previously encountered strange events or the Slender Man in. Tim ends up shoving Hoody off a balcony, killing him. Hoody is revealed as Brian (Entry 83). Tim confronts Alex, who has been attempting to use the Slender Man himself. Tim ends up killing Alex and escaping (Entry 86). The last shot is of Tim visiting Jessica and leaving (Entry 87).

## 5.2 Mytheme breakdown

As is hopefully obvious, or more to the point *less* obvious, this narrative has many elements occurring over a large stretch of time. There are large discrepancies in the chronological order of the material, and video elements not included in the former summary are supposedly uploaded by a different person which alludes to mysteries of other sides of the narrative. To make things slightly easier to digest, we will break down the former story by different elements, primarily mythemes related to or of characters, locations and other story elements.

### 5.2.1 Marble Hornets' characters

We have six characters who appear in the narrative. Four men are working on the film project in some capacity: Jay, Alex, Brian and Tim. We also have two women, Jessica and Amy, who are not quite as present in the narrative as the men. Amy is never seen by the audience and is mentioned by Alex as missing, and Jessica's presence comes in and out. We also have the main antagonist, the Slender Man, who is often referred to as 'the Operator' in this narrative. There are also two masked antagonists, Masky and Hoody, whose identities are later revealed as Tim and Brian, respectively.

Due to the heavily visual nature of the narrative, we have an obvious demonstration of when the Operator is present. The audio and visual tears demonstrate when his influence is present. The affect this has on the characters are thus made more obvious. The coughing fits experienced by the characters are often following the visual and auditory influence of the Operator. Similarly, we see a growing inclination to violence the further the narrative progresses. The beginning starts with concern for a friend, and it ends with violent deaths. We can begin to sketch a dichotomy between different characteristics of the human actors based on whether they are being affected or unaffected by the Slender Man, or the Operator:

| Unaffected | Affected |
| --- | --- |
| Healthy | Unhealthy |
| Friendly | Violent |

The coughing fits as a sign of being unhealthy are found frequently throughout the narrative. The stronger the fits, the more debilitating it is for the character affected. For instance, in an early entry, Tim is seen as having issues with coughing (Entry 20) but despite acting slightly off, is able to function. In contrast, during an encounter with the Slender Man, Alex is brought to his knees coughing (Entry 43). The drastic nature of the more extreme coughing fits demonstrates how close to the level of 'unhealthy' the category can truly reach.

For some affected by the Slender Man, there is also a differentiation of identity. Masky and Hoody both act and think differently than when they are either Tim or Brian. When returned back to Tim, for example, he holds no memory of his actions, or the events held with Masky, making it seem as if these are two different identities which are active or inactive based on the level of affect the Operator has over them.

| Unaffected | Affected |
| --- | --- |
| Tim | Masky |
| Brian | Hoody |

Marble Hornets was one of the first Slender Man-based narratives which introduced the idea of 'proxies': humans who are controlled by the Slender Man and do things, they would normally not do, on his behalf. Tim and Brian acting as Masky and Hoody demonstrate this in action. Tim and Brian act one way, but Masky and Hoody act another despite it being the same physical body. They also retain no memory of their time as proxies. Their entire selves are essentially taken.

The facelessness of the Slender Man is reflected in those he affects. The physical facelessness is brought to the social standing of those left behind. They become stripped from their social position and pushed to the margins. They become faceless. The removal of identity from the proxies, such as Masky, is the next step, and the literal stripping of their face echoes the stripping of their identity.

Essentially, this leaves us with strong differential categories and the differences which exist between those who are affected and those who are not:

| Unaffected | Affected |
|---|---|
| Healthy | Unhealthy |
| Friendly | Violent |
| Tim | Masky |
| Brian | Hoody |

The categorical differences are set between the two: one is either healthy, friendly and themselves; or they are unhealthy, violent and working as a proxy. The characters themselves are unable to move from one category to another freely. When acting as Masky, Tim is unable to remove himself from this position, but can only become Tim again when the Operator wills it. Thus, the Slender Man is acting as a transitory figure. It is only through him one can shift categorical positions.

Like the previous analysis done with Something Awful, the Slender Man is functioning as a transitioning or mediating factor – moving people through categories and placements without the consent or control of the characters themselves. The Marble Hornets given name, 'The Operator', is well suited to his role in the structure – controlling and manipulating from the outside. In our study of the Something Awful forum, we saw the Slender Man acting as a transitional character between the social categories of Untouched, Transformed and Removed.

So far, we have more of a diachronic view of Marble Hornets, splitting up the categories into Affected and Unaffected, while we have a triadic nature in the Something Awful forums (Chapter 4). The Something Awful narratives were focused more on the transition between Untouched and Transformed, and in particular the anxiety of the Transformed category. Marble Hornets, on the other hand, is much more concerned with the transition from Transformed to Removed. Few, if any, of the characters are completely unaware of the Slender Man, though few seem able to understand him or even make reference to his presence, except when he appears, and they feel the urge to run. The question of who he is and what his nature consists of is not a concern for the characters involved.

However, the question remains how similar Marble Hornets is, structurally speaking, to the Something Awful structure we found in the previous chapter. In this section, we focused much more on two of the characters Tim and Brian and their actions as proxies than the others.

### 5.2.2 Mytheme breakdown

As discussed earlier, the various aspects of characters are determined by the extent to which the Operator is affecting them. When affected, they tend to be unhealthy (coughing), violent (random attacks on people once considered friends) and losing a level of self (lack of memory and proxies). The shifting is determined by an outside force, and a character has little control over their own movement. Sketched out differently, these mythemes can be written as:

$$\text{Unaffected : Health : Friendly :: Affected : Unhealthy : Violent}$$
$$\phantom{xxxxxxxxxxx}A\phantom{xxxxxxxxxxxxxxxxxxx}B$$

The characters involved in the narratives are healthy, friendly to one another and essentially unaffected by the presence of the Slender Man. As soon as they become Affected, the other traits also follow; they become unhealthy and turn to violence, even towards one another. The first group, A, can be described as themselves – characters who still have knowledge and memories of who they are. Category B, on the other hand, are those not acting as themselves – the characters are losing their memories and their self-control. Those in Category A are related to those still Untouched – and are seen more clearly in the scenes and episodes of Marble Hornets which show the characters before they are truly affected, or Transformed, by the Slender Man's existence. Category B is more fully seen in those who have already Transformed.

In our former dyad, Category A – associated with being healthy, friendly and seeking knowledge – is our Untouched. Category B – with those being unhealthy, violent and losing knowledge – is most closely related to the Transformed. The Removed are those who lack all descriptors of mythemes. A character's transition from Untouched to Removed, for example, are those who move from being healthy, unhealthy and, finally, to having no health. Despite how the Removed are those lacking mythemes, they are still an important category as that which is in direct contrast to the Untouched. The Untouched is representative of normal society, the Removed are those no longer part of society.

While our first overview of the characters in Marble Hornets alluded to a more diachronic structure, we have yet to introduce the more dynamic last transition: the transition from Transformed to Removed. While all three categories were present in the Something Awful forum, the primary emphasis was on the transition from Untouched to Transformed. For Marble Hornets, we see both primary transitions. The first half of Marble Hornets, like the Something Awful forum, focuses on the transition from Untouched to Transformed. The first half begins with our narrator, Jay, being in the Untouched category, seeing something strange and wanting to know the truth behind the mystery of the abandoned film project. But the notion of the narrative shifts subtly to suddenly focus on the second transition, from Transformed to Removed. The concern with knowledge becomes a concern for survival. These three categories can be detailed as provided:

| Untouched | Transformed | Removed |
| --- | --- | --- |
| Healthy | Unhealthy | No health |
| Friendly | Violent | Removed via violence |
| Themselves | Act unlike themselves | Themselves gone |
| Normal society | Social outcast | No longer in society |

When the normal understandings of society become affected by the Slender Man, or the Operator, they become unhealthy. Coughing fits tend to become the sign the character is becoming affected by the Operator's presence. Some Transformed characters are also found with bottles of pills, a visual demonstration of the unhealthy nature of the category and their position. Sometimes, the concept of unhealthy is also in relation to mental unhealth. Like some of the characters in the Something Awful forum, those who have become Transformed may be also seen as insane.

Characters in Marble Hornets also started friendly with one another, a depiction of university students helping each other for a friend's film project. As the Operator's presence began to affect them more, the characters turned more violent. Some scenes had characters attacking one another without provocation. Proxies attacked seemingly indiscriminately. The movement shifted from friendly to violent, with an increase in violent actions. The more the Operator's presence affects them, the more violent they become, until it culminates in the death of most of the characters.

Marble Hornet's narrative begins with the main character, Jay, seeking knowledge regarding what happened to his friend, Alex. As more becomes revealed, as well as the presence of the Operator becoming known, characters begin to lose memory, moments of time taken away. Jay began filming himself, and not remembering bits of time which were captured on camera as he reviewed the footage. The loss of memory begins to overwhelm more than the sought knowledge. As characters move to the category of the Transformed, they move from those who are seeking knowledge to those losing knowledge – knowledge of memory and of their selves. The loss of self is demonstrated in the actions and appearance of the proxies, which will be discussed in the next section.

This middle category touches the two more stable categories. The nature of the unhealthy has been already discussed, but the touch of death leads to a greater form of a character's unhealthy status. Violence often leads to the Removed category, though this is intermittent, and so the actions go back and forth between the two levels of violence and friendly. Most notably is its connection to the wider society. The social outcasts of the Transformed are still technically present in society, but are ostracized – essentially, they are socially dead. The Transformed category are the mediatory position between the other two. It is stretched out to its own special category due to the importance given to this position in the narratives.

### 5.2.3 Locations in Marble Hornets

Due to the nature of the visual presentation of Marble Hornets, setting and location become almost more important and more present in the narrative than it was in Something Awful. Where Something Awful used pseudo-government documents and emails, Marble Hornets uses easy-to-obtain cameras, simple settings and a pseudo-documentary style presentation. As the narrative of Marble Hornets progresses, the more locations become problematized. The first introduction to this is when Jay begins filming himself, and in a not-remembered stupor, opened one door in his house, walked through, but did not end up on the other side.

Just as characters are affected and changed by the Slender Man's presence, so is the landscape the characters tread. The changing of Jay's rooms is the strongest introduction to this concept. Home is familiar and safe, and the transformation of this to a place which is unsafe, and even somewhere that leads to not-home easily, is a horrific transformation. Like Something Awful, we see a transformation from familiar to unfamiliar, from Untouched to Transformed. The familiar is altered by the Slender Man's presence into something no longer representative of the safety familiarity the character has come to expect.

We see this progression take place as the characters constantly shift locations the more affected, by the Slender Man, they become. The proxies are found to be sleeping in an abandoned building. Abandoned buildings are a physical manifestation of the no-longer familiar. Where once was safety and home (or work, or hospital a place of healing), is now unsafe and alone. The process of abandonment is also reflected in the social abandoning experienced by those *Transformed*. The more the Slender Man has affected Jay's life, the more he moved and becomes transient in transient locations. He moves from hotel to hotel, no longer in solid home, the setting reflects a transitory home, a temporary home, defined by its unfamiliarity. Location, then, also reflects the underlying structure found thus far.

## 5.3 Marble Hornets' structure

The major narrative difference Marble Hornets adds to the Slender Man mythos is the concept of proxies. As the Operator, or the Slender Man, affects some characters, they completely lose themselves within the process. Brian, for instance, loses all aspects of who he is as a person and becomes the hooded and masked proxy figure, sometimes referred to as Hoody. Tim, too, changes into a proxy figure, Masky. Proxies introduce an interesting new element to the narrative of the Slender Man myths. They appear to be a Transformed within the Transformed. But how do they fit in more structurally speaking?

If the Transformed carry elements of both the Untouched and the Removed, so do the proxies to a much stronger extent. The other characters in the Transformed category discussed earlier are those who attempt to still be part of the society of the Untouched – they are still present, as they are not fully removed from society, and still attempting to garner knowledge, therefore demonstrating their slightly more ignorant position. But they are also forever changed by their experience of the Slender Man. Voicing this knowledge, a part of the knowledge the Untouched do not have, separates them from this Untouched society. They are considered as not fully part of 'normal' society. They are kept separate – experiencing a social death while not moving fully into the category of the Removed.

The proxies are a much stronger version of the former. Like the Transformed, the Slender Man's presence affects the proxies. This affect causes them to become violent. The violence is also present in non-proxy figures in Marble Hornets. For example, we see Alex attacking Jay even though Alex is not seen as a proxy. Jay also attacks Brian for the tape being kept from him. The main difference between the two is the agency involved in this violence. Even though the change in Alex and Jay to become violent is caused by the Slender Man's influence, they still actively choose to attack who they do and how. In contrast, the proxies retain no memory of their actions (which will be discussed later), with the implication being the plan for the attack and attack itself were not fully of their cognitive doing. Here, they are the embodiment of the lack of agency characters have over their structural movement. Their actions are purely of the Slender Man's scheming.

The proxies are also just as separated from society as those seen as Transformed. They have been removed from the workings of society in a more manifest form than we have seen in Transformed previously. While the Transformed still attend events, go to work and so forth, but they are only considered insane, different or strange by the outlying society, the proxies are fully removed from society but not removed to the point of death or disappearance.

The masks and hoods shield their identity, their social identity, and removes an aspect of their humanity, stripping them both physically and metaphorically of their face and identity. Masks are often related to transformations of identity. Leenhardt sees the person who wears the mask as someone who disappears, or ceases to exist, when the mask is worn (Leenhardt 1979, 125). Napier follows this line of thinking and demonstrates in his work on the paradox of masks. He illustrates how masks help to transgress the boundaries which allow for an experience of the supernatural (Napier 1986). John Emigh, too, saw masks as a way to play with confusions of identity (Emigh 1996), though his focuses more on theatrical uses of masks rather than more ritualistic takes, and thus sees the masks as more of a combining of the identity of the wearer and the life in the mask itself (ibid., 275). This, more the first two approaches than the third, reveals much of what we see for proxies. The mask is a symbolic demonstration of their identity removal, and thus their social removal. No longer are they simply marginalized, they are removed without being fully removed. Unlike those fully Removed, however, they can still return to their place as Transformed. Tim is the only character who successfully returns from being a proxy. When un-masked, and back to being Tim, he admits he does not carry any memory or knowledge of his time as proxy. Like the Removed, during their time as proxy, they have no knowledge.

Most of the Something Awful forum narratives focused more on the transition from Untouched to Transformed, with the threat looming of Removed. For Marble Hornets, the movement from Untouched to Transformed is quiet and quick. The Slender Man as a figure is clearly present, but not discussed as openly, even in hidden confused tones, as the narratives discussed before. The importance instead is on being in the Transformed category and navigating what it truly means while trying not to be fully Removed. For Marble Hornets, then, proxies are the mediator within the mediator. The proxies are the mediator which is closer to the Removed. The lack of humanity is stronger with the proxies, marking them as being further Removed than the Transformed. Perhaps the best way to depict such an element of the structure is with the following (Diagram 5.1).

Tim's ability to shift back from being a proxy is an interesting element to consider. Unlike Brian, Tim can return to being a proxy, the contrast made all the more portent by how Brian and Tim were once good friends. The shifting back also denies an element of the structure found thus far. The triadic formula we have so far discovered is a one-way movement: once Transformed, one cannot go back to being Untouched; once Removed, one cannot go back to being present. Proxies are still an element of being Transformed, so it could be argued Tim is not moving full categories. However, the fact that Brian is unable to return from his position as a proxy is a relevant contrast to Tim, who shifts between the two several times. Over the course of the narrative, it becomes revealed that Tim has had a connection with the Operator/Sender Man since he was a child. Perhaps it is the long-lasting connection to the Slender Man which both allows Tim to return after his time as a proxy and to survive at the end of the narrative.

Mediation exists in two primary ideal types: negative and positive mediation. In a negative mediation model, the cultural equation is built around the inability to bridge between the categories, and any element which consists of characters of both is often rejected. When there is positive mediation, there is overlap between the structural categories (as depicted by the overlapping circles in our diagrams) and allow movement between these categories.

Marble Hornets, as well as the structures of Something Awful before, demonstrates a positive mediation, as characters move from one category to

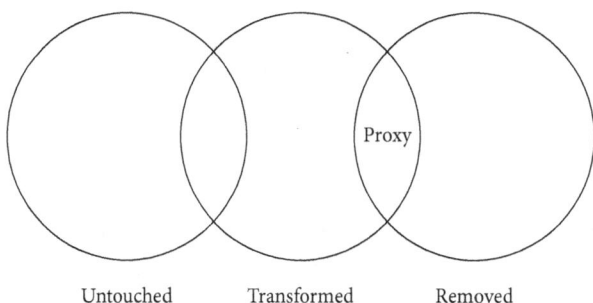

**Diagram 5.1** Marble Hornets' structure with proxies.

the other. The mediators here, however, only sometimes are the vehicles for the movement to occur. They mostly are responsible for setting up the situations in which the Transformed characters then move based on their own actions or exposure to the Slender Man. Jay, for instance, was tied up near the end of the series by Tim, in Tim's attempt to protect him by keeping him out of the fray. Hoody, Brian as proxy, comes around and gives Jay a knife to free himself, leading to Jay getting into the middle of a fight and dying because of it. It is not the proxy, therefore, who is directly responsible for the death, or Jay's transition from Transformed to Removed, though it is because of him Jay was able to find himself in the situation which led to his transition. Proxies play a more covert and strategic role in the transitions of characters.

The true transition vehicle as it was for the Something Awful forum is the Operator/Slender Man. Because the structure is truly no different from Something Awful, the structure still represents characters who have had different levels of exposure to the Slender Man. Although the characteristics of the various categories, such as healthy/unhealthy/no health, do not mention his direct presence, the process of transition is often marked by exposure to the Slender Man. Also, like the Something Awful forum, there is still no place for the Slender Man to exist within the structure.

## 5.4 The Slender Man's structure

Like the trouble with Something Awful in the previous chapters, we still do not yet have a place within the structural equation for the Slender Man. In the previous chapter, the potential for the Slender Man to not have a place within the structure was discussed, an element which is consistent with his nature as a 'monster'. The categorization of a 'monster' for the Slender Man relies primarily on Cohen's famous seven theses, primarily the one which sees the monster as a transgressor of categories (Cohen 1996). This categorical crisis monster was also used anthropologically when Mary Douglas saw the pig as abominable (Douglas 2001). Now that we are beginning to complicate the structure, and see its possibilities as reaching past just the Something Awful forum, we can give more attention to the location of the Slender Man within our structure.

We should first consider the general characteristics of our structure. Our first category, the Untouched, is representative of a 'normal' society. They are ignorant of the Slender Man entirely and are considered healthy and present. These stand in direct contrast to those Removed. They are no longer part of society. They consist of those who have no amount of health and are no longer present: the dead and the missing. When a child is taken by the Slender Man, the child moves to the Removed. Most of the information regarding the Removed is gone, as they fall into the segments of society we have no knowledge of, like where they are, or where one goes after death. But there are those in between: unhealthy, but not yet without health; removed from society but not yet missing or dead. These are the Transformed, altered by their experience, often seen as mentally ill by those outside. They are not as dead as those Removed but are socially dead.

If we consider these various characteristics, we see no place for the Slender Man. We have no knowledge of his health, and perhaps his health is not important to him as a character. He is not in normal society ever, but present and definitely not dead. He is not socially dead either, but he is not part of society to begin with. The knowledge he holds, or the extent of it, is not revealed to us, nor does it appear to be important. His primary characteristics in relation to those in our structure are either not present at all, as in his relationship to society, or not considered important enough to consider.

No matter how we look at him, or the structure, the Slender Man does not seem to fit. Instead of residing within the structure, embedded in one of the categories, he works outside the structure – forcing movement when it is unwanted. He is the catalyst for migration through categories, his influence which shifts the change. Discussing him calls what others know – and even their sanity – into question, pushing them on the fringes of society. This push requires these characters to seek out the truth to what they saw, seeking their knowledge. It is his influence in Marble Hornets which pushes characters to be unhealthy. While these elements themselves are what defines these categories, these elements are obtained through the Slender Man.

We, therefore, can agree with this consideration of the Slender Man, as resting outside the structure but controlling it through simply his presence, acting as a true 'Operator'.

## 5.5 Conclusion

In Marble Hornets, we see no structural change from what was found at the end of our review of the Something Awful forum. The triadic structure, which moves from Untouched, to Transformed, to Removed, is a one-way movement. The addition of proxies, while a definite shift on the more narrative level of the mythos, still fits into what we have seen as they hold characteristics of the

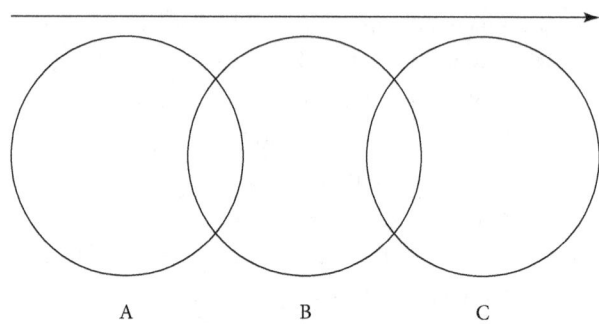

**Diagram 5.2** Structure found in Something Awful and Marble Hornets.

Untouched and the Removed like the Transformed, though on a level much closer to that of the Removed, a collection of both characteristics which are not in balance. On a more pure structuralist view, we can simplify this structure another step by removing the categorical names. Theoretically, this structure should hold in the creepypasta community at least, as their understanding of cultural construction and ways of categorizing the world will fit the same structure, which is the purpose of Chapter 9 (Diagram 5.2).

There are two primary ideal types for categorical relationships. A positive relationship allows possible overlap – movement between the two categories is seen as possible. In Diagram 5.2, this is demonstrated by the overlapping circles of each category. The other relationship possible is negative, meaning movement between the two categories is culturally considered impossible, and elements which exist as mediators of the two categories are considered abominations.

Our movement between the categories here is slightly more complicated. The one-directional movement (represented by the one-sided arrow) restricts movement between categories. Category A (Untouched) can move to B (Transformed) and finally to C (Removed). One cannot directly move from A to C without first passing through B, nor can C move to A. Therefore, A and C have a negative direct relationship – it is impossible to move directly from A to C, or from C to A. Most of the narratives we have discussed so far demonstrate the easy transition from one to another (A + B). The more complicated transition is that between B and C. As both Something Awful and Marble Hornets have shown, many characters do shift from B to C, from Transformed to Removed. This last transition is met with an interesting mix of feelings. While there is some fear in the action of being Removed, for many this may also be met with relief with the true horror as left in the middle unstable and social outcast category of the Transformed (B). This fear is made horrifically real by the truth that some characters, most notably several in the Something Awful forums, as well as both Tim and Jessica in Marble Hornets, do not make this last transition. The unsure state of Tim, who is sometimes proxy, and most clearly affected by the Slender Man, means the social question of the second category does not leave the character. So movement between B and C is possible, especially as this is the only transition which is possible for those moving from A all the way to C, but it is not necessarily made, as characters and even locations are fully able to be trapped in the transitory category.

We see this restrictive structural movement as being present in both the Something Awful forum and Marble Hornets. However, we have only truly begun to follow the train of narratives the Slender Man mythos leaves in its wake. The attempt to discover these narratives is a rabbit-hole of stories, images and virtual narratives. One of the greater moments of the Slender Man's life is the birth of the Slender Man video games, a media form which strengthened its presence further by spreading his narrative to new audiences. The video game storytelling form's relation to structuralism, and the Slender Man video games themselves, will make up the contents of the next chapter.

# 6

# Playing the Slender Man

The progression we are taking through the Slender Man narratives in the development of the online mythology has now taken us to look at the video games which contributed to the Slender Man's story. These two video games, *Slender: The Eight Pages* (2012) and *Slender: The Arrival* (2013 [2015]), helped to propel the Slender Man mythology into a different area of the digital world.

While internet memes are interactive in the way they are created (Chapter 2; see also Chapter 8), the interactivity is differently experienced in the case of video games. Video games are, by their nature, interactive. While the interactivity on the Something Awful forums and Marble Hornets was a choice in the creation, interactivity on a video game is an essential part of the experience of the story. In order to be an audience member, one must also be a player. Where interactivity was once a choice for the mythos, it is a necessity here. Interactivity also makes it a difficult medium to study as a mythographer. Each player can have a different interpretive experience of the game, emphasizing different elements, while ignoring others. Individual player agency suddenly makes the narrative a more individualized experience, making the mythographer's work much harder.

In that vein, this chapter is divided into two main approaches: the first, a theoretical overview to understand how structuralism can fit with a video game, and the second, an analysis of *Slender: The Arrival*. In order to fully explore the role of interactivity and agency in the context of the video game while also maintaining the structural analysis, a revisit of Lévi-Strauss's concept of implicit mythology will help to explore the various aspects of how the narrative is experienced. A fuller breakdown of how this analysis can work has been explored in a previous article (Asimos 2019), but a brief summary will follow.

## 6.1 Screaming at webcams in the dark

Three years after the first creation of the Slender Man, a game *Slender: The Eight Pages* (2012) appeared. The game is in first-person point of view, where the player explores a forest to gather eight pages of scribbled drawings. Two years later, Blue Isle Studios released *Slender: The Arrival* (2013 [2015]), a cross platform (meaning it was released on multiple gaming consoles) Slender Man video game which continued the legacy of *Eight Pages*. The first part of *the Arrival* was even a direct replication of the forest location page gathering of *the Eight Pages*.

These video games grew in popularity over time, at least in part due to the presence of Let's Plays. Let's Plays are a form of web videos which rose to popularity on sharing sites such as YouTube; players play a video game and record the gameplay while also recording their voice, and sometimes, although not always, with a camera recording their face. Horror is a popular genre for Let's Plays, particularly those with footage of their faces (Markiplier n.d.; Pewdiepie n.d.).

The impact Let's Plays have on video game sales is a contested debate in the video game industry. While some developers argue Let's Plays damage their sales (Green 2016), video game sales are often not reported, and when they are it is difficult to tell why certain sales occurred. Video game company Bethesda, for example, clearly sees a benefit to the impact of Let's Plays and other gaming-centred personalities as they decided to no longer give early copies of games to game reviewers, and instead give them to these online personalities (Steinman 2016).

Whether or not the horror Let's Plays favourably impact the sales of the games, the videos are immensely popular themselves. Multiple Let's Play channels almost exclusively upload playthroughs of horror games. For example, horror games make up a large amount of Backwardz Compatible's catalogue (only accessible for members on Rooster Teeth, Backwardz Compatible n.d.), and Jesse Cox has a side group of YouTubers who upload playthroughs of horror games called Scary Game Squad (Jesse Cox n.d.). Markiplier, one of the most popular Let's Players on YouTube, has a large amount of views on his horror gameplays. Markiplier's channel has over eighteen million subscribers at the time of writing (Markiplier n.d). His first episode of *Slender: The Arrival* has close to three million views (Marikiplier 2013a). His first episode of *Alien: Isolation* (2014), another survival horror game, has close to six million views (Marikiplier 2014).

### 6.1.1 Video games and online narratives

Video games and online storytelling have a symbiotic relationship. For example, one of the earliest internet memes was based on the poorly translated game *Zero Wing* (1989) on the SEGA Mega Drive. The participatory culture of video games is similar to the participatory culture of communal narrative creation. Video game content often creates the backbone of various memes, such as the All Your Base Are Belong to Us. Similarly, the image of Vault Boy, a cartoon figure from the *Fallout* series, became a thumbs-up meme, often used in more sarcastic circumstances.

Similarly, video games provide a foundation for the creation of other online content. Machinima, for example, is a form of web video in which the scenes are all filmed in a game world. This form of filming allows for individual content creators without access to expensive filming hardware and software to create video content. One of the longest lasting web video series, *Red vs. Blue*, is a machinima series whose jokes often create online memes themselves, such as the insulting cry out of 'cock bite' which later led to the company's name Rooster Teeth.

While machinima uses video games as a creative tool to create web video content, Let's Players use video games in a purer form to create a source of entertainment, as mentioned previously. These Let's Players often use memes and other online jokes within their own content, a primary source of Twitch streamer BrownMan, for example (Brownman n.d.), but also create their own memes for their community. Jesse Cox, for instance, is a YouTuber who created the idea of a space butterfly who dreams up existence during a sleep-deprived playthrough of the game *Terraria* (2011). The space butterfly became a constant meme in the community and is even sometimes used to refer to the community themselves (this narrative is discussed in further length, with analysis, in Chapter 10). While these more specific memes are only circulated among a smaller audience than some of the other online memes featured in earlier chapters or even the All Your Base Are Belong to Us meme, they are still ideas able to be remixed and spread among a community.

Early debates in game studies led to the division between narratological and ludological approaches to video games. The narratological approach thought of games as something which can be 'read', equivalent to books or film (Jenkins 2004; Kirkland 2005). This approach was led by scholars in film studies and literary studies. The ludological approach, on the other hand, thought of games as something you 'play', using primarily theories from game studies (Eskelinen 2001; Aarseth 2004) such as Caillois and Huizinga. The various advantages and issues with these two approaches have been described in detail for many years, as well as the arguments which exist between the two approaches. Others have stated it was a debate which is either already over (Murray 2005), or never even happened in the first place (Frasca 2003). The extent of this debate is not the purpose of this discussion.

The purpose, and the reason for referencing the ludological/narratological divide, is to paint a fuller picture of the divide which is often understood to exist between a story and a play in the study of video games up to this point. However, video games are both narrative and game simultaneously. We 'read' and 'play' at the same time and to the same extent. It is not that one approach is less important or relevant, but both are accurate.

The importance of both game and narrative together is what often leads to gaming narratives being felt strongly by the community. For example, the beginning of the game *Bioshock: Infinite* (2013) necessitates the main character accept a baptism in order to enter the game world. This is not something presented in a cut-scene (or a movie-like sequence cut in between gameplay), but requires the player to push a button to accept the baptism. This combination of gameplay and narrative strengthened each aspect. Some players felt this move forced them to accept a baptism, and claimed this broke their own faith, and demanded a refund (Hernandez 2013). This move means the combination of game and narrative created a stronger experience of the narrative for these players.

An Inuit Tribal Council joined up with a game developer to create a video game which would retell their folklore in this powerful medium. The game *Never Alone* (2014) was created, where players would take control of a hero from Inui folklore, playing out the various adventures and solving the puzzles. The gameplay is what kept the players interested in the narrative – the two work together to create a powerful experience and allow for players far away from the original source to experience these narratives in powerful ways.

Video games fit our understanding of myth quite well, particularly in how it demonstrates narratives, and interactive narratives, which individuals use to understand themselves and the world around them. *Never Alone*, for example, indicates how myths can still hold power in different formats. Research I have previously undertaken on fans of *the Legend of Zelda* series also showed a power in the narratives, including individuals who tattooed images from the games to remind themselves to live their life according to the importance of the game (Asimos 2019).

## 6.2 Implicit myth

The full theoretical exploration which backs the understanding of the application of structuralism to video games has been detailed out by myself previously in an article in *Implicit Religion* (Asimos 2019), which will be summarized here.

In order to provide the best analysis possible for video games, it is important we embrace an aspect of Lévi-Strauss's own work on what he called implicit mythology. For Lévi-Strauss, explicit myth consisted of stories and narratives, both oral and written. Implicit myth, in contrast, is ritual action. He saw explicit myth as complete, while implicit myth as fragmentary (Lévi-Strauss 1981, 669). For him, explicit myth, the narrative or story myth, is superior to the ritualized implicit myth. Ritual, for him, is removed from the language centre of culture, and the more removed ritual is from language, the more it becomes fragmented. The more movement is incorporated, the more separated from language it is, as Lévi-Strauss sees objects and gestures in the ritual sphere as substitutes for words (ibid., 671).

This hierarchical divide, in which implicit myth is regarded as less important than explicit, has been revisited, and denied, by neo-structuralists (Munz 1973; Galinier 2004; Kunin 2012). Jonathan Miles-Watson (2015) demonstrates how the same concept of implicit myth can be utilized in a slightly different way in his research on the Shimla Hills. He sees implicit myth as that which both inspires and develops personal narratives of experience. In fact, for Miles-Watson, the implicit mythology is seen as more contextually situated, and therefore capable of dealing with the problems involved in navigating the world (Miles-Watson 2015, 38). Miles-Watson's focus on personal experience, and Kunin and Galinier's assertion of explicit and implicit myth's equal footing, can guide us in an application of these terms to the complicated notion of video games, and how to begin the approach of a structural analysis of this medium.

While video games are important forms of contemporary myth-telling today, the way in which people engage with this technological storytelling presents mythographers with a small complication. Video games are, by their nature, interactive. Approaching the game as a script of a straightforward narrative would be a misstep, as we would be ignoring *how* these stories are being performed and received. The way the narrative is revealed and experienced by the player is as important to the mythic structure as the scripted narrative.

But implicit and explicit myth work simultaneously and are equally used by the audience to understand themselves and the world around them. In the act of playing a video game, the myth of the game is being revealed to the player both implicitly and explicitly. Explicit myth is a more scripted narrative, making it more evenly experienced by the community overall, while the implicit myth is more individually experienced. The explicit textual myth is the scripted narrative of the game, sometimes rendered in cut scenes – cinematic sequences literally cut in between the action of gameplay – and in written dialogue. The implicit myth, in contrast, would be the direct experience the gameplay has on the player. As Jonathan Miles-Watson puts it, implicit mythology is 'the narrativization that both accompanies and contextualises ritual action, as well as being the trace of that ritual action. Moreover, I take implicit mythology to be operating where there is material and action that is tumescent with meaning' (2015). This is how we see the way implicit mythology is present in video games – they are the other elements of the narrative which contribute to the full experience of the myth. There are two sides of implicit myth: one being the personal narratives which give the more individualized experience of the scripted narrative; the second is the gameplay, understood elsewhere as ritualized action. The implicit myth in games is the personal narrative of the experience, while the explicit myth is the scripted narrative. This gives us an implicit myth which functions as a combination of Lévi-Strauss and Miles-Watson. The direct action of gameplay echoes the direct action of something like a ritual, though this action gives an avenue to elucidate personal narratives, bolstered by the explicit myth. The implicit myth's emphasis on more personalized experience is what often gives the more explicit myth personal connection and emotional interest, and so the two are tied together. Each of these represents a facet of our previous definition of myth. The player actively engages with the complicated interweaving of these two sides of video games. Explicit and implicit myth rely upon one another and often work together, such as in the process of world building, or the presence of narrative backstory hidden in the game world itself (for a further exploration of this in mythology, see Asimos 2019).

The two work together, flowing on a continuum. This can be considered on a grid. To assist this idea, we can think of the explicit as being the vertical axis, and the horizontal axis the implicit. Each quadrant would represent an ideal type of the levels of emphasis given to implicit and explicit myth engagement. While we can think of ideal types which can possibly exist in each quadrant, we can also keep in mind the variety possible within each quadrant's understanding of emphasis. This process is simply to help visualize the dynamics possible (Diagram 6.1).

Within these quadrants players have agency in which they can emphasize or de-emphasize aspects of the game, or certain sides of the myth. A player has the agency to de-emphasize the explicit while emphasizing the implicit, for example. Or the player can choose to experience the full spectrum. The player's agency within this is important. The graph provides us with a starting point to understanding the game itself, and the avenues to which it can go.

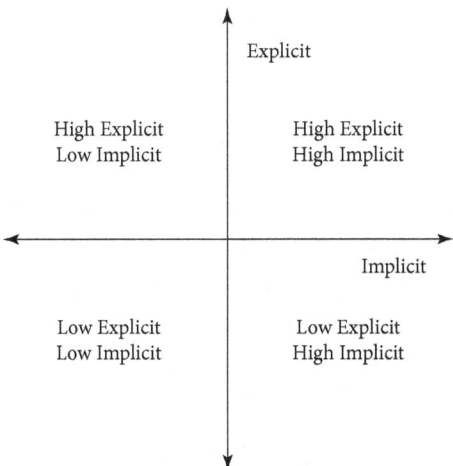

**Diagram 6.1** Graph of ideal types regarding implicit and explicit myths in video games.

## 6.3 Introducing *Slender: The Arrival*

The complexity of video games is well demonstrated in *Slender: The Arrival*, which has scripted events, locations and dialogue, with the backstory and gameworld information hidden in notes scattered throughout the world. This means some players may gather all the information, while others only some, and even others none at all. *Slender* also has sections of the game which can only be accessed if the player obtained a certain number of items, looked at a specific piece of the gameworld, or directly chosen to access this aspect of the game. Although these elements are scripted, and can therefore be thought of as explicit myth, the way in which they are revealed to the player is more personalized, thus in line with implicit myth. This demonstrates the claim made in the previous chapter regarding how implicit and explicit myth work together – they are woven together in a mythic tapestry the player plays within.

The game, thus, has a high influence and importance of implicit myth. The ways in which a player encounters the explicit myth, as well as the way in which one discovers the history of the game world, is entirely personal and wound around implicit myth. The horror genre itself tends to lean more towards personal narratives as well (Asimos 2019).

The writing of *Slender* is in many ways familiar because the writers of the video game are the same who wrote Marble Hornets. Some of the elements introduced in Marble Hornets continue here, such as proxies. The concept of a proxy was first introduced in Marble Hornets. Some of those on who Slender Man has a very strong influence over can mentally change, and they start to work for the Slender Man. They are often completely removed of all social identity (Chapter 5). While this will inevitably affect the scripted, written explicit myth, we have less understanding of how this will affect the more personal implicit myth. In order to have a look at the personal experience of the game myth, some quotes from players as well as Let's Plays will be used in a future section. Let's Plays also introduce a more performative element, though this will be given a much more in-depth look in a future section.

## 6.4 *Slender*'s explicit myth

The explicit myth we will be looking at in this section is simply the game actions. The following notes, including the playable character's name and other more specific information, may or may not be obvious to the player, as information on characters and connections to the Slender Man are all to be found by the player in the game world. They are included for ease of reference. A more detailed look into the more direct narrative will begin in the following section. The explicit narrative is broken into five sections:

1) **Prologue:** The player, playing as a young woman named Lauren, searches her friend Kate's house. She finds a room filled with strange drawings and in the distance hear a scream. The house is surrounded by a forest, and the player goes to investigate the scream.
2) **The Eight Pages:** The player wanders around the forest collecting eight pages which have scribbled drawings on them (a reference to *Slender: The Eight Pages*). The Slender Man begins to stalk the player, getting gradually more aggressive with each drawing obtained. After obtaining all of them, or failing to, the Slender Man directly attacks.
3) **Into the abyss:** The player wakes up outside in the forest, just outside some abandoned mines. The player must find six generators and start them, all to power the lift and escape. During their hunting in the mines, the player is stalked by both the Slender Man and a strange hooded figure acting as proxy.
4) **Flashback:** The player is once again in a forest. Along a path, they have the potential to come across a teddy bear. If the player looks at the teddy bear, a flashback of a missing child's memory is then played, in which

the player has control. Back in the forest, following the path, the player comes into a small tunnel with an old television and some video tapes. One of these tapes is of another woman drawing, who then quickly grabs the camera and has to shut all the windows and doors in the house (the first one we encountered in Part 1) to keep out the Slender Man. Another video the player could watch, though is not required to continue the game, is a flashback of a character by the name of CR who is wandering around a burnt-out house while being stalked by both the Slender Man and a proxy.

5) **The Arrival:** The player is now in a forest which the Slender Man is setting on fire. The player can see him moving between trees. The player must run to the radio tower. Here they find a burnt body of a man and are attacked by a proxy. The game ends with a shot of the playable character's legs being slowly dragged away (Blue Isle Studios 2013 [2015]).

In this explicit myth, there are two flashbacks which can be missed: that of the child and of CR. The implications of these will be discussed in a later section (Section 6.5.2), as well as a more detailed rendering of what these flashbacks are. Regardless of their accessibility for players, they are scripted events, ones which encourage personal encounters as well as demonstrating how intricately the explicit and implicit myths are woven together. While these events may be technically elements of explicit myth, their connection to implicit myth is why we will be discussing them at length in a later section.

### 6.4.1 Locations

There are four primary locations: house, forest, mines and tower. The progression moves in this order as well: from house, to forest, to mines, back to forest and finally to the radio tower. The movement alternates between human and natural locations. The forest is also the only location in which replaying, or revisiting certain actions or events occur. The movement gradually transforms from emotional safety to perceived safety. The game is encouraging the player, both in world building (which will be discussed later) as well as game progression, that the location for endgame, and perceived safety, is the radio tower.

The house's beginning of emotional safety and the tower's element of perceived safety are connected through their notion of safety. Two points, in which danger or the forest, lie in between. The emotional safety of the house is not a unique idea to *the Arrival* (Bachelard 1964). The emotional safety of the house, however, shifts away as the intensity of the darkness and the presence of the Slender Man creeps in. The odd drawings on the wall are few, but as soon as the player enters Kate's bedroom, the intensity of the drawings increases – the walls are covered in the drawings, and the window is broken. The player hears a scream, and upon that moment must leave the house to progress the narrative. Like characters we have seen in past narratives, the Slender Man's presence influences a shifting from one category to another. This is also present in the locations – his presence transforms the location from one of safety to one of danger. The character mimics this movement as well – leaving the house and going into the forest, the area of wilderness and danger. Progression of location is also progression from our previously established categories of Untouched to Removed.

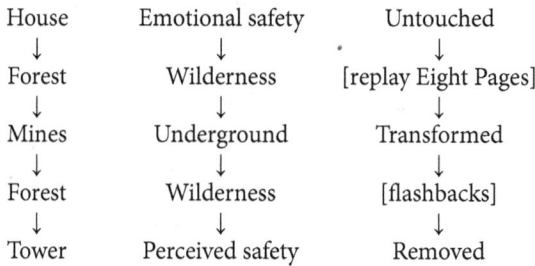

The role of the mines is a point of question here. The mines are neither a place of safety, either emotional or perceived, and nor the same as the wilderness of the forest. We have this location noted as the point of the Transformed category. Its primary difference as a location is in being underground – the rest are on the ground or above. The mines are abandoned – separated from the social environment in a similar way the characters in the Transformed are equally separated from the social environment.

The mines are also powerless – both literally in terms of electricity, and emotionally for the character. The player is being sought by, and attacked, two foes, for the first and only time in the game: both the Slender Man and the proxy are present. The result is an intensification of the player's powerlessness. The mines are also out of electric power – in order to escape the player must activate six generators, which powers the lift out of the mines. The lift brings the player out of the mines and back into the wilderness. The trip to the underworld – the underground mines – is like a death which is not a death. There is separation from the social, particularly in the interaction with the proxy, but the rise at the end lifts the character back to the wilderness.

The wilderness and the forest are present on both sides of the trip to the Underground. The home's original position of Untouched and the tower's position of Removed are each separated from the Transformed Underground by the forest. The forest is a common symbol found in folklore, legend and myth (Porteous 2002). In the Germanic folklore recorded by the Brothers Grimm, the forest was a great transformational place, due to how society's conventions do not hold in the wilderness (Zipes 1988). If this convention holds true here, the forest would be the avenue through which the other transformations occur, the wildness of the location which rests on either side is the transformational avenue which leads to the large categorical shifts for both the locations and the playable character.

Even without the addition of the implicit myth in our analysis, we can see a similarity of the explicit myth to the structure we have already seen. The character begins either with no involvement or knowledge of the Slender Man – there is nothing present in the world building which demonstrates this. The player, however, may have prior knowledge of the Slender Man. The implications of these various nuances all impact the implicit myth rather than the explicit. It is not only the playable character which moves across the categories, but the locations as well. Home moves categories from Untouched to Transformed. As the home moves from safety to not-safety, the perceived safety of the tower remains. In order to progress to redress the balance of the structure (Lévi-Strauss 1973c), the player character is attempting to move back to the realm of safety – the perceived safety of the tower. However, when the player character gets to the tower, it is revealed the perceived safety of the tower is not a safety at all, as the proxies attack and the game ends. The game concludes with the realization of the danger – there is no safety, only danger. All rests in the unstable location then. The only safety realized is in death.

## 6.5 World building: implicit and explicit myth

As described previously, implicit myth is that which rests outside the scripted narrative. World building establishes rules and history of the gameworld, often expanding upon characters who are not necessarily main protagonists or antagonists. This often happens through side quests, or activities other characters in the world give the playable character, which does nothing to advance the main story. It can also occur through exploration in the game world, where players can find small clues, symbols or architecture which gives life to the game world.

World building is, thus, a combination of both implicit and explicit myth: these narratives and elements are scripted, and thus part of the explicit myth, yet are discovered in an individualized and personalized manner. The fragmented approach to the narrative leaves room for a variety of knowledge regarding the underlying narrative. The player's knowledge of outside influences also plays into this, especially the player's personal experience. The latter, the player's specific personal experience and knowledge, is an incredibly difficult thing to study. Due to this complication, we will be taking each type of implicit myth separately in stride. The structure found in world building is similar to the structure found in the previous details.

### 6.5.1 CR and Kate

The most prominent form of world building in *Slender: The Arrival* is the story progression between Lauren (the player character), Kate (Lauren's good friend) and a man by the name of CR. All the notes are from CR's point of view, written to Kate. According to the notes, CR and Kate were childhood friends, and reconnected after the death of Kate's mother. The notes at the beginning hint Kate and CR used to go out to the forest at night as kids. The next note begins to detail out the specifics of the effects they have been feeling since children. They are sharing hallucinations and, according to CR, electronics act strange around them. Both these elements which have become definitions of the Transformed category in both the Something Awful forum narratives (Chapter 4) and Marble Hornets (Chapter 5). The notes shift between handwritten notes and emails, attributed to this issue with electronics. CR writes about the shared hallucinations as possibly due to a 'shared traumatic event' when they were children. They are both hearing strange noises outside their homes as well. CR, with a doctor, comes up with an idea to confront their 'traumatic event' with the idea that 'seeing nothing will help get rid of these stupid problems' they have been experiencing. This idea backfires: the two get separated, and CR experiences either a seizure or a true supernatural attack. He wakes up and makes his way back to Kate's house and finds her in a fugue state but leaves her. The next note from CR is strangely different, writing to Kate that the woods are 'beatiful [sic]'. Later, CR finds Kate in the woods behind her house passed out with 'a bag full of weird drawings' and takes her to the hospital. At this point, the notes from CR begin to take a turn. He writes he knows a place that is safe and does not feel his home is safe anymore. The next note truly demonstrates a sinking into paranoia and apparent insanity, and the one following alludes to a possibility that CR burnt his home. This firmly moves CR's home to be no longer a place of safety, in a similar way to Kate's house in our exploration of locations. CR himself has demonstrated firm positions of the Transformed. The final note from CR says he knows how to fix all of it. In the last segment of the game, the player (Lauren) finds CR's body where he attempted a double suicide, and only managed to kill himself (Blue Isle Studios 2015). Kate somehow managed to escape CR's attempt, but did get badly burnt, and it is assumed by some in the community the burnt image of the proxy attacking in the mines was Kate (FalcoFanBoy 2013).

The CR and Kate story is at the heart of *Slender: The Arrival*'s game. The notes are scattered throughout the game's progression, slowly building up to demonstrate the reason the player character is there and connecting the player to the story and the mystery of what happened between the two characters. Like the Something Awful forum narratives and Marble Hornets, the world building narrative also follows the triadic structure found previously.

At the time of their reconnection, the first note, nothing strange appears to exist for either character. Finding it in the abandoned and ransacked house gives that sweet, not yet strange, narrative an eerie feeling. The second note is found very soon after and begins to explain how the two were not as Untouched as may have been previously thought, as they are sharing the same 'hallucination'. The description of them both – or at least just CR – hearing odd sounds outside his home is apparently spurred by this 'shared traumatic event' which occurred when they were younger. So, the note of nothing strange occurring in the beginning with their re-finding each other is not as accurate as originally thought.

The 'shared traumatic event' is clearly connected to an experience of the Slender Man, and the attempt to confront it only made the presence stronger. The player, as well as the playable character, experienced a transformation along the various categories of the gameplay in the explicit myth. Here we see characters even not directly interacted with, only experienced through the discovery of various notes scattered throughout the world, also experience a movement across the triadic structure.

Although they do not start at the point of the Untouched, Kate and CR start the game already in the Transformed category. They have already had an experience of the Slender Man as children playing in the woods, though they did not recognize it for what it was. For that reason, we can possibly conceive of them as existing in the overlap between the Untouched and the Transformed. They can still retain some sense of social identity, still remaining an element of society without being pushed out. However, the shared hallucination (although not known to be shared, but apparently still considered to be hallucinations) set them aside from the Untouched due to the connection of the consideration of 'insane' which is a designated factor of the Transformed (Chapter 4).

As the notes progress, CR decides to confront the 'traumatic event' which gave both he and Kate the hallucinations as well as 'the noises' they would hear 'outside my window at night now'. The severity of the movement to the Transformed occurs the night in which the two attempt to confront their event. CR's description of the supernatural attack he suffered intensely describes the amount of fear felt at a confrontation with the Slender Man. Immediately following is a strangely written text regarding the woods (see Figure 6.1). The paranoia grows after this, the places in which they feel safe shrinking. The growth in paranoia and the fugue states CR describes Kate as being in at times, moves them from the border between Untouched and Transformed, to firmly Transformed.

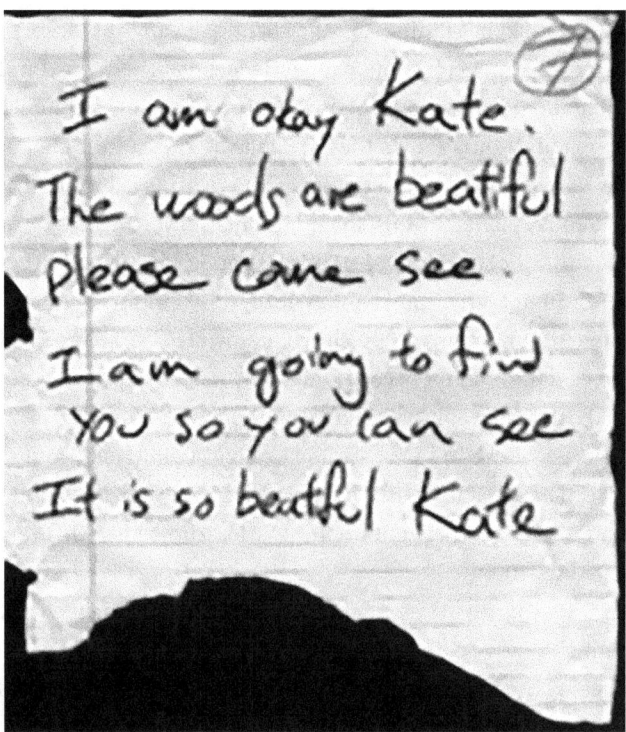

**Figure 6.1** Image of Note 7 from CR. Screenshot from own playthrough (Blue Isle Studios 2013 [2015]).

The movement is one way, and so the only solution for the characters in order to be no longer Transformed is to be Removed. Transformed is often considered by both those outside and themselves as insane as they suffer with what they think to be hallucinations, and increased paranoia. The fear of being stuck in the Transformed state can be intense for the characters. CR's solution for a double suicide is thus considered the only solution in order to properly save them both. Death becomes a perceived safety.

In most narratives we have looked at until now, the only character in the narrative who has agency in movements between categories is the one character who does not have a category for themselves: the Slender Man. CR's agency was thus important. In his suicide, he took control over his own movement to the Removed category. However, his plan to also move Kate along with him ultimately failed, as he does not have the same power as is embodied in the Slender Man.

### 6.5.2 The flashbacks

*Slender: The Arrival* has several more secret levels, which are able to be missed during normal playthrough time. These chapters are flashback chapters. Charlie Matheson Jr is playable in one, and CR the other, called 'Memories' and 'Homestead', respectively. These are only triggered by specific actions taken in-game. For Charlie's flashback, the player must find a teddy bear in the second forest area outside the mines and interact with it. CR's flashback is activated by choosing his VHS tape at the same point you play Kate's tape, but you must choose CR's tape first.

Charlie's flashback is the simplest and shortest section to playthrough in the game. Charlie is on a beach and finds small sections of a toy train in the sand. Following the trail, Charlie gets farther and farther away from his family and into the woods. Once he is far enough from his family, the Slender Man's shadowy tendrils appear and take him.

In contrast, CR's flashback is significantly longer, and details the history of Charlie's family, who has a history with the Slender Man. This narrative mimics that which was found in the Something Awful forums. The family invited the monster in by thinking about him and interacting with him. This causes him to slowly take the children in the family, culminating in the family trying to kill him in fire.

The structure here does not differ strongly from what was found previously. The Charlie story gives us little to work with, but like previous narratives a child is taken, and the woods are a source of the Slender Man's presence. For CR's flashback, children continue to disappear, with no apparent end once the Slender Man's presence is known. Both the difference in treatment of various ages, as detailed in the early Something Awful chapter (Chapter 3), and the progression of movement are echoed in Diagram 5.2.

## 6.6 *The Arrival* implicit myth

Discovering and studying the implicit myth of any video game is complex. If we are to follow Lévi-Strauss's claim that a myth is made up of all its variants (Lévi-Strauss 1963b, 217), then a video game's implicit myth is made up of all the various personal experiences of its audience. To plan for this is daunting and the task impossible. Adding to this issue, the more time which passes between the game's release and act of research, obtaining any emotional feedback directly from players can have added difficulty. The drop-off number of players means the feedback you would be receiving as a scholar would be skewed in favour of those still playing the game several years after release. Others will have several years of space between playing and participating and will thus have a different type of narrative than if talked about much closer to the time of game release.

The issue for the current study is just this. *Slender: The Arrival* was first released in 2013, seven years before the time of writing. In order to solve this, I am also taking personal narratives from YouTube videos released closer to the time of game release. The YouTube videos are from Let's Players, people who record their playing of a video game and share these online. I used multiple playthroughs: Achievement Hunter, a Let's Play group from internet company Rooster Teeth who only had a single video and never finished the game; Markiplier, a single Let's Player who is known for his playthroughs of horror games and who completed the game; and Scary Game Squad, a group hosted on YouTuber Jesse Cox's channel who play and complete horror games. These three various playthroughs and their commentary on the game while playing has been added to the personal narratives of players talked to on gaming discussion forums, as well as my own playthrough of the game.

These playthroughs are also forms of entertainment, as Let's Players fight to obtain and retain an audience. Because of this, these Let's Plays not only provide us with implicit myths but also different variations on a myth's performance. The two are linked – a personal connection to the narrative can lead to different ways in which the narrative is told. The following three Let's Plays not only demonstrate different ways in which people can emphasize or de-emphasize certain elements of the myth, but these various levels can be compared to the different ways a myth could be performed. Lévi-Strauss himself focuses more on the myth as if it was written then on the performances of the myth. Other structuralists, however, have shifted focus to more performative aspects. Galinier, for instance, described how the Otomi's connection to mythology is much stronger through the ritual rather than in formal telling (Galinier 2004). The ritual, then, is the performance of the myth. Turner, too, insisted on studying myth as it is told or performed by the people it belongs to (Turner 2017). Kunin has connected structuralism to the way people talk about a myth and ritual, in a similar way to our understanding here of implicit myth, and the performance of these (Kunin 2009). Of course, Miles-Watson's concept of implicit myth, which was used to form our own understanding in relation to video games, also looks at the personal connection, which could also be the personal performance, of a myth (Miles-Watson 2015). Some other structuralist approaches to performative storytelling rely more on Kenneth Pike and Eugene Nida (see Hymes 1985, as example), rather than Lévi-Strauss. However, we will stick to a Lévi-Straussian approach to the material when looking into this more performative side of the *Slender: The Arrival* implicit myth.

### 6.6.1 Achievement Hunter playthrough

Achievement Hunter's playthrough of *Slender: The Arrival* differs considerably from the other Let's Plays to be discussed because it is a single episode, and the players did not seek to complete the game. The playthrough began at the beginning of the game, but the players stopped after their first exploration into the mines. However, like the other Let's Plays, Achievement Hunter was not simply playing through the game in the same manner a normal player is. Successful Let's Players consider a large portion of their job to be more than simply playing but also needing to entertain. More on the impact this has will be discussed at the end of this section.

Achievement Hunter began in 2008 as a subsidiary of online production company Rooster Teeth. Started by Rooster Teeth co-founder Geoff Ramsey, Achievement Hunter at the time of this writing is comprised of six primary on-camera personalities, several extra personalities occasionally featured and several behind-the-scenes workers including editors. At the time of the *Slender* playthrough, the team was growing, but had not quite reached the number of background workers as the team currently has. At the time of writing,

Achievement Hunter is comprised of two main YouTube channels: Achievement Hunter and Let's Play. The Achievement Hunter channel has over 1.4 million subscribers (Achievement Hunter n.d.), and the Let's Play channel has over 3.7 million (Let's Play n.d.). The *Slender: The Arrival* Let's Watch video has over one million views (Let's Play 2014). These numbers, even with their height, is also sometimes lower than what could be accurate, as Rooster Teeth hosts all their videos, and some exclusive videos for paid members only, on their main site. The YouTube views do not reflect the views also featured on their site.

Achievement Hunter's *Slender* playthrough is part of a series called Let's Watch – a Let's Play style in which only one person plays, and the other members of the team watch the playthrough and give commentary or react. The video specifically features founder Geoff Ramsey playing the game, while team personalities Michael Jones, Ray Narvaez Jr. (who later left the company in 2015), and co-founder of Achievement Hunter, Jack Patillo watch.

Like most Let's Plays, and especially those featured from Achievement Hunter, humour is prominent in their playthrough. The choice in Geoff playing the game was made due to how he gets scared much easier than the others, resulting in more funny jumps, frequently at nothing, and more hilarious reactions when faced with the Slender Man. One main repeated joke is Geoff's insistence that he is not scared, and jokingly putting down the game to being 'boring', most repeated when he becomes both visibly and audibly scared. The phrase 'I'm bored' became synonymous with fear: during the gathering of *the Eight Pages*, when scared by the Slender Man, Geoff would cry out, while his character ran, 'I'm so bored right now!' (Let's Play 2014).

Like the former example, and as we will see in the other Let's Plays of *Slender* and horror games in general, fear and humour work together simultaneously. Often, people watch these videos for the humour involved in watching others get scared. Fans of Achievement Hunter Let's Plays have commented on this level of humour involved in horror game playing. One said they love seeing how others react in the same position they were once in while in their own playthrough. Another simply said: 'watching other people get scared is just funny'.

Achievement Hunter also represents the type of gamers who de-emphasize explicit myth. Despite finding several lore fragments, they were unconcerned when they missed a numbered letter which, lore wise, was between Kate and CR, nor were they interested in piecing together the story of what was occurring. Exploration was seen as foundational – less from a search for lore aspect as an experience of gameplay. From this playthrough, as well as through watching many of their others, Achievement Hunter preferences gameplay itself, and the implicit myth experienced through this rather than the explicit myth of the scripted narrative. They may connect at times, though this is rare.

While exploration was emphasized, especially in the prologue section, the eight pages hunt led to a different kind of exploration. Those watching, especially Michael Jones, pulled up a walkthrough and began to attempt guiding Geoff through the game by informing him where the pages were located. The others even went so far as to look up a map to guide from one landscape marker to another. The need for this was due to the ease in which the player, Geoff, was lost in the landscape. The ease of getting lost was due to this exploration, but also an aspect of the game – the forest all looks similar, no tree looks different from the others, and so the player is easily lost. The darkness is often frequently intense.

The primary mythemes in their implicit myth is the darkness, being lost, exploration, horror and humour. How these mythemes work in the full structure will be looked at in the next section. First, we should look at the mythemes, and how these mythemes are formed, in the other Let's Plays of *Slender*.

### 6.6.2 Markiplier playthrough

Unlike Achievement Hunter, and Scary Game Squad which will be looked at in the next section, Markiplier is not comprised of a group, but a single person. Mark Fischbach, known as Markiplier online, first joined YouTube in 2012, and since has quickly gained heavy prominence. He currently has one of the most profitable YouTube accounts (Lynch 2017), and his channel has over 18.7 million subscribers (Markiplier n.d.). Although he also makes vlogs and other non-gameplay videos, his channel is mostly known for his Let's Play videos, mostly in playing survival horror games.

In stark contrast to Achievement Hunter, Markiplier not only finished *Slender: The Arrival* over the course of five videos but also went back to record more as more content was released to the game, and to replay the game on hardcore mode. Due to how it was his first experience with the game, Markiplier's initial playthrough of *Slender: The Arrival* is all which will be discussed here.

Again, humour takes a centre point in the videos. These include jokes regarding the horror aspects of the game, as at one point excitedly calling, 'let's all die in the woods' (Markiplier 2013a), as well as joking about some YouTube comments saying he should soak up the environment more, to which he responded by just looking at a tree and commenting only on the tree (Markiplier 2013b). His humour is present in most of his horror playthroughs, due to his extreme reactions and screams. These include insults thrown at both the Slender

Man and the proxy when they scared him, over-the-top yelling and cursing, and excitement for when he finished a section.

The darkness also came into account in Markiplier's Let's Play, though less so than in the other playthroughs. His commentary on the darkness, as well as the music, was positive. In the beginning of his playthrough he explains how for horror games, 'atmosphere is paramount' and comments that *Slender: The Arrival* truly nails it (Markiplier 2013a). This is picked up in music cues, which stays typically low until when Slender or some other danger seems to be near, or they wish to intensify the emotions. Sound cues were also present, including the sound of footsteps behind the character or static noises at the Slender Man's approach. All feeds into the implicit myth aspect of atmosphere, the gameplay and experience for the player. All impact Markiplier's experience of the game.

Due to the longer playthrough here than Achievement Hunter, the full gameplay of *Slender:The Arrival* also came with aspects of frustration. For Markiplier, this did not hit until his time in the mines. When the proxy begins to attack, the confusion of this and the ignorance of how to fight him sets in to frustrate Markiplier. Getting lost in the mines, and thus not knowing where he was, only assisted the frustration (Markiplier 2013b). The mine area took over more of his playtime than any other section and took two full videos to complete. The combined actions of getting lost, the confusion of how to combat the proxy, and the lack of control over the speed of the playable character, all led to a great amount of frustration. The first video of the mine area ends with a death just as he finished finding all the generators. When the next video begins, he has to explain he has since 'calmed down' from his frustration and anger at the ending of the last one (Markiplier 2013c).

Markiplier is the type of player who gives emphasis to the explicit myth, though did not seek out these elements and notes exhaustively. Unlike Achievement Hunter, he reads through each of the notes found, and gives thought and discussion towards what he believes is occurring in the narrative (Markiplier 2013a; Markiplier 2013d; Markiplier 2013e). However, when he misses a few of the notes, he does not backtrack to discover the ones missed. While he clearly emphasizes the explicit myth more than Achievement Hunter, he does not emphasize it over the implicit. His experience playing the game is much more prominent, given more of the commentary, and emphasized more by both player and audience. His commentary is more on how the game makes him feel: frustration, excitement over progressing, anxiety at what is happening next, fear of the Slender Man and the proxy attacks, and the frustration of being lost or failure in progressing. The explicit myth here helps drive many of these experiences but is not seen as more important than these elements or emotions. For him, the explicit myth drives the implicit, emphasized but not on equal footing.

The mythemes here are very similar to the mythemes in Achievement Hunter's implicit myth: darkness, being lost, exploration, horror and humour; Markiplier's playthrough adds frustration, an emotion echoed in multiple videos in his *Slender* series. Again, a fuller structure involving these mythemes will be explored in the following section. Beforehand, it will be useful to compare these mythemes to what occurs in our last Let's Play example: Scary Game Squad.

### 6.6.3 Scary Game Squad playthrough

Scary Game Squad was founded by YouTuber Jesse Cox, and hosted on his channel. His channel has over 900,000 subscribers (Jesse Cox n.d.). Their *Slender: The Arrival* playthrough has over half a million views collectively (Jesse Cox 2015h). The group is a collective of various YouTubers playing a horror game in a similar way to Achievement Hunter's Lets Watch – one plays through while the rest watch. The *Slender* playthrough is comprised of Jesse Cox; Jirard 'The Completionist' Khalil, from YouTube channels That One Video Gamer and Super Bear Bros; Greg Wilmot, who worked for That One Video Gamer until 2015 (after being replaced on Scary Game Squad by Alex Faciane from The Dex and Super Beard Bros.); and Michael Davis, a member of YouTube group Warp Zone.

Again, Scary Game Squad played through the entire game like Markiplier. Also like Markiplier, they struggled with emotions of frustration. The intense darkness often contributed to this idea, though what should have been present for the atmosphere was intensified by what might have been a faulty setting on their monitor (Jesse Cox 2015e; Jesse Cox 2015f). Like where Achievement Hunter stopped and Markiplier got frustrated, Scary Game Squad also had lots of issues in the mines. A primary concern was the speed in which the character moved. Jirard, who was playing the game, commented: 'the fact I can't run is the fucking worst' (Jesse Cox 2015d).

Scary Game Squad also got frequently lost and confused within the landscape. First during the *Eight Pages* replay section, the other members often had to guide Jirard in the right area (without a walkthrough), and sometimes guided incorrectly (Jesse Cox 2015c). In the mines, the group was frequently at a loss for where they were actually located in relation to the generators, and even where they had been (Jesse Cox 2015c), and after leaving the mines, while wandering the second wilderness, Jirard's comment 'I would just want a map in all this'

(Jesse Cox 2015e) clearly demonstrated the frustration he felt at his almost constant state of being lost.

The issue of being lost is perpetuated by the need for exploration. Scary Game Squad's approach to *Slender*, and their other playthroughs as well, is the antithesis of Achievement Hunter – the group actively searched for lore, and often backtracked to areas they already had been in attempts to fill the gaps they knew were present. For example, before entering the mines, the numbering of the notes resulting in them knowing one had been skipped, so the group decided to exhaustively search the surrounding area to make sure they had the notes in order to help fill in the narrative of the game (Jesse Cox 2015d). During load screens, or quiet exploratory moments, the group would discuss what they thought was occurring in the explicit myth, piecing together the puzzle of the narrative (Jesse Cox 2015a; Jesse Cox 2015c; Jesse Cox 2015g).

Like the other two playthroughs, the videos uploaded were also meant to be a form of entertainment. As such, the Scary Game Squad, like the others, had a high level of humour involved. Sometimes these were in relation to the levels of fear felt, such as Davis's reaction to a scare by saying 'I have pee' (Jesse Cox 2015f). Sometimes these were purely contextual. At the start of CR's flashback section, Jirard, in control of the playable character, began to move it backwards, away from their main destination, while saying 'I don't want to do this mission' (Jesse Cox 2015e).

The mythemes in Scary Game Squad is like the previous two implicit myths: darkness, fear, horror, humour, being lost and exploration. Despite their difference in emphasis of interaction with the explicit myth, the experience of the implicit is mostly similar. In the following section, the structure we have found will be explored more in depth.

### 6.6.4 Implicit myth structure

As previously stated, there are six primary mythemes: darkness, fear, frustration, being lost, exploration and humour. Aside from humour, much of these have already been explored in previous iterations of the Slender Man myth. Our previously understood three categories often reflect some of these, most clearly the second category, the Transformed. The Transformed is associated with being lost, being frustrated and an intense fear. The frustration and aspects of getting lost are often related to elements such as darkness and exploration.

The mytheme more complex to fit is humour as, until now, humour has not factored into any arena. It is tempting to immediately contrast humour and fear, as they appear to be a dichotomy. However, this is not only a poor representation of humour, but specifically a poor representation of humour found in these implicit myths. The humour was often dark or absurd, such as Markiplier directly asking why the playable character is even wandering into the mines to begin with (Markiplier 2016d), or Jesse Cox in Scary Game Squad playing on the fear of Slender Man in the house by calling out 'He is in your house . . . he is playing with your silverware!' (Jesse Cox 2015g). The humour is present because of the fear. These Let's Plays are technically forms of entertainment, and humour is a popular aspect of this. The way in which the humour works with the fear, however, demonstrates how fear and humour, in this situation, are not binary oppositions. The humour is dark and absurd, in many ways reflecting the frustration, absurdity and fear found in this Transformed category. The humour is used to reflect the absurdity of self and situation, a position reflecting the middle, Transformed, category.

The sound cues experienced in the act of playing also reflect the sensory codes found in the first half of the Something Awful forum. Here, we found sensory codes fell into three primary categories: prohibited senses, sound and obscured senses. Prohibited senses, in Victor Surge's post (Chapter 3) which initially posed these elements, related to sensory codes which directly relate to the relationship between post and audience, often one in which the audience is told they cannot look. The sound cues were solely related to the Slender Man himself, and the obscured senses are those either hidden or in lack.

The prohibited senses are demonstrated in the characteristic technological glitches of the Slender Man. One of the signs of his being present is the camera beginning to get static, and a noise of technological issues sounding. These technological issues double as not only providing a sense of fear of the Slender Man's approach but also prohibiting the player from fully viewing the Slender Man. In Victor Surge's performance post, the audience is told they cannot look at the Slender Man (Victor Surge 2009d). We are not directly told this prohibition in the video game, but rather it is implicit in the technological glitches which automatically prohibit the player from fully viewing.

Sound cues work similarly in the game as they did in the previous use of these sensory codes. The sound cues are almost solely related to the Slender Man. The most obvious phenomenon are the sound issues which arise from the technological glitches described earlier. More quietly, music and sound effects also influence the sound, all related to the Slender Man. The music is often quiet and low in the background and increases in volume when danger is near in order to increase tension. In the Scary Game Squad playthrough, for instance, one member referred to this as 'Slender Man's theme song' (Jesse Cox 2015b). The only sound effect not directly in relation to either the Slender Man or his proxies is the player character's footsteps. The effect, however, makes the player pay attention to extra footsteps, which sound when the proxy is near enough to attack.

These sound cues and atmospheric elements are picked up by other players of the game as well. One player I talked to told a story of initially playing the game with a group of friends as they got scared in a group. They said that the 'music and atmosphere are so incredible' which 'never fails at keeping me afraid. [. . .] I hear the wind in the prologue, and I get actual chills'. Similarly, another said they 'like to just walk around in the woods for whatever reason [. . .] the ambience and music and what not is great'. Two players agreed the gameplay itself was not the best they experienced, but the connection was to the story it told, and the mood of the game.

In my own personal playthrough of the game, I also found most of these same experiences in my own implicit myth as those found earlier, aside from the humorous aspect. I attempted to gather as many of the notes as possible, though missed some. I got lost frequently, got frustrated, and even with brightness settings up, the darkness was intense. The locations fit the same progression as the locations mentioned in the previous section in the explicit myth.

The Diagram (5.2) given earlier is the same structure we have found and subsequently refined over the last several chapters. Nothing we have explored in this chapter appears to alter things. The majority of the game situates both player and character in the middle category of the Transformed, experiencing the slow process of becoming Removed. When the character is in some way Removed, the specific way is incredibly vague: the player character is no longer played. The player is removed from the game.

The act of playing is thus following the same pattern as the written myths which have come before. The player plays through the transformations of locations – moving from one category to another as they shift locations. The character's death is an act of safety; the player is forced away from the myth – the game ends.

## 6.7 Conclusion

*Slender: The Eight Pages*, and its replication and larger exploration in *Slender: The Arrival*, helped to spread the Slender Man's narrative into new virtual arenas. Let's Players, such as Markiplier and Achievement Hunter, helped to spread these video games and their subsequent reception. Perhaps due to similarity in writers and producers who worked on the video game, the structure we found previously continues to remain intact. The game focuses primarily on the transition from the second Transformed category to the third Removed category, in much the same way as the early Something Awful forum stories did.

The elements of the myth we have looked at thus far are those all actively involved in the horror storytelling which feed the Slender Man myth. As the story grew, however, so did the possible variants one could find. A long-lasting internet meme Rule 34, an internet adage in so-called Rules of the Internet, asserts that 'if something exists, there is porn of it'. Whether or not this is a true statement of the internet is yet to be discovered, but it does summarize the ways in which the online community transports stories to new contexts, even those sometimes unasked for. The next chapter examines how the Slender Man fits into these types of narratives, when he becomes transported out of the horror realm. In the following two chapters' cases, these are the realms of both romance and humour.

7

# Loving the horror, romancing Slender

As the narrative of the Slender Man grew to various locations online and in a variety of virtual spaces, the different influences of various writers and contributors shifted the appearance of narratives. The popularity of the video game and web series, for example, exposed new units to the mythos. Several more writers took the mythology to another perspective, shifting the narrative from horror to romance, and combined the two into a form of horror–romance. The shift came with a new focus on female protagonists who find a more misunderstood Slender Man, and who grow to love a monster.

This chapter represents the transition of both the narrative and us, as mythographers, to potentially a second community which shares and tells the Slender Man's story. Each of our chapters in some respect demonstrates this – the way the narrative spread to different group of people on the virtual geography of the internet. Each time we see a different kind of narrative, told more or less by different people, we have to question where the boundaries of the Slender Man's narrative lies, or if there are boundaries at all. The greater question will be addressed at the end of this study (Chapter 11). But to test these points, and thus know what kind of structural purpose the Slender Man is providing for the fanfiction and romantic narratives, we must give them a full study, which we shall do in the following chapter.

This chapter focuses on these narratives. All were found on fanfiction.net. The first, and one which will receive more attention in this chapter due to both size and content, is a romance story between the primary female protagonist and Slender. The others are more erotic takes on the Slender Man, which depict him both as a misunderstood carer and just as vicious as previous narratives. First, however, we must explore the realm of fanfiction writing.

## 7.1 Fanfiction

Due to where these stories were found, as well as their treatment from both audience and writer, the narratives discussed in this chapter are frequently considered 'fanfiction', a form of online storytelling yet to be explored in this work. This is primarily due to how fanfiction fits into more of a traditional model of writer and audience, rather than mass communal storytelling which has formed much of the processes and narratives we have studied up until now. Despite this difference, there are a few interesting notes regarding fanfiction's connection to the Slender Man which is important to note before our analysis of these narratives.

A historical overview of the history of fanfiction is too detailed and unnecessary for this section, and has been done much more effectively than would be possible here by Henry Jenkins (1992). For fanfiction, narratives stand in contrast, or in comparison, to a canonical work, such as a television show or novel – a major difference to the starkly non-canonical nature of mass communal storytelling. Despite this, there are more fundamental similarities. For one, as Jenkins (1992) illustrates, fanfiction also demonstrates readers not as a passive audience, but as Michel de Certeau's 'poacher' ([1984] 2013), using their creativity and agency to engage with the narratives they love.

Here is a connection to our understanding of memes, as seen earlier in this manuscript (Chapter 2). The creation of memes, through a process of mass communal storytelling, similarly draws on the concept of readers as 'poachers', or through Lévi-Strauss's *bricolage*. Writers grab from their environment for a process of creation, in both inspiration of content and form. Fanfiction, like meme-making, demonstrates the ability for ordinary readers and audience members to take an active role in reshaping known narratives to suit their own interest (Duffett 2013, 171). Both mass communal storytelling and fanfiction mimic this process, though in slightly different ways and on slightly different scales. Fanfiction writers see their writing as a starting point for getting into more traditional writing, while memes in mass communal storytelling are intended to be anonymously spread online. Fanfictions themselves have also become bestsellers, such as *50 Shades of Gray* which was originally a fanfiction of the *Twilight* series (Bertrand 2015). Ika Willis has also demonstrated how fanfiction, and amateur writing, can still be considered mythology (Willis 2016).

The more romantic takes on the Slender Man cross the boundary between fanfiction and mass communal storytelling. Unlike many other fanfictions, there is no set canon in which the authors play, as the Slender Man's narrative has no canonical narrative (Chapter 2). Because of this, the romantic takes, therefore, do not rest outside of the canon, as other fanfictions do, although perhaps it is better to consider these narratives as making no attempt to add to the widening circle of narratives in the same way as the previous narratives we have analysed

(Chapters 3-6). That being said, these reshaped narratives are essential to understanding how the authors here creatively influence the Slender Man mythos, and what this creative reshaping means for the mythology as a whole.

The stories gathered in the rest of this chapter were found on fanfiction.net, a website dedicated to the writing and reading of fanfiction. People searching for various fanfictions on the site can narrow down their searches by clicking on specific categories such as 'web shows', or more specific categories like 'Harry Potter'. One such category is 'mythology', the category in which the Slender Man fanfiction is frequently found. These narratives also partake in what is often called 'cross-universe' fanfiction (Duffett 2013, 170), or narratives in which characters from different shows or fictional worlds are together, such as *Harry Potter* and *the X-Files*. For the Slender Man, this cross-universe writing is frequently between different creepypastas, or other shared online horror narratives, re-shared and spread online. One example is the primary romantic analysis which follows, 'The bride of the Slender Man'.

## 7.2 The Bride of Slender Man

User Kimori94 on fanfiction.net wrote a horror-romance story called 'The Bride of Slender Man'. The website allows for updates to the narrative after publication, so while the first section of the story was published in December 2012, it was last updated – at the time of writing – in March 2016. The story, consisting of a prologue and eight chapters, tells the story of a young nineteen-year-old woman named Auraelia who finds herself protected by the Slender Man. The story also draws on another creepypasta character called Jeff the Killer, who is typically depicted as a psychotic killer who, like the Batman's Joker, carved a smile into his own face.

The story centres on young Auraelia, who met the Slender Man as a child, though for some reason was not taken. After her high school graduation, she gets into an argument with her mother who was trying to marry her to the son of a rich businessman, causing her to run into the wilderness where she finds the Slender Man again. At first scared, she soon remembers the character from her childhood, when she had considered him a friend, though is still unsure of the relationship. She is rude to him at first, but after being attacked by Jeff the Killer in her own home, she begins to accept the protection Slender Man and his proxy Masks (derived from Marble Hornets) offer. Auraelia's mother surprises her by forcing her to house another young woman in her home for a few months, a blind woman named Rose. Both Masks and Jeff are living at the house as well, causing some issues and trepidations. Jeff is immediately unsure of Rose's lack of sight and acts strange around her. Due to anger, Auraelia leaves Rose alone in the house with Jeff. Jeff physically attacks Rose and rapes her. Wracked with guilt, Auraelia gets drunk and the Slender Man, after physically attacking Jeff as punishment, takes Auraelia away to his own small house in the forest. Their attachment grows with the time they spend alone together. She gets bitten by several black widow spiders, and Slender Man takes her back to her own home, where he and Masks together bring her back to health. When sharing a moment after her recovery, Slender Man and Auraelia kiss. Rose recovers from her wounds, forgives Jeff and moves back into the house. Jeff seems no longer interested in harming her. Rose begins working for a large and influential business, and Auraelia is faced with a choice: to abandon her other choices and live with the Slender Man, or to leave the Slender Man for a normal life. She chooses the Slender Man.

### 7.2.1 Transforming the Transformed

From the surface, there are several major differences between the the Slender narratives we have looked at so far and 'the Bride of Slender Man'. For one, this is the first narrative we have in which the Slender Man is given a voice. Multiple sections shift the narrative point of view, and there are three primary ones: Auraelia, Jeff and the Slender Man. The nature of Slender Man's violence is also very different. While he is rather ruthless when it comes to both Masks and Jeff, there is no violence directed towards anyone else in the narrative. He also demonstrates anger towards Jeff's attack of the blind Rose. This is also the first narrative with primary female characters. Women in the previous narratives were not highly represented. In fact, when we previously looked at the role of different ages and genders in relation to the natural and the supernatural, the position of adult women was in question, primarily due to there not being enough reference to build on (Chapter 3).

We should take a moment here to address the role of rape in these narratives. The sexual nature of these narratives is in stark contrast to the narratives we have looked at prior to this chapter. Its presence here requires two comments: first, the importance of trauma in relation to storytelling; and second, that the narrative level may not be relevant.

The first comment requires us to, at least briefly, address 'rape play'. At first glance, it is possibly surprising to see the word 'play' in direct relationship to rape, but, as we have already seen in this study (Chapter 2), play does not necessarily mean frivolous, or childishness. Rape play refers to individuals, often in the BDSM (bondage, discipline, sadism, masochism) community, who enact or re-enact rape and sexual assault (Halena 2011). Often individuals who engage in rape play are those who have experienced sexual trauma in the past. They see rape play, with its negotiation and consent, as providing a level of agency to the event which they did not have in the past (Hammers 2012). Essentially, rape play helps individuals who have experienced sexual trauma to heal from their previous experience.

Rape play is similar to what is occurring in the process of horror writing online. While rape play is much more active than the process of writing, it helps to demonstrate an element of what is occurring for many of those who engage with the process of horror writing online, and quite possibly elsewhere. When talking with those in a more contemporary horror writing community, primarily those on the subreddit r/nosleep, a participant described in great detail how writing helped him cope with a history of abuse and trauma. In many ways, this participant is using writing in a similar way to the individuals engaged in rape play – both confront their issues by reliving them, but on their own terms.

However, there is also the role of the narrative level itself. The sexual violence as we have seen it prior to any analysis is on the N level, the narrative level of the narrative. It may or may not affect the underlying structural levels, and the extent of this, if at all, will be explored in the rest of this chapter. When we pull back to survey the other narratives, violence in a more general sense is heavily present. We have already analysed the role of such violent actions as disembowelling and impalement. The rape present in these narratives, while sexual rather than the pure physical in the previous chapters, is still a form of violence. We will see if, in the following sections, this violence remains purely on the narrative level, or if it filters down to influence the structure underneath, which is more of our concern.

Before tackling the larger questions such as Slender Man's voice, we should first focus on the female human protagonists in the narrative. 'The Bride of Slender Man', like other more romantic takes on the Slender Man, does have an adult female as its primary character. In our previous look, humans' fit in the natural/supernatural scale left adult females as a question. After Jeff attacked her, Auraelia responded by both forgiving him and demonstrating she has no fear. Similarly, after Jeff's attack and rape, Rose also forgives him and shows no fear. The previous scale from natural to supernatural had adult females as somewhere in between the two, but mostly because there was little knowledge with where they truly rested. Now, we can see how this position may be an accurate positioning.

At the end of the narrative, both Auraelia and Rose have an affinity with the supernatural, though this was not something which automatically began this way. Our previous narratives demonstrated how children have a more innate affinity with the supernatural, in contrast to adult males who were both treated and regarded as more aligned with nature. This separation was mostly due to treatment the Slender Man inflicted: adult males were found viciously killed, while children simply disappeared. The position of women was more in question, primarily due to the lack of women in the narratives to give sufficient evidence. The most direct reference to women was in Victor Surge's narratives, where the captions under the first image referenced a female photographer, who was missing (Victor Surge 2009a). In these narratives, women's affinity with the supernatural was not as innate as children, but the lack of violence inflected by the Slender Man to them reveals some form of similarity to the supernatural disappearance of the children. For both Rose and Auraelia, the relinquishing of fear is what unites the two, and causes their shift to a more supernatural consideration.

This also creates an interesting dynamic regarding the violence the Slender Man inflicts in regard to these female characters. As mentioned before, the Slender Man in 'the Bride of Slender Man' acts violently to a few of the male characters, more specifically Jeff the Killer and Masks. He often reacts in anger, resulting in him violently attacking these two. His reactions towards Auraelia, however, tend to be softer even when in anger. This reflects the different standings on the natural/supernatural line between adult men and adult women. Despite the softer presence, and therefore a lack of violence on the Slender Man's part, the women are not precluded from violence more generally speaking, especially sexual violence. The Slender Man does not have a role in this, though he will in the more erotic narratives later in this chapter. In previous narratives which depicted the Slender Man taking children, no obvious sign of violence was shown, nor were children's bodies ever found. Children simply disappear; they get a strongly different treatment than adult men, who are found impaled on trees or dissected. Somewhere in between these lie adult women, who are not treated as severely as men, but not quite as silent and calming as that directed towards children (see Diagram 3.1). Women's violent treatment more generally seems to push them more to the side of nature, though, at least in this narrative, the Slender Man's protection seems to protect them slightly. For now, we can place adult females in the middle.

Rose, as a blind character, also orients us once again to the sensory codes and their relation to Slender Man. In our previous studies, we saw three primary modes of the senses: prohibited senses, which directly affect the relationship between the narrative and the audience; sound, which is directly related to the Slender Man himself; and obscured senses, which are often more related to the Transformed, mostly related to Slender Man's original place in the background of photographs (Chapter 3). Rose's lack of sight immediately precludes her from being of the obscured senses, as these have often been linked to fooling sight, such as Slender Man being hidden in pictures. The removal of one sense has heightened her other senses, most specifically her sense of hearing and touch (Kimori94 2012 [2016]). These made it easier for her to be aware of the Slender Man in the house, even though she could not see him. Once again, this connects sound to the Slender Man.

The romance narratives present a different understanding of our initial triadic structure. Our female characters have a movement of categories, and like the characters in our other narratives, the characters here move from Untouched to Transformed. They are unable to move once there, unless through a process of becoming Removed, either through death or proxy. For the first time, however, being trapped in the middle category of Transformed is no longer seen in a negative light, nor one to fear. In fact, it is almost a positive position, as Rose had an opportunity to either be Removed through death but chose instead to return to the house and live there as Transformed.

The progression from one category to another also comes with shifts in understanding of power relations. While previous progressions saw a loss in the social self, the progression here has an added level. Both Auraelia and Rose have lost their more social self but have gained a greater self-understanding and have become more comfortable with their lack of power.

Prior to the events of the narrative, both women view themselves as ultimately powerless in their lives. Rose is neglected and abused by her parents, and Auraelia is heavily controlled and abused by her mother. After Jeff's attack, Auraelia's reasoning for forgiving him quickly was 'because I am a woman. We are tools in which men use to satisfy their needs [sic]' (Kimori94 2012 [2016]). The lack of power over the self is evident. As the two women move to the Transformed, their strength comes from both an abandoning of fear and a regaining of more comfort in the lack of power truly had. While they began with a lack of power of self, and continue a lack of power over self, there is a greater comfort in this when moved to the Transformed category. The Transformed is connected to powerlessness one felt throughout different narratives. It is a powerful mytheme which impacts the movement of the structural categories – individuals move without power or agency in their own placement (Chapter 4). The power is shifted though from others, to exclusively the Slender Man. The Slender Man is still in control of their movements, and whether they are pleased with their position, they are nevertheless stuck there. The women in 'The Bride of Slender Man' are comfortable with this shifting of power in a way other narratives have not portrayed.

As mentioned at the beginning of this section, the Slender Man has a voice in this narrative, a stark departure from the previous tales. As he has no direct place in our current structure, his sudden voice is a stark contrast to the quiet firm figure which once directed the structural flow. His voice lets the reader into the mind of a monster, but mostly gives him more empathy as a character. But if we, as readers, can empathize with him, does he still hold his omnipotent place in the structure?

The characters are moving from one category to another purely based on their interaction or knowledge of the Slender Man. Once progressed, there is no returning to previous categories. Instead, the characters are forced to either remain or advance. Their movement is based on the Slender Man, which means they do not have power over their own movement. So, like the previous sections, the Slender Man is a mechanism for the structure. His voice appears to not change this.

The other supernatural or creepypasta entities also fall into the pre-set categories of the structural diagram. The proxy, Masks, does not act like our previous proxies who existed in the Transformed category, though very close to the Removed (Chapter 5). In 'the Bride of Slender Man', Masks is constantly dying and being resurrected by the Slender Man. His humanity is thus stripped. Masks, then, is fully Removed. While Jeff the Killer is technically a human, his nature as a creepypasta character, and his separation from normal society, is fully Removed as well. He is not fully removed by being dead but is, like his separation from social setting as the proxies. More telling for their position as Removed is their connection to the Slender Man. More affected than typically possible, they seem to stay lingering around him, as if somehow a part of him and his presence, though not so much a part of it as to be omnipresent in the structure.

Thus, every character has a position in the triad, and the main protagonist moves within it, all through her relationship with the Slender Man. This is similar to other narratives from before, although the relationship with the Slender Man previously was less romantic. This shifting makes the Transformed position not something to be feared – in fact, fear has little place in it. Instead, the characters find love instead of fear.

## 7.3 Slender Man erotica

'The Bride of Slender Man' by Kimori94 represents a more subdued romance. The focus is on the relationship between Slender and Auraelia, as she learns to not fear, and he protects her from other acts of violence. Other romantic takes on the Slender Man slipped into much more erotic forms. Erotic narratives are not uncommon in fanfiction, as there are various terminologies and categories of narratives which differentiate both erotic narratives in general and specific types of erotic narratives. For example, 'slash fiction' tends to portray two characters of the same sex in intimate and/or erotic situations (Duffett 2013, 170). Similarly, some writers and fans like to 'ship' characters together, or imagine two characters who are canonically not in a romantic relationship as being together. The Slender Man is not immune to this part of online storytelling. In fact, when finding case studies for this chapter, it became difficult to find narratives which were not in some way erotic. Their prevalence is the reason for a separate section.

As these narratives tend to be relatively shorter than the longer romantic piece of 'The Bride of Slender Man', I have chosen four examples from fanfiction.net: '50 Shades of Slender' by Kingdomheartlover123; 'It's Not Real' by laglycerine; 'The Slender Man who tied me to a tree' by OpaliteMoon; and 'Be at Peace' by Chooboo.

The plot of these narratives, like most erotic short stories, is not overly important functionally speaking. What is relevant for our purposes are references, metaphors, symbols, use of sounds and so forth. The plot is often short, simple and only vaguely complete. The rest of this section will give a quick overview of these narratives, and the following section will give a more specific analysis.

'50 Shades of Slender' by Kingdomheartslover123 is a story about a young woman who, while walking home late one night, begins to find scribbled notes in the woods. After taking several of these notes (similar to both *Slender: The Eight Pages* and *Slender: The Arrival*; see Chapter 6), the Slender Man appears, and she falls unconscious. She wakes to find herself captured. The Slender Man steals her voice, so she is unable to scream while he sexually tortures her.

'It's Not Real' by laglycerine similarly begins with a young woman walking home at night, after a university class on mythology in which she first heard of the Slender Man. Along the way, she gets attacked by the Slender Man, who sexually accosts her. She at first resists, but then changes and becomes interested in the act. When Slender begins to strangle her, her fear returns. She dies but joins the Slender Man in death.

'The Slender Man who tied me to a tree' by OpaliteMoon is our third narrative which centres on a young woman. Our protagonist is walking through the woods when she encounters the Slender Man. She falls unconscious and wakes up tied to a tree. The two engage in sexual activity, in which the protagonist begins to enjoy the process. She wakes up again after, with no sign of him and no longer on the tree.

'Be at Peace' by Chooboo is slightly different from the three previous ones. For one, the primary protagonist is a young man, not a woman. Second, the narrative is the least overtly sexual. Our male protagonist has been stalked by the Slender Man for just over a decade. When finally facing the Slender Man again, he gives in to his fate. Although he dies almost immediately, his spirit is meant to be forever with Slender.

### 7.3.1 Sensory codes

Similar to several analyses before, including previously in this chapter, we will start with the sensory codes. In the four narratives briefly described earlier, the sensory codes continue to fall into the three categories described in previous sections related to the senses: obscured, sound and prohibited. In both 'the Slender Man who tied me to a tree' and 'Be at Peace' the protagonists' vision is obscured prior to a direct and more obvious encounter with the Slender Man. The direct sight of the Slender Man is obscured (OpaliteMoon 2012) or it is too dark to see properly (Chooboo 2013). Similarly, darkness is often associated with other encounters with the Slender Man in these narratives, such as wandering through the woods at night (laglycerine 2013; Kingdomheartslover123 2015).

Sound is once again directly related to the Slender Man. This is sometimes in what the character hears which signals the monster's coming, for example hearing children's screams when he is near (laglycerine 2013). In most of the narratives, the Slender Man is given a voice, in a similar way to 'the Bride of Slender Man' (Chooboo 2013; laglycerine 2013; Kingdomheartslover123 2015). In the case of '50 Shades of Slender', the Slender Man's voice does not come until the voice of the female protagonist is removed (Kingdomheartslover123 2015). The removal of one's ability to sound allows his to flourish.

Prohibited senses are also present. Both '50 Shades of Slender' and 'Be at Peace' refer either directly or indirectly to the notes found in the Slender video games, some which directly reference the prohibited senses, such as 'Don't look or it takes you' (Chooboo 2013; Kingdomheartslover123 2015), as well as reference to the prohibited notion of the Slender Man in the mythology recap notes in 'It's Not Real' (laglycerine 2013).

The prohibited senses are those typically recalled and associated with those Untouched, or, as referenced at the very beginning of this book before the term was used for a particular category, with those uninvolved or ignorant of the Slender Man's presence. The prohibitions are in place in order to allow for those to remain within the category of the Untouched. In contrast, the obscured senses are those which cause the audience member to seek the unfamiliar, the supernatural, the Slender Man. The presence of obscured senses, thus, keep the Transformed within their category (Chapter 3).

### 7.3.2 Locations

The locations of each narrative are similar. 'The Slender Man who tied me to a tree' and 'Be at Peace' both take place entirely in the woods. '50 Shades of Slender' begins in the woods, and then the female protagonist is moved to an abandoned building. 'It's Not Real' takes place along a countryside road.

The presence of woods is something we have grown incredibly familiar when it comes to the Slender Man narratives. His presence in the woods goes back to the Something Awful forums, with the digitally manipulated photos of the Slender Man lingering menacingly behind trees (Victor Surge 2009c, Chapter 3; genesplicer 2009, Chapter 4). The film students of Marble Hornets find connections to the Slender Man in national parks (Marble Hornets 2009-2014, Chapter 5). Players flee from him as they gather pages in the woods in his video games (Parsec Productions 2012; Blue Isle Studios 2013 [2015], Chapter 7). The woods are an essential part of nature, one which some victims are forced to become a part of through treatment, such as disembowelment or impalement through the trees (Chapter 3). The woods harbour the unfamiliar (Zipes 1988).

We see similar treatment here. The woods are where the Slender Man hunts, and the avenue through which he shifts others' categorical position. It was the woods which the player had to cross before moving to a new categorical position in the video game (Chapter 7).

For 'It's Not Real', the protagonist is walking along a countryside road – a position which borders both civilization and wilderness. Similarly, the primary character in '50 Shades of Slender' begins in the woods but gets taken to an abandoned house. The house itself is similar to the country road in its position of both wilderness and civilization, but it is more similar to the position of the mines which we saw in *Slender: The Arrival* (Blue Isle Studios 2013 [2015]; Chapter 7).

While not underground, the abandoned house is equally as separated from the social. Similar to the movement found in *Slender: The Arrival*, the abandoned house demonstrates the past movement from the Untouched to the Transformed – the house, once a place for emotional safety (Bachelard 1964), has been left by the social and human interactions. It has been relegated as only a reminder of the part it once played yet not truly part of the system, in much the same way human characters in the Transformed are both a reminder of what was once a social element, but has been marginalized from this and is no longer as present in the social while still being present physically. Thus, the locations which are not directly the woods still exist in the border between the country road and the abandoned house. Best represented is the waking of the protagonist in 'The Sender Man who tied me to a tree' who wakes on the edge of the woods – the border between the unfamiliar and the familiar.

### 7.3.3 Mythemes

Most of the mythemes found in these narratives are ones found in other Slender Man narratives we have already explored: death, unhealthy (first from Marble Hornets; see Chapter 5), gender positions such as male and female, and fear. Similar to 'The Bride of Slender Man' analysed previously, there are some additional mythemes which cause an interesting second look to the narratives. In contrast to fear, we have a letting go of fear, and love. There is also a present obsession through the Slender Man's eyes of ownership.

What is interesting to consider is the connection of fear and death to both its antecedents: letting go of fear and life. In 'The Slender Man who tied me to a tree', the female protagonist is afraid at first but relinquishes her fear as the enjoyment of the moment overtakes her. At the end of the narrative, the protagonist is left on the edge of the woods still alive. In contrast, the character in 'It's Not Real' does not fully let go of her fear. She begins the encounter in fear, and begins to relinquish in enjoyment, much like our character on the tree. But as the Slender Man wraps a tendril around her neck, the fear comes back, and she cries out against it. She dies at the end of this encounter but is chosen by the Slender Man to 'live' this life-after-life as his bride. It seems the relinquishing of fear is connected to a continued life, while continuing to live in the fear leads to death.

But how does this compare with our other two narratives? The character in '50 Shades of Slender' does not die at the end, but there is no clear indication whether she has died or will. Granted, we have only the amount of story present, but we must assume we have the full finished narrative. Fanfiction.net allows writers to update stories after their initial publication, which leads to many unfinished narratives in which only the first section has been uploaded. While I have decided to choose narratives which appeared 'finished', it can be difficult to tell if a narrative has gotten its last update at the time of reading. '50 Shades of Slender' has other interesting added elements, some of which we have already discussed such as the removal of voice, and so perhaps it would be best to return to this narrative once the others have been given their proper study.

The other narrative left out of the fear/death question is 'Be at Peace', a complex narrative for its relative short length, which is also our only narrative with a male protagonist. Here, there is a letting go of fear as well – the protagonist seemingly willingly gives himself up to the Slender Man, tired of being fearful and running for years after a childhood encounter. Fear is given up for ownership, a relinquishing of control of self (an interesting notion which we shall return to). While death is met, there, like 'It's Not Real', is a life-after-death with the Slender Man. The primary protagonist sees this as a form of 'eternal love' (Chooboo 2013). Even though he let go of his fear, he still met death.

But this brings us back to the position of adult males, adult females and children on the supernatural/natural scale. The more erotic takes of the Slender Man stories have given us an understanding of the placement of adult females, a more complete knowledge we have not had until now due to a lack of female protagonists to truly garner an understanding. We can ideally place female protagonists in the middle – their gender/age does not automatically relate to them a particular supernatural/natural understanding as it has for adult males and children, but is rather seemingly up to choices the female protagonists make. Our male protagonist, then, in 'Be at Peace' must be treated back to the natural regardless of his choices. His gender positions him more than his choices.

Despite this, there is a release when dead and a return to a different emotion – love. This is something that, until this chapter, we have not seen as a mytheme at all. Love is only directly present in two of the narratives, both of which the character dies: 'Be at Peace' and 'It's Not Real'. Again, we see the progression from Untouched to Removed, the one-way progression which is normally met with fear. Once in the Transformed category, the way of re-establishing balance is to become Removed – or, essentially, to die. Perhaps this is why our character in 'Be at Peace' relinquishes the fear and control readily – because he seeks the balance death brings. In past narratives, such as those found on the Something Awful forums and in Marble Hornets, the progression, even when it establishes balance, is met with fear. The progression, and every movement through it, is a horror. Here, in both 'The Slender Man who tied me to a tree' and 'Be at Peace', the movement is not feared. The characters relinquish their fears for their transition – one from Untouched to Transformed ('The Slender Man who tied me to a tree') and one from Transformed to Removed ('Be at Peace'). For 'It's Not Real', in contrast, we have a protagonist who fears, relinquishes fear and then fears again. The progression still occurs but is met with negative emotive experiences. This is the same for '50 Shades of Slender': the progression still occurs, but the experience is full of fear and pain. For the protagonist here, the process is drawn out – the Slender Man plays with her in a way not portrayed in the others. But the others relinquish much faster than the protagonist here.

And this is where the mytheme of ownership comes in. The ownership mytheme is only one directional – it is only the Slender Man who owns. The monster in 'Be at Peace' refers to the protagonist as something that is 'rightfully mine' (Chooboo 2013). The act of an intimate relationship is also associated with ownership – the moment the protagonist first releases fear in 'It's Not Real' is when she 'wanted to be his' (laglycerine 2013). While it is not directly described in '50 Shades of Slender', the Slender Man's treatment of our female protagonist demonstrates a form of intense ownership – he strips her voice, and thus a way of expressing self. He mentions near the end wanting to 'break' her mind – wanting to strip what it is that makes her herself. Ownership for the human protagonists means relinquishing control and the idea of self.

Relinquishing of fear is thus associated with a relinquishing of self – a giving over of ownership. The Slender Man already has control over the progression movement of characters, the relinquishing of control is only a demonstration of the lack of control the characters truly have over their own location. When the characters relinquish control, they are met with something almost positive: relief, love and, in one case, life. In contrast, the presence of fear is also a presence of an attempt of control over self, and this is often met with more negative ends, either death or a prolonged torture before death.

This also helps to, more permanently, position women in the middle position on our natural/supernatural scale (see Diagram 3.1). We initially positioned them in the middle due to violence being inflicted upon them, though in our first narrative it was not perpetrated by the Slender Man, but by being spared from the Slender Man's bringing of death or disappearance. Here, we can see the sexual violence the women suffer through is present in almost every narrative. When the women let go of their fear, in essence letting go of any semblance of control or power – in other words becoming more child-like – they are spared, and can be more aligned with the supernatural.

### 7.3.4 Slender's erotic structure

What has been demonstrated through the last chapter is the lack of change from our current structural understanding. The structure is still triadic – an extending of a middle category which is both present and not present, alive and dead, all at once. This Transformed middle category has, in the past, been met with fear – and a greater fear of being trapped in such a position. The progression, eventually ending in the Removed, or in death and complete loss of self, while returning to a balanced state, is also one which is feared as well. This progression still occurs: the categories are still associated with similar mythemes, and the final state remains a form of death, or complete removal from the social (as is demonstrated by our female protagonist in 'The Bride of Slender Man') as the only way of establishing balance once again. The emotional attachments to these categorical changes, however, are slightly different.

Perhaps here it is best to repeat an important understanding of structuralism which was last discussed very early in this study: the nature of structuralist analysis (Chapter 1). Lévi-Strauss more implicitly laid out the idea of structural levels (Lévi-Strauss 1969, 12), but this has since been more fully sketched out by neo-structuralists (Kunin 2004, 7–15; Miles-Watson 2009b, 11–13). Essentially, a myth is made up of several structural layers.

The N level, or Narrative level, is the one which we are presented with when first encountering the narrative. This is the story told by the storytellers around the fire, or the narrative read on the computer screen from Something Awful late at night. The Narrative level is full of cultural and social contexts, often flowing from the particular place and time the narrative is told, full of detail and description and the need to entice readers or listeners. For structuralism, this is the least important structural element of the myth.

The $S^3$ level is the first step below the N level. At $S^3$, the description, detail and emotional renderings of the N level is boiled down to mythemes and the relations between them: how one relates to the other and the categories we have listed and understood. So, for example, our rendering of the Transformed category and the mythemes represented therein make a part of this $S^3$ structural level.

The $S^2$ level boils this down even further. The detailed categorical names, such as Untouched, Transformed and Removed, are brought down to A, B and Cs. They are understood as categorical spaces, which could be replaced by a multitude of others depending on the mythos or narratives to be experienced or read at that time. The structural equation should remain the same when looked at within the same cultural context.

The first layer, $S^1$, is most often seen as the potential for structure – the human potential for structure. Lévi-Strauss in the past attempted to paint this as the Canonical Formula (Lévi-Strauss 1963b, 228), though it has since been reformulated by Mosko (1991). This book does not seek to find this level, as it is fraught with too many questions best answered by a very different study than the present one. A fuller discussion of the structuralist $S^1$ level and its relation to the Slender Man is best reserved for the end of this study, especially in helping to answer the question of where the Slender Man's culture resides (Chapter 11).

The reason for the repetition here is to serve as a reminder that the most important structural element we seek to find is $S^2$ – the structural equation boiled down after our mythemes and their connections. So far, we have dabbled between $S^3$ and $S^2$, occasionally dipping down into the deeper layer to ensure the equation still holds true before we move along to the next group of narratives. This is important to consider since the differences we initially saw in the more romantic and erotic takes of the Slender Man are those more emotionally present – the romantic connections to the feared monster, for example. Most of the differences we initially saw are on the N level – the mythemes are rarely changed, and the structure is not altered. The structure is not even an inverse. The primary differences found were mostly on the N level, and the few additions to mythemes have only solidified, or clarified, positions rather than altering them.

Despite having a voice, and more involvement in the narratives than typical, the Slender Man's presence in the structure is also not different. His presence is a mechanism through which the structure functions. He still has no place within the structure he works. He moves people along and defines categories themselves.

## 7.4 Conclusion

Throughout this study, we have given consideration for many of the narratives which make up the Slender Man's mythology. We started with the first instance of the narrative on the Something Awful forums. We spiralled out from there to other narratives, like Marble Hornets, and other forms the narratives take, such as video games. We have also looked at other genres, stretching out from the horror genre to more romantic genres.

Throughout these various narrative changes and alterations, the structure first refined from the Something Awful forums has remained the same. It has become somewhat refined and solidified but has not completely shifted or altered the understanding. So far, however, we have remained within the Slender Man's mythos, so perhaps this is why the structure has remained largely unchanged. While we have moved between what is, theoretically, different groups of people, the Slender Man is still present in all, meaning there must be, historically, someone who brought the story forward. According to Lévi-Straussian structuralism, the structure on the $S^2$ level should be the same even when the specific narrative is different (Lévi-Strauss 1963b). That is the case for the same cultural group, which begs the question, what is the Slender Man's cultural group? If the Slender Man is simply a representative of his cultural group, then theoretically the structure should remain the same, even when the Slender Man is left behind. However, on the online sphere, the virtual geography does not lend itself to an easy distinguishing of community groups, especially when the speed of social 'movement' is as fast as it is online. This means we must find the culture for ourselves. The first step to this would be to test the boundaries of the Slender Man's mythology realm.

In that vein, we shall begin moving closer to other narratives. This chapter took us one step closer to this by shifting the locus from horror to romance. The following chapter pushes this even further, dabbling into emotional relations and, touched by the Let's Players of Chapter 6. As the Slender Man narrative grew, more humorous takes on the monster arose.

8

# Laughing at the horror

So far, our spiralling exploration of the Slender Man has brought us to a large amount of different narrative forms and expressions. We have chased through a variety of virtual geographic locations to find different forms the mythology touches. We have looked at images where his form lingers in the background (Chapters 3 and 4), read newspaper articles about his abductions (Chapter 3), watched films of his proxies (Chapter 5), played with him in video games (Chapter 6) and seen the women who love the monster (Chapter 7). But there is still one other narrative form and community who took control of the Slender Man's mythology. Like most things online, humorous takes on the Slender Man rose alongside the various web series, video games and images which we have already seen. The humorous, like the pure horror elements we have seen, come in a variety of forms. Images styled similarly to the image-based memes, written stories and web videos all helped to spread the funny side of the horror.

The move to humour does not alter our mythic approach. To review our definition of mythology, a myth is a narrative or something similar to a narrative which an individual uses to understand themselves and the world around them. So far, we have seen at least a certain level of the structure of the Slender Man around the different narratives he appears in. To see the connection to how humour and jokes could be considered mythology, we can first see how jokes are used in a more folkloric understanding. For Alan Dundes, different forms of communication which make social commentary on folklore, most prominently jokes, are considered 'meta-folklore' because they are still forms of folklore which make commentary on the folklore they reference (Dundes 1966). Meta-folklore has also been used to reference images (Fineman 2003; Mechling 2004). In a similar way, the jokes which follow in this chapter are commentary on the mythology we have analysed so far. The jokes are, in some way, meta-mythology, and are myths in their own right. The jokes reveal a social understanding or comments on the myths, which means they reveal, to a certain extent, the understanding an individual who created the joke, or the community who spreads the joke, understands themselves in relation to their world and myths.

In this chapter, we will look at several of the more laughable sides of the Slender Man. We will explore the more fashionable critiques of the mannequin who resembles him, and the sparkly happy version which celebrates and dances. Both of these forms led to the creation of the Enderman family, to which we will give some consideration. A revisit to fanfiction, this time the humorous side of the community, leads us to a version of the fanfiction which crosses different universes. What happens when the Slender Man becomes part of the *My Little Pony* universe?

## 8.1 Parodying the Slender Man

Most of the more humorous approaches to the Slender Man take a parodic approach. The images, with words chosen, shift the narratives from horror to humour. These different humorous parodies take a variety of forms, from memes to videos. Each one of these adds to the larger myth of the Slender Man, despite some of the difference in narrative for comedic purposes. The myth grows and changes to even incorporate these alterations. Several examples of these will be looked at, including the Trender Man and the Splendor Man.

Similar to how much of the Slender Man's narratives were told in a highly visual way, the jokes regarding the Slender Man are also highly visual. As mentioned in a previous chapter, more visual forms of storytelling do not preclude a structuralist analysis from the outside. Lévi-Strauss himself demonstrates a connection to not only reading narratives but also aesthetics both visually and in music (Lévi-Strauss 1997). He also looked at actions and ritual as action (Lévi-Strauss 1963a). Galinier also proposed a connection to ritual, which is primarily movement, music and visually centred (Galinier 2004). Similarly, Will Wright attempted a structuralist analysis of Western films, a primarily visual experience (Wright 1975). Seth Kunin connected not only ritual but also personal narratives of ritual, myth and religious experience as a form of mythology and cultural understanding (Kunin 2009). Similarly, Jonathan Miles-Watson's conception of implicit mythology, which we used in our own formulation of the concept in Chapter 6, saw personal narratives and connections to myth as being a form of mythology itself (Miles-Watson 2015). If we see jokes, as described earlier, as a form of commentary on the mythology, than in many ways it fits both Kunin and Miles-Watson's view of personal narratives and mythology, and others have demonstrated the visual nature possible in the study of mythology. In other words, the visual nature of jokes is not outside of either the conception of mythology or the ability to practically apply structuralism to it.

### 8.1.1 Trender Man

An image of a mannequin wearing a brown sweater and white shirt underneath was posted on the social media website Tumblr by user Conjured Charisma. Posted in 2012, three years after the Slender Man's first appearance, the image was captioned: Slenderman's Casual Friday (Know Your Meme 2010 [2018]). Another user commented that it was, in fact, Slender Man's more fashionable and sassy brother, the Trender Man. The image became popular on Tumblr, and eventually spread to other websites as its own meme.

The Trender Man meme followed the format of most early text-related memes – with typical unspoken or unwritten layout rules and guidelines. The history of memes is fuzzy, as the word has changed meaning in its more casual usage. Its stricter definition which has been used in this study before – spreadable media able to be remixed by users (Wiggins and Bowers 2015) – was its earlier online understanding, and the one associated with textual memes like Trender Man. This sits in contrast to 'viral' – just one image or video which is immensely popular. A meme is more than just viral, it demonstrates individual creativity by allowing variations to exist. To understand a meme, you must see several iterations, not just one video or image.

More textual image-based memes typically use a single image, with set, yet unspoken, guidelines on the proper use of the image. After the *Lord of the Rings: Fellowship of the Ring* (2001), the quite simple line the character Boromir delivers in the scene of the Council of Elrond – 'One does not simply walk into Mordor' – became a popular internet meme, taking on several different iterations. Starting on Something Awful, the full line was repeated, with replacements of the word 'walk'; users would photoshop Boromir doing other actions. This version of the meme began with 'One does not simply drive into Mordor'.

The more common Boromir meme, the 'one does not simply' begins with the text at the top being the beginning of the quote ('one does not simply') with the second half being the phrase of the meme. The image backdrop is always the same still image from the *Fellowship of the Ring* movie, at the primary moment the line is delivered, so the actor's hands and face are in the moment of explaining something. An example is featured in Figure 8.1: one does not simply explain memes.

**Figure 8.1** One does not simply explain memes to someone (quickmeme n.d).

As you can tell from Figure 8.1, the format of the wording is important for memes like this one. Not just any words or phrase will fit. The words fit the original context of the image. The humour comes with the flipping of the phrase to fit the context the individual meme-maker wishes it to fit. The meme assumes knowledge of the original context – the joke means little to someone who does not know the context of the 'one does not simply walk into Mordor' line. The meme is based on a 'remixing' of this – a product of the meme-making *bricoleur*. Within the one joke meme, there are two different contexts: one of the original image and/or saying, and one of the social commentary the joke is referring to. The reference to the second necessitates a subversion of the first.

As Ryan Milner points out, the connection does not end with the meme-maker. Rather, the meme-maker's act of connecting the meme to areas of knowledge outside creates a social group with social identity. He claims this makes the internet feel more like 'a place' (Milner 2016, 33). Limor Shifman also points out how memes may, on the surface, appear to be trivial and mundane, but they reveal deep social and cultural structures (Shifman 2014, 15). This is not unique to memes but is also applicable to jokes and mythology. Mythology must, by both our definition and structuralist thought, reflect the cultural structures and understandings in which the myth arises (Lévi-Strauss 1963b; see Chapter 1). In jokes more generally speaking, cultural references and structures are necessary for the subversion they represent and invoke (Douglas 1968; Lincoln 1993).

Trender Man fits this type of meme-telling. The original image reflects the concept of the Slender Man, the beginning words reflecting the type of horror storytelling typically reserved for him. The bottom half of the phrase shifts away from the typical horror and violent actions, and towards fashion-sensitive commentary. The humour comes from the shift between the two – from the more serious actions of the Slender Man, to seemingly over-exaggeration.

Figure 8.2 gives us an example of how the Trender Man meme looks. The simple image of the mannequin is still present. The top line is the threat typically associated with the Slender Man. The second part of the text, however, shifts this away from the threat to a question of fashion. Figure 8.2 exemplifies the Trender Man meme well, as it also represents a commonly found joke within the Trender Man memes: the wearing of crocs. The time in which the Trender Man meme arose is around the time the wearing of crocs (plastic-appearing shoe) was a topic of constant discussion, and often the butt of jokes.

The Trender Man meme, as a joke, is a parody of the Slender Man myth. Like most parodies, the humour necessitates a previous knowledge of the original narrative. The humour of the Trender Man is lost for those who do not know the original context of the blank-faced monster who lurks and threatens. Even the original post of 'Slenderman's Casual Friday' relies on a knowledge of the basic Slender Man narrative: most notably the blank face and the suit. Like

**Figure 8.2** Trender Man meme example (memegenerator n.d).

our previous studies, the audience is already placed in a mediatory position of the Transformed, living both in normal society, but with the knowledge of that outside. Folklorist Barbara Babcock uses the idea of symbolic inversion, which she defines as 'an act of expressive behaviour which inverts, contradicts, abrogates or in some fashion presents an alternative to commonly held cultural codes, values and norms' (Babcock 1978, 14). Following Mary Douglas's assertion that 'jokes are expressive of the social situations in which they occur' (1968, 366), we can see jokes as a symbolic inversion of the social situation the joke is found in. Jokes, and their performance, whether it be oral or visual, are intricately wound up in the sociocultural power relations and categorical structures they both embody and may attempt to disrupt. A disruption of the structure does not necessarily mean, however, it is a complete shifting of this. Lévi-Strauss found structural inversion actually reflects the original structure through its process of inversion (Lévi-Strauss 1973a). Here, the process is more likely one of subversion than inversion, but the extent this affects the structure has yet to be seen.

### 8.1.2 Splendor Man

In 2010, YouTuber 'Neil Cicieraga' posted a video which began in a similar way to the Marble Hornets videos (Chapter 5). There was no sound, and words appeared in white on black, informing the audience that the following footage was taken when attempting to make a short film. The video shows two young women sitting on a picnic blanket eating berries and talking about pleasant things. The video, at times, glitches. And suddenly, behind the two, a looming figure slowly approaches. At first the audience can only see the long black legs. When the two girls look up at the figure, they cry out 'Splendor Man' with glee. The stilted figure has a joyous face painted largely, and proceeds to dance and throw glitter at the girls (Neil Cicieraga 2010).

The Splendor Man is similar enough in basic appearance to the Slender Man, though with small differences. He wears a suit, but one covered in bright buttons and with a bowtie. One of the original depictions of the Slender Man was with odd proportions to the face, for example in Victor Surge's performance post (Victor Surge 2009d; see Chapter 3). The Splendor Man mimics this by a smile which is too largely proportioned, and with a top hat.

Like the Trender Man, Splendor Man is a parody of the original conception of the Slender Man. Here, the set-up is similar to Marble Hornets specifically – drawing on a pseudo-documentary style approach, especially with the plot detail of the group having tried to shoot a short film. The narrative plays on the expectations previously established by Marble Hornets and other Slender Man narratives. Like the Trender Man, the Splendor Man ended up growing the Enderman family. Considered Slender Man's older, and nicer, brother, Splendor Man is often given the role of a similar narrative to the original YouTube video: he throws glitter and dances and celebrates.

The Splendor Man is a great example of the turn towards what became deemed as 'HappyPasta'. The opposite of creepypasta, happypasta became the joyful parody of the narratives and characters often existing in the creepypasta sphere. For example, the happypasta version of the creepypasta character Jeff the Killer, which we saw depicted in the previous section's story 'The Bride of the Slender Man', is Jeff the Hugger (HappyPasta Wikia n.d).

## 8.1.3 Parodies and the Enderman family

The happypasta of the Slender Man and the meme Trender Man are, as has already been said, prime examples of how parodies of the Slender Man eventually increased the narratives of the Slender Man. Despite their original intent based on humour and shifting the narrative of the Slender Man in more funny ways, the mythos grew to incorporate these parodies.

The growth of the narratives grew into the formation of the Enderman family. The Trender Man is considered the Slender Man's younger brother, more fashionable and with a bit more of a sassy streak than a vicious one. The Splendor Man is the older but much happier brother. Essentially, these parodies start simply as a form of humour – a joke to flip the content of the story to make a comedic point. The effect, however, was that these jokes were incorporated into the mythos by extending the understanding of the Slender Man to include the variations.

Mahadev Apte described humour as consisting of four stages: the first being the cognitive experience which could result in a mirthful state of mind; the second being external sociocultural factors which triggers this cognitive experience; the third, the pleasure derived from the experience; and the fourth is the external manifestations (1985, 14). These four levels are similar to the levels of structure we have previously looked at in structuralism.

The N level, of the narrative structure, is related to our last section of humour, where the effect of the external manifestation occurs. The laughter which occurs after the joke does not demonstrate to us the deeper structural levels of the joke, as the N level is not as revealing of the underlying structure for the myth. On the opposite side of the spectrum, the $S^1$ level, which was the potential for structure typically on the biological level, is the first section of humour – the unconscious experience which 'could' result in a mirthful state of mind. Essentially, the structure of the joke is not any different than the structure of myth. This should not be a surprise, as we have already addressed at multiple points in this chapter, the function jokes play in the culture which tells them is the same as mythology, so the structure being similar should not be a surprise to discover.

Like the meme-maker, the humour-maker also works using the same techniques of the *bricoleur*. The humour draws on surrounding sociocultural factors which trigger the happy experience, in the same way our myth-makers, crafting memes, fanfictions and images, draw on the sociocultural surroundings to craft their narratives. Humour is built on these factors as well, giving it their $S^2$ and $S^3$ levels. Humour, as this form of narrative, is also revealed as myth – built in similar ways, on similar factors, and revealing the underlying cultural structure in similar ways.

Parody, as a form of humour, is used in a way which is 'repetition with difference' (Hutcheon 1985, 32). It takes the set form and shifts it to suit its own needs. As a form of narrative, it is derivative, yet unique. As a form it incorporates new into old, and often leads to new forms. *Don Quixote*, for instance, was a parodic work which led to be representative on its own. Some parodic texts free themselves from the background text, and thereby create new and autonomous forms (Hutcheon 1985, 35). Parody is transformational in its relationship to other narratives (Genette 1982, 34).

Even though parody creates difference, these differences remain an authoritative form. The form it parodies gives the authority it carries (Hutcheon 1985, 75). In this case, the narrative takes the same structural equation as the original contexts, though the differences are important to note, especially in how this difference may impact the cultural and structural levels. As mentioned previously, Lévi-Strauss demonstrated how narratives, which appear very different on the narrative level, still reflect the same cultural structure, even when an inversion of the structure is present (Lévi-Strauss 1973a). Many anthropologists and those who work with child play see jokes as a form of play which focuses on both reversals and inversions (Douglas 1968; Erikson 1972; Lincoln 1993). Parody, while subverting the structural understanding, often is also still reflecting the underlying categories and structure which it attempts to subvert.

For example, another Slender Man parody added an element to the Slender Man's attacks. In 2009, YouTube channel brett824 used the sixth entry to Marble

Hornets to add to the narrative. The original episode of Marble Hornets had no audio, and brett824 said they 'discovered' the missing audio. In his video, whenever Slender Man appeared, it played the song 'Gimme 20 Dollars' by Ron Browz (brett824 2009). It grew into a separate meme, or sub-meme, related to the Slender Man. The reasonings for his attacks were because he needed $20.

The authoritative background of the parody, found on the formation of its origination, gives the users the ability to more easily incorporate these narratives into the greater mythos. Each of the parodies, including $20, has been incorporated into the general understanding of the Slender Man for the larger mythos. The growth of the Enderman family, and the incorporation of $20, is present in various narratives and variations.

The Trender Man, Splendor Man and Slender Man's $20 are all parodies of the various narratives which the community has grown to know and connect to. These parodies have not simply existed in themselves, but also have grown the narrative. The authority of the background narrative has also grown the original narrative, the parody retreating on itself to help give even more versions and myths to contribute to the full mythos.

## 8.2 Comedic fanfiction

In the previous chapter, we gave attention to fanfiction – narratives crafted by individuals with a more traditional authorship understanding, based on a set of canonical work. This attention was primarily focused on more romance or erotic narratives. This was beneficial as we got to see a different side of the Slender Man narratives, one in which love and women enter an equation in a way we had previously not seen.

Not all fanfiction is romantically or erotically focused. To demonstrate a different side, we are here going to see a more humorous take on fanfiction. As discussed in the previous chapter, there are several different types of fanfiction, and an important one is 'cross-universe' fanfiction (Duffett 2013, 170), which are narratives where different characters from different shows or fictional worlds are depicted together. The following narrative is a cross-universe fanfiction, combining the Slender Man with the figures from *My Little Pony*.

The newest instalment of the *My Little Pony* franchise started in 2010, with Hasbro recruiting animator Lauren Faust. Faust designed the *My Little Pony: Friendship is Magic* show to move away from the stereotypical clichés present in young girls' television shows. She wanted to change the way shows, toys and comics were geared towards girls, as what is present for girls is not compelling to them; the low sales are blamed more on gender than the content: 'Too much stuff for girls is about tea parties and holding hands and skipping down the lane' (Faust, in Ohanesian 2012). A similar view of children's narratives was detailed by Laycock (2010). He discussed how children have much more discerning taste when it comes to the narratives of what they are consuming. His work was more focused on narratives geared towards boys, with *Masters of the Universe*, but the understanding is similar to Faust's primary complaint.

The shift in *My Little Pony* led to users on the sharing site 4Chan watching the episodes together to give commentary, more as an ironic statement. This ironic viewing led to more posters beginning to watch the shows in an earnest and less ironic manner, which has been dubbed 'neo-sincerity' (Robertson 2014, 25). The viewers who were more adult, and typically male, were dubbed 'Bronies', a combination of Bros and Ponies. This 'Brony' fanbase led to a proliferation of creative endeavours, like fan art and fanfiction.

Fanfiction.net user Dark_Spectre2013 wrote a cross-universe fanfiction between Slender Man and *My Little Pony* titled 'Cutie Mark Crusaders Slender Man Hunters!'. The narrative reads like an episode of *My Little Pony: Friendship is Magic*. The language is playful and fun, and the characters move like cartoon characters. The narration also echoes the language used both in the show and by the fanbase, which 'ponifies' the English language: *everybody* becomes *everypony*; *somebody* becomes *somepony*; *handmade* becomes *hoofmade*; and so forth. The narrative also draws on characters in the show, though not the primary six main (or 'mane') characters. In the show, the ponies are marked by a symbol on their hip which depicts what their primary job, love or skill set is in. Several of the primary characters' younger siblings have yet to receive their 'cutie marks' and have forged a team they call the 'Cutie Mark Crusaders' in which they try to do new things to see if this marks their new interest.

Dark_Spectre2013's narrative follows these three Cutie Mark Crusaders who attempt to hunt in the forest for a missing pony, as they want to be heroes. The pony Dinky Doo has been missing, and her sister Ditzy Doo had stumbled out of the forest and collapsed in Ponyville Town Centre. She has no memory of her time before – the only clue being a note glued to her back. The three – Applebloom, Scootaloo and Sweetie Belle – all sneak into the forest at night to try to find the lost pony. As they walk through the forest, they begin to find some notes in the forest. Seeing them as clues, they begin to collect these notes. The more notes they collect, the more lost they get, and some begin to get scared of the dark surrounding them (Dark_Spectre2013 2012).

And suddenly they found an extraordinarily tall stallion in a black suit and tie, whose face was flat and smooth without any eyes or nose. Dinky Doo is with him. Apparently, Dinky Doo had got lost in the woods and found the tall stallion, who he called Slendy. Slendy is helping him find his way back to Ponyville. The three go back to town with Dinky Doo, leaving Slendy in the forest where he lives. As he walks away, he called one more time to ask for $20 (Dark_Spectre2013 2012).

Like all the narratives before, 'Cutie Mark Crusaders Slender Man Hunters!' set up the story to have all the similarities of the Slender Man. The notes scattered in the forest are heavily reminiscent of the two video games, in which players must hunt for the notes, and each additional one causes the Slender Man to hunt the player more vigorously (Parsec Productions 2012; Blue Isle Studios 2013 [2015]). The narrative continues in a similar manner. After several notes, one of the ponies gets a headache – a similar response of being unhealthy from Slender Man's presence like Marble Hornets. They also hear footsteps all around them before seeing Slendy.

It is upon seeing Slendy that the narrative turns. Slendy is not the monster depicted in the previous narratives, but a misunderstood stallion who lives in the forest and who, like the video from brett824, just wants $20. He is not a monster at all, and the great fog of worry and fear becomes the basis for the joke. There was nothing to fear in the narrative at all.

## 8.3 The structure

The parodies and humorous stories told in these last few sections are built with, as described earlier, repetition with difference (Hutcheon 1985, 32). The difference is the subversion of the cultural norms and structure (Douglas 1968). The humour is built on familiarity and given the twist of difference to cause the humour. The set-up of the narrative, then, is built on the same foundational structure as the other non-humorous stories. But humour is transformational. It shifts the narrative in the way it is told, transforming through the simple action of being told.

We can assume, then, the humour narratives discussed in this chapter are built on the same structure. They reflect the same social and cultural norms. Humour builds on this, but causes shifts both narratively and structurally, to alter the expectation. We have come to know the narrative of the Slender Man to be built on a triadic structure, where the second mediatory category is prolonged

– anxiously so. The effect is a level of anxiety, fear and concern associated with not only existing in that mediatory middle, but being forced to remain there, unable to return to a more stable location and placement. If this is our narrative's starting point, then what is happening, more structurally speaking, when the joke shifts our expectations?

Our joke begins by assuming we have prior knowledge of the Slender Man. We know the video games, the web series, and we have seen Victor Surge's images. We have read the stories and seen the pictures and are familiar with our extraordinary tall and thin monster. If we are unfamiliar with him, the joke does not work. The Trender Man appears to be a strange reaction from a mannequin, the Splendor Man something to shrug at, and the fanfiction narratives just strange. Without the prior knowledge, the joke fails. But this is typically how jokes work. If they are built by surrounding sociocultural factors (Apte 1986, 14), then lack of knowledge of these factors cause a loss of the humour.

Like our previous narratives, then, there is an assumption of the reader's position in the structure as well as the characters. The memes and parodies are not retellings of characters and the like but are directly spoken and inclusive of the audience. The audience is part of the joke. Our expectations are played against us as the punchline. Even the fanfiction narrative of the Cutie Mark Crusaders works in a similar way. While this story does have characters who we read and follow, the joke only plays due to the audiences' expectation. The narrative itself is not the joke, but the thoughts of the audience while reading. Our own anxieties, therefore, are played against us. We are the anxiety-ridden mediator, seeing the horror around us of our position. Our anxieties and fears dictate how we believe the joke will play out. And the shifting means we are surprised, reversed and find it funny.

The joke, then, plays with the structure itself. It anticipates our placement in the prolonged middle category – the mediator so anxiously pressed we extended its presence. The jokes dance within this idea, putting stress on the first category of normal society, while playing with the expectation of the third. The middle category does not exist in these stories aside from our presence in them.

It may seem, at first, strange that those who have agency would choose to use it to transform the narratives of horror and trauma into a joke. But there is a deep connection between trauma and humour, and memes are not immune to this. There have been several studies of what are called 'disaster jokes' (Dundes 1987; Oring 1987; Davies 1999; Ellis 2001; Kuipers 2002). Elliot Oring (1987) and Christie Davies (1999) both argue the way we witness horrific disasters strangely place them alongside other media images and videos that are much less horrific. Oring suggests these disaster jokes are an act of rebellion against the way these events are presented (1987). Giselinde Kuipers has extended this study of disaster jokes to online memes, specifically in relation to 9/11 (Kuipers 2002; Kuipers 2005). While Kuipers, Oring and Davies focus on the way real-world trauma is translated to humour, a similar idea can be extended to the more fictional consideration of the Slender Man mythos.

Our acknowledgement of the possibility for agency means storytellers can emphasize and de-emphasize elements of the structure to suit their needs, though they are not necessarily self-aware of the structure itself. A continuation of this can eventually alter the culture's structure itself. Seth Kunin called this process *jonglerie*, where people juggle different aspects of their personality (2001; 2009). In this, people emphasize and de-emphasize different aspects of their cultural structure, either consciously or unconsciously. The structure itself does not change, just certain points, categories or elements are emphasized either more or less.

Kunin's idea of *jonglerie* is most attached to his work with Crypto-Jews, where the different levels of emphasis – either given to their Catholic identities or Jewish ones – were differently especially connected to identity (2001; 2009). While still involving in this process, the *jonglerie* of the storytellers of joke versions of the Slender Man are not emphasizing and de-emphasizing as a matter of identity, rather for the effect of humour. The shift is not a matter of thoughts regarding identity, but an idea of play and playfulness.

The structural effect of the humour is a de-emphasizing of the full triadic nature of the structure. Each element is present, but the mediatory category is suddenly less important. Unlike the narratives which have come before, little attention is paid to this category except in acknowledgement of the audience member's expectation and position. The normally third category is present as the threat, but the transition from one position to the other never occurs. All these examples demonstrate a shifting in which the horror and removal from 'normal' society never occurs. The threat is dangled in front of the audience, but never taken.

The change from triadic to dyadic has the effect of shortening the extent of the mediatory category. The number of categories has not changed. Instead of our middle category being a third separate section, it exists in the overlap between the two more stable categories. The initial question which may arise is why this more dyadic model was not chosen to begin with. The answer is in the extent of that mediatory category for the narratives. While being a full mediation – a category which consists of mythemes and elements of both of the other categories at the same time – it is also so lengthy a position, and one viewed from the perspective of the other two categories as not wholly of them while still being a part, that it is deserving of its own position. Here, in the humour sections, this middle category is much less emphasized as it has been in the past. Rather, the difference between the two more stable categories is of import, with the audience position as mediators as the payoff of the joke. Without the middle position, the joke would not work. But unlike all the other stories, this mediatory position is not given as much emphasis as the others.

While the middle is present in both these structures, they function in vastly different ways. In one, the mediatory category is a temporary position, a spot of transition for the actors involved. In the others, the mediatory category can become permanent. In Something Awful, Marble Hornets and even in the video games, the mediatory category was almost the sole categorical concern of the narrative – the fear in the final transition. The transition for the humour is the difference from Untouched to Removed, with the Transformed as only having the information available to finish the puzzle of the joke. Movement across the categories are still the same. It is still a one-way movement, with no going back. Once moved from one category to another, there is no ability to return (see Diagram 8.1).

For the Trender Man, the threat is present in the first couple words of the meme, the top phrase. It is the second one which flips the threat to a simple over-exaggeration of the 'sassy' fashion-centred character of the Trender Man. The Splendor Man video is similar – the threat is in the set-up of the picnic, near the woods and filmed like the Marble Hornets videos. Video glitches and auditory tears leading up to the sight of the long black legs leads audience members to expect something like the Slender Man's attack, or at least in appearance. We believe something bad will happen. So, when Splendor Man dances and throws glitter instead of attacking, our expectations are denied. Similarly, the pony version of the Slender Man is revealed not as the monster the Cutie Mark Crusaders may first expect, as well as what the audience expects, but instead it is

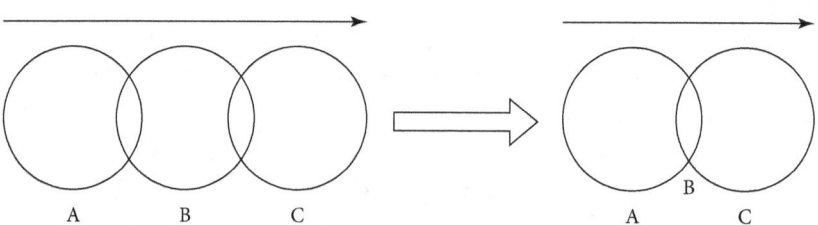

**Diagram 8.1** Structural alterations.

a simple misunderstood stallion. The agency in the narrative not only shifts the expectations to cause humour, but also emphasizes and de-emphasizes to cause these shifts in expectations on the structural level as well.

Agency is important not just in considering neo-structuralism and Kunin's *jonglerie* (Chapter 1), but especially in past views of meme-making as well. The entire point of memes, in which individuals are able to put their own version and spin on it, means the entire 'mythos' of a certain meme is built upon the individual agency of individual meme-makers: memes are based on agency (Knobel and Lankshear 2007; Burgess 2008; Shifman 2012, 2013, 2014; Milner 2016). This agency and interaction leads to the meme as a 'performative act', in which choices to follow or change the story or formation lead to both self and collective identity creation, contributing to what becomes considered the 'norm' (Butler 1990; Shifman 2014).

The humorous versions of the Slender Man meme, then, are the product of the individual agency of writers and meme-makers who impact not only the formation of this meme but also the formation of what is potentially 'normal'. The normality of these memes has the potential to form the basis for change. Perhaps their presence as humorous memes means they cannot alter the larger narrative not related to this humour; though that remains to be seen, as according to Kunin, this change will happen as time progresses (Kunin 2009). While the online social infrastructure changes at an accelerated rate, it has yet to be seen whether sociological effects, such as Kunin's *jonglerie*, also happen at this accelerated pace. And even if it has, it is much more difficult to change the effect of this in older stories – and new narrators are constantly returning to these early narratives to craft their own.

Transformation based on *jonglerie*, or even just structural difference in a more general sense, cannot simply be based on genre. So, when the structure here appears differently, it cannot simply be brought up as a matter of humour over horror. Typically, we see change happen gradually over time, especially in the matter of *jonglerie*. While time has passed between the beginning of the Slender Man narrative and the proliferation of the joke memes based on him, it is only over the course of a few years. This raises our first question on cultural difference. Up until now, the structures we have found have all been similar, with only the addition of mythemes or the stressing of some transformations over others. The Slender Man narrative may not be a culture in and of itself but is a narrative which started as a part of the creepypasta community. Are the memes, then, coming from a different cultural group than the creepypasta community's culture? The cultural boundaries of the Slender Man's original cultural group are beginning to get questioned. Future questions on cultural boundaries and the Slender Man's culture specifically will be the focus of our last chapter (Chapter 11). But before we can attempt to see anything definitive, we first must continue to explore boundaries by pushing past the Slender Man narrative more generally speaking.

## 8.4 Conclusion

Essentially, though, in these more humorous memes, we have a shifting of structure which is built upon the expectation of the previous one. The structural subversion has altered the structure slightly, mostly in shortening the experience of the mediatory category, so it no longer is the middle of a triadic structure, but a dyadic one. The alteration of expectation is what gives rise to humour. In some way, this is reflected in our own study of this material as well. In going into this portion of the Slender Man mythology, I expected, to some extent, for the structure to be vastly like what we have established before. When first approaching the more romantic and erotic takes of the Slender Man, I expected more of a shift, so when the shift did not happen, I expected the humorous takes to be quite similar as well. Maybe there would be small changes but nothing massively significant. The reversal of expectation happened not only structurally for the narratives but in my own approach to the story as well. The structure itself is not hugely different, but the agency individual writers take with the structure reflects a shifting for the sake of humour.

As mentioned earlier, the discovery of a different structure, even one of shifting the experience of the mediatory category, calls for a question of cultural boundaries. We have, for the first time in our study, discovered a different structure. This calls for our spiralling study to begin to take into consideration narratives which are not directly about the Slender Man, but who have connections to the Slender Man mythology in some other ways – either by the original community group or by the way the audience formulated the narrative. Our initial question of where our cultural boundaries exist, when it comes to our choice in the structuralist method, is beginning to come forward. Is creepypasta writing more of a subculture, which the structure reflects? And can it be pushed even further outwards. In the next chapter, we will discuss these questions by looking at other creepypasta narratives, to test if they have a structure similar to what we have already found.

9

# A dog, a video game and a monster

The Slender Man is one of the most well-known creepypasta characters. The online horror storytelling community took to the variety of narratives and interactivity of his story with a fervour. The agency given to the community has led to a wide array of narrative types, formats and even content. The Slender Man has lived in photographs and written narratives on the Something Awful forum (Chapters 3 and 4); he has been depicted in a variety of web videos (Chapter 5) and even directly interacted within video games (Chapter 6). The narrative has been flipped to depict more female-centred narratives (Chapter 7), and even more humorous takes on the Slender Man led to the horror being subverted to laughter (Chapter 8). Finding a common structure among these has demonstrated that the narratives, up to this point, do carry a similar underlying structure. But the larger question to ask is where the boundaries lie. The previous chapter on humour demonstrated some structural difference, bringing this question of culture and cultural boundaries to an immediate point.

For Lévi-Strauss, one cultural group will share one structure. He often drew the lines dividing cultural groups on linguistic boundaries. For Lévi-Strauss, linguistics is a frequent marker point for culture, but has been rejected as a marker point by Bloch (1991). A greater discussion regarding the idea of culture, both from the linguistic standpoint and from a more Lévi-Straussian approach, will be analysed further in Chapter 11. The primary issue for our studies is how the online environment is technically accessible across multiple physical geographic areas. It crosses national and ethnic boundaries. Most of the Slender Man narratives are in English, so linguistic boundaries are not as easily crossed; however, it is not limited to native speakers. However, Lévi-Strauss did not always stick to his concept of language and geography as the primary marker points, as he often compared his primary studies in the Americas with Japanese mythology (Lévi-Strauss 1973b).

The first step to addressing this is to begin to test the possible boundary lines, especially in relation to the different types of stories the Slender Man epitomizes. The first step, to push boundaries, is to turn our attention to the original community which gave him birth: the creepypasta community. As the spiralling outward continues, we can look to the specific social group which both gave birth and continues to contribute to the thin monster. Considering the Slender Man is one of the most prominent creepypasta narratives, our first step is to look at other creepypasta narratives in order to test the structure. This chapter will look at three other creepypasta narratives: *The Curious Case of Smile.jpg*, a chain mail-styled creepypasta involving an image of a smiling dog which drives its viewers insane; *the Rake*, another 'crowdfunded' creepypasta like the Slender Man about a humanoid wild monster which can kill those whose name it speaks; and *Ben Drowned*, a creepypasta about a haunted Nintendo 64 cartridge of the game *Legend of Zelda: Majora's Mask*. Despite having mentioned another popular creepypasta character, Jeff the Killer in a previous chapter (Chapter 7), I have chosen to not include it here for several reasons. Smile.jpg is an early creepypasta, started around the same time as the Slender Man, and therefore it is important to include it as a starting point. Ben Drowned is connected with other forms of virtual storytelling – video games – which gives an insight to more visually based narratives like those also looked at it in Chapters 5 and 6. Jeff the Killer, while circulated widely, often only involves one narrative, and the Rake, by contrast, is a more community-sourced monster similar to the Slender Man. The three presented here, therefore, are chosen with the specific purpose of connecting to the Slender Man's creation and spread in other forms of creepypasta.

## 9.1 The Curious Case of Smile.jpg

The initial beginnings of Smile.jpg is unknown but is mostly tied to the forum site 4chan. The story revolves around a singular image of a dog, resembling a Siberian Husky, with a strange human-like smile (see Figure 9.1). The image is said to drive its viewers insane. Where the image originally came from is unknown, but at some point in its history, a story became attached to the image. Mr. L goes in search of more information on the 'cyber-legend' of the image Smile.jpg. The only history of the image known is that it appeared on 4chan's /x/ boards, which are paranormal-based subforums.

The Curious Case of Smile.jpg is not a mass communal story, in the same way as the Slender Man, but is akin to an email chain. While the Slender Man

**Figure 9.1** Smile.jpg (Creepypasta Indexer 2013a).

thrived on the ability for users to remix and alter the narrative to their own creativity, while still staying within the parameters of what is recognizable as a Slender Man story, the image of Smile.jpg was spread in the way-early email chains, or forwarding lists. True to its original creepypasta name, the Smile.jpg was literally copied and spread in this fashion. The narrative also utilizes this type of narrative historically and socially – referring to 'Bulletin Board Systems' and sites like Usenet (Creepypasta Indexer 2013a).

Email forwardables were a common occurrence in the early stages of online communication but was not completely new with the advent of the internet. Jan Brunvard has recorded instances of forwardables in the form of handwritten mail, most notably his collection of the 'Red Velvet Cake'. This story is about the sharing of a recipe for Red Velvet Cake, which supposedly came from the Waldorf Astoria Hotel. The story goes that a woman, after having the cake at the hotel, requests for the recipe in a letter. The response comes back but with a bill for a sizable amount of money (which varies with each story). The woman decides to circulate the recipe as a form of revenge on the hotel which charged her for the recipe. The recipe, and the story accompanying it, was circulated, sometimes handwritten, sometimes simply shared, and even appeared in newspapers (Brunvard 1981, 154–60).

The email forwardable, then, is not so different than other forms of storytelling which occurred prior to the inception of the internet. The popularity of forwardables reached such a high that users were often inundated with large amounts of forwardable email, so much so it rivalled the infamous spam mail. Some were related to anti-virus programmes, wanting the narrative to be shared through a variety of forwarded messages. Some people share these because they find, if it is a humorous one, it to be funny enough to share, while some share from a genuine, if misguided, attempt to contribute a solution to some given problem (Kibby 2005). The format of the email forwardable, therefore, was one which would be familiar for the audience of the Smile.jpg image.

The written story of Smile.jpg follows a 'Mr. L' who goes in search of more information on the Smile.jpg, as the image is only occasionally seen in various places online, and few others have described ever seeing it. He finds a 'Mary E' who encountered the image on a Bulletin Board System for her neighbourhood. The conversation with her is strange as she remains in a different room, and he never sees her, communicating mostly through a door while her husband attempts to calm her. In further attempts to find out more after, Mr. L reaches out for more information on a variety of sites. Mary E then sends an email, pleading for him to stop, describing the image as something which gets in your head, haunts your dreams and pleads for you to 'spread the word' and 'share the pain' with another. She almost immediately after commits suicide. Mr. L then receives an email with an attachment, describing it as giving information and 'spreading the word' (Creepypasta Indexer 2013a). The end of the story has an image of an oddly human-like smile on a dog, lit only by a flash of a camera on what appears to be a polaroid (see Figure 9.1).

A few elements stand out immediately with this story. The first of concern is the consistent separation of those 'afflicted' with the smile dog from what can be deemed as 'normal' society. This is something we have already seen multiple times in relation to the Slender Man. For the Slender Man, separation was mostly social, where the Transformed's element of the Removed was in their social death, and their marginalization from 'normal' society. Here, it happens both physically, with Mary E in a separate room during the initial interview, and psychologically by deeming them mentally ill in some way. The narrator Mr. L, for instance, at one point speculates Mary E 'was not on effective medication', and the effects of the Smile dog is said to be closely related to epilepsy

(Creepypasta Indexer 2013a). The relationship with mental health demonstrates both a continuation and separation from 'normal' society. These members are still present but deemed different. Mary E is thus socially dead and remains so until she takes her own life to become fully dead and thus transition fully to this category. Those affected with the image, then, are both present and dead, part of society and yet separated. The depiction of them as somehow 'unhealthy' is the way in which they are described as that which is separate.

Interestingly, there is an importance of words and voice. The Smile dog is described as speaking to those who are affected. In her email to the narrator, Mary E describes her nightmares since seeing the image: 'I do not move and do not speak.' During these dreams, the Smile dog talks to her (Creepypasta Indexer 2013a). The image, then, has primacy and voice over her own. The stress on words and speaking is repeated in the need to 'spread the word', which also echoes missionary commitments. Sound, here, continues to be an important sense. For the Slender Man, where we first encountered the importance of sound, it was directly related to him. Here, we see the importance of sound in the hearing of voice, and the spreading of words. Thus, the sound is still directly related to the monster, whether it be a smiling dog or a tall man in a suit.

What is most interesting about the Smile dog's necessity to 'spread the word' is in its direct comparison to the Slender Man's prohibition. The Slender Man kills or takes those who know about him with what appears to be the need to silence the knowledge. An early image by Victor Surge claims 'don't look . . . he doesn't want to be seen' (Victor Surge 2009d). This led to a theory among the audience and storytellers that the Slender Man attacks are centred on those who know of him. Smile dog works in an opposite way – the need to 'spread the word' is what drives the image both in the narrative and outside it.

The technology involving the image is in some way alive. Mary E's husband finds the disk drive she described as having the image saved on it. He refused to check it and immediately burnt it. He described that it 'hissed' like some sort of animal when it was burning (Creepypasta Indexer 2013a). The image also lives on in the dreams and nightmares of those who view it. It speaks to those it has inflected. The image, in some sense, is alive, even if only in a virtual sense.

## 9.2 The Rake

The Rake started in 2005 and/or 2006 on 4chan in a similar way to the call on the Something Awful forum which led to the Slender Man. An anonymous poster created a thread with the call 'let's create a new monster' (in a title incredibly similar to the 'create paranormal images' which gave birth to the Slender Man). There were many ideas circulated, but a combination of a couple different ideas led to the creation of the Rake. One of the primary narratives which began to spread was one written on the blog of Something Awful user Brian Somerville in 2006 (Know Your Meme 2012 [2017]). This narrative was quoted and repeated on the Something Awful forum which gave birth to the Slender Man by user Clockspider, which is what will be used as the narrative analysed here.

The story begins with the mythology that the Rake has been around for many hundred years. The narrative compiles different 'archives' of various accounts of the Rake throughout the years, the earliest being a log from 1691, and the most detailed from 2006. As the introduction to the collection details, there was a compilation of over two dozen documents spanning that length of time and four continents. The stories are all slightly varied, with different levels of information given on the Rake, but with a connecting piece of the power and fear of his voice.

The Rake spread from 4chan to a variety of other online locales, including LiveJournal (hauntings 2008), and even appearing on Something Awful on the forum thread which gave birth to the Slender Man (Clockspider 2009). The creepypasta is now present on a variety of paranormal and creepypasta websites (GunRecon 2012; Creepypasta Indexer 2013b; reddit n.d.). The Rake was also featured as a prominent figure in the web series EverymanHYBRID, which is also a Slender Man web series (EverymanHYBRID n.d.). The following narrative is one which was quoted as a copy-paste job on the Something Awful forum in the thread which gave birth to the Something Awful thread, directly taken from Brian Somerville's original post.

The thread on the 4chan board started with a list of elements which users had, collectively, found terrifying, including a being humanoid who 'usually crouches and walks on all fours' and how he simply watches unless provoked to attack. The discussion eventually formed what became the Rake, but was, at first, called Operation Crawler. The primary characteristics which came about led to the colour of its skin, the fact it had no nose, that it attacks when provoked but normally simply stares and it is seen in suburban areas (Know Your Meme 2012; see Figure 9.2). In many ways, he attacks and moves similarly to the Slender Man, though in a more animal-like fashion than Slender.

The longer narrative involving the Rake is narrated by a woman who details an account of the Rake. She woke to find 'At the foot of the bed, sitting and facing away from us, there was what appeared to be a naked man, or a large hairless dog of some sort. It's [sic] body position was disturbing and unnatural, as if it had

**Figure 9.2** Image of the Rake (Creepypasta Wiki n.d).

been hit by a car or something' (Clockspider 2009; see Figure 9.2). The creature moved and said something to the husband. It then ran to her daughter's room and attacked the young girl. Both the husband and daughter died in a car crash that night, when the husband was rushing her to the hospital. The woman then sought to assemble information on the Rake from a variety of other people, alluding to the collection of materials connected to the Rake (Clockspider 2009).

In our early look at the Slender Man, we saw the importance of sound. Sight was often either obscured in some way, or completely not present. But sound was directly related to the Slender Man, whether it be the absence of it or the creation of it (see Chapter 3). The Rake has a similar connection to sound, particularly its own vocals. The Rake speaks to their victims before something happens. There is an added importance to the speaking of names. One of the suicide notes in the entry logs writes 'I have prayed for you. He spoke your name' (Clockspider 2009).

Seeing the Rake, like seeing the Slender Man, automatically changes a person. The Rake's appearance and voice is what shifts people. Hearing the voice, or seeing him, moves a person from living a life which was once lived in ignorance, untouched by the monster's presence, into a place of being Transformed. They are part of society, moving and living in the everyday moments, but forever seeking answers. Like the Slender Man, the Rake holds an importance with the sense of hearing, and primarily the use of sound. While the Slender Man's association with sound was in a way which signalled his approach, the Rake's association with sound is his own voice. The voice of the Rake sometimes changes the transition again. The voice, and the name it speaks, leads to the removal of the person, often in some violent way. Those who are in knowledge of the Rake, then, are both present and yet separated: moved from ignorance to seeking knowledge and yet constantly losing knowledge at the same time. Sometimes victims feel insane, and brought to suicide, as the suicide note excerpt insinuates. The fear is both in the placement of the second, mediatory category, extended, in question, and owning elements of both more stable categories; as well as the movement which occurs from this to the stage of complete removal.

Nowhere in this structure does the Rake stand. He moves the agents in the structure, and his unknowable nature seems to be a specific element of the fear which keeps the agents from being able to control their own movement. The Slender Man, as we saw in Chapter 4 and again in the following chapters like Chapter 5, also stands outside the structure. His presence controls the structure and the flow of movement between categories. The Rake, then, also has this omnipresent position in the structure – lingering outside of every category, while having the only agency and control over movement and categories.

## 9.3 Ben Drowned

In 2000, Nintendo released *The Legend of Zelda: Majora's Mask* on their Nintendo 64 home consoles. *Majora's Mask* stood, and still does stand, as a stark contrast to the normal format of *Legend of Zelda* games. Following both *Link to the Past* (1991) and *Ocarina of Time* (1998), Nintendo had begun to establish a system which would stand for several decades in the *Legend of Zelda* series. The games are strictly narrated, with little wiggle room for the player to follow their own course. The player is led to a variety of dungeons, or temples, in which they solve puzzles, often gain a particular weapon, and use that weapon to defeat the boss of that temple. And then the process continues a set number of times, until the player faces the final boss.

*Majora's Mask* (2000), on the other hand, is different for a number of reasons. The most obvious is how the developers had a very short time for its development. Because of this, *Majora's Mask* uses the same engine, graphics and character models from *Ocarina of Time*. The world is also a little smaller, with only four different main regions, with four temples, for the player to battle through. One of the primary differences with *Majora's Mask*, however, was the introduction of a timer to the game. The whole game has to be completed in three game days. A clock is introduced to the interface of the game, and players were always reminded with how much time was left. If players played a particular song, the game clock, and many other elements of the game, reset with only a few things lasting.

This clock, as well as some of the background story to the game, is what makes *Majora's Mask* stand out as a rather different game to the rest, and more importantly, especially for our purposes here, a strangely dark game. The game takes place immediately after the events of *Ocarina of Time*. An imp from the woods, called Skull Kid, has stolen a magical mask from the Happy Mask Salesman, a mask which is said to harbour a dark power. The Happy Mask Salesman enlists our main character Link to get the mask back. The game must be completed in three game days from this request, however, as Skull Kid is bringing down the moon to crash into the town in three days.

Because the player is essentially repeatedly replaying the same three days, the player learns the schedules of the various townsfolk, and can solve many of their problems throughout the course of the three days. This is in combination with completing the four temples in the four various areas, as there are guardians there who, once freed, can come to help stop the moon from falling. Even though many steps are taken to solve the city's problems, and many people and areas are helped, at the end of the solution, the player must reset time, and all the solutions to the problems are reverted to the beginning of the three-day cycle. The player only keeps the reward item, and everyone and everything returns to the beginning one more time.

The reuse of character models, the continuous replaying of days and the darkness of the narrative of the moon falling, all lead to a darker version of a familiar game. Masks are acquired in the game which cause the main character to change shape, but the transformation sequence played is one of utter terror and pain. The whole mood led to a popular fan theory that Link, the main character, has died, and the game is playing out a version of purgatory in a nightmare-esque world (Game Theory 2013).

This information on *Majora's Mask* as a game is important background knowledge to a popular creepypasta called Ben Drowned. The horror narrative follows a haunted Nintendo 64 cartridge of *Majora's Mask*. The game is glitched beyond a recognizable old glitched game, and with a fear and creepiness which makes it feel like there is something much greater occurring. The previous owner of the game, Ben, was a young man who died in a drowning accident, and the game at first seems to be haunted by him. As the narrator delves further into the questions of the game, something even stranger is occurring.

The narrative of Ben Drowned started with an online user named Jadusable posting on multiple online forums in 2010 about his finding of a weirdly glitched cartridge of Majora's Mask. He uploaded on his YouTube page videos of his various attempts to play the game. In each attempt, something strange would occur, including Link bent strangely, and a statue randomly appearing behind him. The music is also altered. Instead of the various music which typically plays in the game, a version of 'The Song of Healing', a song played when soothing troubled spirits in the game (which turns them into masks), plays in reverse. In town, all non-playable characters were gone (Alex Hall 2010a) which gave Jadusable a growing sense of loneliness (Jadusable 2010).

Most of the text for the first two videos is either garbled, or segments of written text from different points in the game. The last two videos change this, so the dialogue boxes become changed to attempt conversation (Alex Hall 2010c, 2010d). Strange sound affects also occur, including the Happy Mask Salesman and the Skull Kid's laughter.

Again, we see lots of similarities between not only the Slender Man but also the previous two creepypastas looked at earlier in this chapter. The sound element – like the Rake, the smiling dog and the Slender Man – is equally as important here. The strange music seems to give a signal that this game is not the normal, or Untouched, game. The sound cues from the Happy Mask Salesman or Skull Kid also signal transitions in the game's glitches. The longer the narrator engages with the game, the more he feels his sanity slip away (Jadusable 2010).

Like what we saw with Marble Hornets, and Smile.jpg, the narrator Jadusable begins his journey in the place of those in normal society. He begins his experience with the game without any thought of it being different. As he continues to play and engage with the game, his mental state slips, and he begins to retract himself from 'normal' society. In the uploaded file 'TheTruth.txt', Jadusable wrote 'This semester I really didn't have any friends, or rather, I stopped paying attention to them' (Jadusable 2010). The Transformed category is also often marked by being unhealthy. For Marble Hornets, the mark of this ill health was coughing (Chapter 5), and the effects of Smile.jpg was associated with epilepsy. Jadusable commented how he gets random 'inexplicable' headaches (Jadusable 2010).

In both cases, we see markers of the mediatory, elongated, category of the Transformed. The separation from society is marking the more 'social' death, in which the character is both technically present and functioning in society, and yet is seen as different and separate like those who are dead. Those Removed, on the other end, are often those dead; when the world of the living is touched by it, unhealthiness occurs.

## 9.4 Creepypasta structure

As has been demonstrated briefly earlier, there are similarities in what we have seen over the past several chapters in the Slender Man narrative to the narratives here: similar themes, concepts, placements and mythemes. Characters move across categories in similar ways, lingering in the extended mediatory category with the fear and trepidation experienced in our previous studies. They also share many elements with each other.

Between the four narratives, the three summarized here and the Slender Man, there is a consistent theme in a life and agency where there is typically no life and agency. For the Curious Case of the Smiling Dog, the image itself seems to be somewhat alive, talking to its audience and living within drives which hold it, hissing when these drives are burnt (Creepypasta Indexer 2013a). Ben Drowned has a video game cartridge which thrives outside of the way a typical gaming cartridge thrives (Jadusable 2010). It moves, lives and talks through the cartridge. The Rake, and our primary case study of the Slender Man, is less about technology living, and more concerned with monstrous bodies and supernatural figures who inflict their agency on the world around them. Of all the creepypasta creatures, the Slender Man is the most humanoid – resembling at first glance a tall man. In fact, many of the narratives detail calling out to him in the incorrect assumption that he is a regular passer-by. The Rake, however, appears much more like an animal, but one which is still somewhat strangely humanoid. The Rake stands as a cross between the natural, the human, and the supernatural – capable of living throughout many centuries, appearing beside beds and whispering names in an inhuman voice.

These Supernatural Others are always in the shape of something familiar yet twisted to be the unfamiliar. The Slender Man's humanoid form fools others into thinking, at first, that he is a tall man. It is not until the second look, or closer examinations, that his inhuman proportions and, sometimes, extra appendages are revealed. Smile.jpg is similar. The image shared is that of a dog, but one with a very human smile. The addition of something which should not be in the familiar image warps the familiar to something unfamiliar.

These representations of the monstrous are not new with the internet or creepypasta. Noël Carroll defines the monster as that which is a fusion both in a physical sense and as a transgression of categorical distinctions (Carroll 1990, 43). His concept of categorical distinctions is echoed in Mary Douglas's concept of danger and the monstrous as that which demonstrates issues in cultural categorization (Douglas 2001). The monstrous, and the grotesque, is a concept which either occupies multiple categories when that is unjustified, culturally speaking, or falls between categories and are thus not accommodated in the structure (Douglas 2001; Harpham 1982). An aspect of this is also echoed by Edmund Leach when he discusses taboo in relation to categorical distinction – those outside of categories are considered by Leach as 'non-things' (Leach 1972). The Slender Man is the impure monster who falls outside of categories, and reveals categorical issues, resulting in him as representative of the Supernatural Others, like the Rake and Ben Drowned, who exemplify the monstrous categorical issues.

In all the creepypasta cases in this chapter, the supernatural figure, whether it be technological or otherwise, is the figure which controls the structure through which everything else is either situated or moves. Those affected, or those which have moved into the Transformed, are regarded as being without their full faculties and are dismissed. As we saw most notably in the Something Awful forum narratives of Mr. 47 (Mr. 47 2009) and genesplicer (genesplicer 2009), those who speak of what they saw or experienced of the Slender Man are disregarded as either having seen it incorrectly, as in the case of the children depicted in the earlier narratives, or insane, as in Aleph Null's narrative (Aleph Null 2009b). Jadusable, in their narration of Ben Drowned, described themselves as feeling their 'sanity slip away' (Jadusable 2010). The Rake's victims experience 'traumatic levels of fright and discomfort' and one even said the thoughts made him feel he 'cannot ever wake' (Clockspider 2009), and even the narrator of the more written-out narrative of Smile.jpg describes those who detail their experience as being possibly 'off her meds' (Jadusable 2010).

This middle category is the last step before full removal. The last category is reserved for those either taken, in the case of the children the Slender Man takes, or dead. These are fully removed from society, completely gone and with nothing anyone left can do about this. Once you progress to one category, there is no returning to the previous. On our previous studies, the only movement to the last category is through the Slender Man himself – either through him taking or killing. In both Ben Drowned and the Rake, we see a different kind of self-propelled movement: suicide.

Some of the narratives of the Slender Man, particularly those on the Something Awful forum, did present suicide as a matter of progression out of the mediatory category separate from the option of death or disappearance via the Slender Man (BooDoug187 2009, for example), though these were not given a spotlight here. The Rake's presentation of suicide as an out was more implicit, in the presentation of a section from a suicide note (Clockspider 2009). In Ben Drowned, the option of suicide was equally as implicit, this time more present in the game world itself. During Jadusable's playing, he said he thought that if he drowned his character, perhaps things would reset to normal (Jadusable 2010), potentially echoing the thoughts of those who committed suicide in the other narratives.

The option of suicide is an interesting one, as it seems to question the full agency of the Slender Man, or the supernatural in general in the case of the Rake and Ben Drowned, over the structure. In these cases, the characters have taken agency over their own movement, no longer content on waiting for the movement to happen to them. However, the control is still present and character agency is not as actually present as may appear at first. Their need to escape is due to the placement in the Transformed in the first place, controlled in thought, social position and structural position by an outside force. In this way, they are essentially compelled to suicide by this force. Thus, even when characters enact agency over their movement, this agency is only allowed in the direction the outside force, the Supernatural Other, has over them.

Essentially this means there is still the triadic model we have seen in the past. The progression is still one way, and the primary figure in the narratives, the horrific supernatural element which has nowhere to go in the structure, controls the structure itself (Diagram 9.1).

In this case, the mythemes representative of these categories still stands. The first being the more ignorant and yet more safe (seemingly) normal society. This is the category for those unaware of the mechanisms of the supernatural creatures, or even their presence in this world. We sometimes get a glimpse of our characters in this world prior to their first transition. In Ben Drowned, we see him driving from neighbourhood garage sale to garage sale, shopping for cheap video games. In Smile.jpg, we see a university student interested in simply doing the research necessary for a quick story, mostly for fun while attempting to also get a grade.

But the experience with the Supernatural Other moves them – shifts them to a realm apart from this place of ignorance. They get glimpses of knowledge, only small pieces of the puzzle, and the need to find more consumes them. They either choose to or are forced to be separate from the normal society of which

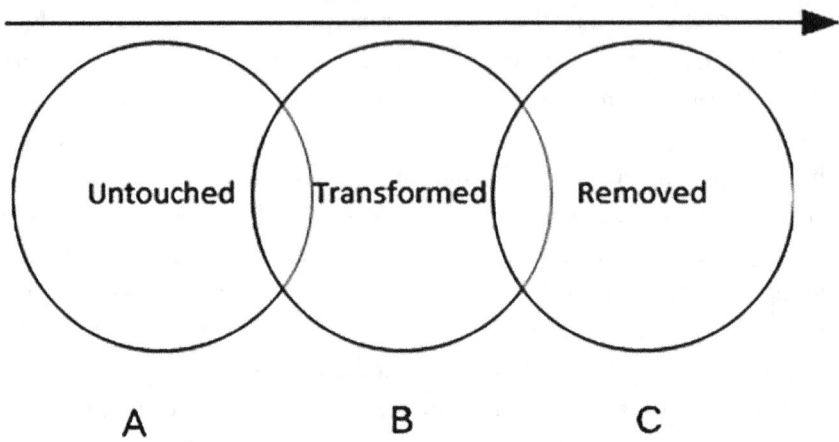

**Diagram 9.1** Full structure.

they were once accustomed to be a part of. Mary E, our primary character's informant in our narrative of the Smile.jpg image, was once a normal woman who encountered the image on a Bulletin Board System which was small and local. Her separation from this is marked by her relation to mental illness, and physically representative in her interview with the narrator when she is not even in the same room. Jadusable separates themselves from friends and family. Those marked by the Rake have their voices silenced.

## 9.5 Conclusion

Perhaps it is not a surprise that other creepypasta narratives echo the same structure as the Slender Man. Not only do they share structure, but even some of the mythemes carry over. Admittedly, the study here on Smile.jpg, the Rake and Ben Drowned are brief. Each of these narratives are deserving of a significant study on their own. Unfortunately, space in this particular study is not large enough to accommodate such detailed studies on each of these narratives alongside the analysis already present for our primary case study of the Slender Man. This is an avenue for future research which would assist in furthering not only a more detailed look at the stories themselves but also furthering the more specific details of the structure, and the mythemes more specific to the narratives themselves.

The creepypasta structure has continued the triadic structure in a one-way progression in which an outside force controls this progression, rather than the agents which move within it. The triadic structure is also relevant here. Each category is represented, either directly or in an important implicit position. The player in Ben Drowned presents his life as Untouched prior to his movement to Transformed, and the threat of the Removed continues to linger in his narrative. The fact the user never continued to post alludes to some form of Removal at the end of his narrative. This is also seen in the story of the Rake. The shifting of characters as their world is revealed to be something greater than they thought, with the lingering of the Supernatural Others. The smiling dog drags those who are unsuspecting online browsers to become Transformed. The extended mediatory category, brought out to be its own section in the structure, is a large element of the fear, trepidation and the centre of concern point for the narratives themselves. All the narratives are based on this category's existence.

What this means for our purposes is we have an added element of narratives who are structurally similar to the Slender Man narratives. The creepypasta community seems to have narratives which hold the same structure as the specific mythos we have studied thus far. This means that the full creepypasta community seems to have the same cultural structure. The Slender Man's structure has now reached out to encompass the creepypasta community as a whole.

At the beginning of this study, we asked the question of who owned the Slender Man, not in an authorial or copyright sense, but in a cultural or social sense. Which community or society can really claim the Slender Man as something they did, and that represents them, especially pertinent as the Slender Man mythos began to spread to different arenas online? We are getting closer to answering that question. The creepypasta community at least gives us a solid idea of where the narrative finds its cultural home. A more in-depth study of the culture of the Slender Man is found in Chapter 11.

As our previous chapter on humour demonstrated, not all narratives online are horror narratives. Our next chapter shifts focus from the furthering extension of creepypasta to other mass communal narratives. The nature of the Slender Man narrative came from the way many people gathered together to tell the story. The mythos grew through the amount of people telling it, contributing and retelling these contributions. The non-canonical nature of the narrative helps contribute to its spread. This mass communal storytelling, as detailed in the beginning of this study (see Chapter 2), makes up many of the ways stories are told online. Narratives which are told through mass contribution, especially those which are not focused on the horror genre, are going to be our focus on the following chapter.

10

# The online hive mind's stories

The Slender Man is a product of mass communal storytelling, as has been referenced especially at the beginning of this book (Chapter 2). Each member's contribution to the narrative grew the story until it became a larger mythology. The contributions fed the creature like a true Tulpa, giving strength to the character in the way the community thought about him, wrote about him and photoshopped him. While unique in the specifics related to its birth, the way a community gives birth communally to a narrative is not something unique to the Slender Man alone, and especially not online. Online group narratives are a common way in which stories are created and disseminated on the internet, though the specific ways these take form are always slightly different.

This chapter seeks to test the boundaries of the Slender Man's community, and the structured thought process behind the mythos, by expanding our study to other forms of these communally created narratives. Our boundary testing is not only structural, but also cultural. We are seeking to find the Slender Man's culture, or what cultural or subcultural group can claim ownership over his narrative. What we have found so far is a connection, structurally speaking, to the creepypasta community. But does the structural culture extend to other areas of the internet, including the way the narrative is put together?

Our two case studies for this chapter are vastly different in scope and formation. While the Slender Man's narrative was created over time, and over the course of a variety of stories, the mythology of Twitch Plays Pokémon happened incredibly quickly, almost spontaneously, through simply the communication of chaos. The narratives arose mostly in the form of communication and a variety of visual memes. Also formed through communication, Jesse Cox's narrative of the Great Space Butterfly, is much less massive in both scope and community. Formed gradually over time, the Great Space Butterfly narrative represents more of a 'top-down' perspective than the spontaneous development of the Twitch Plays Pokémon phenomenon.

The two present examples of other ways communities create narratives as a collective online. The exact formation of the Slender Man is not easily replicated, and the intent here is not to find a direct replication, but a similarity within the relatively free circumstances of the internet. The first two sections will explore each narrative and their formation. A group structure will follow, and a discussion of how this relates to that found previously on the Slender Man.

## 10.1 The internet plays Pokémon

In 2014, an anonymous programmer put together an emulation of the game *Pokémon Red* (1996) to the video game streaming website twitch.tv. The concept is that anyone in the chat could participate by inputting commands to the game, which would respond as if someone pressed the command on the controller. A participant puts A, the game recognizes it as a player pressing the A button and responds accordingly (see Figure 10.1). The point was a 'social experiment', as all participants are essentially playing the same game at the same time. The goal was to see what would happen when 100 people are all trying to play the game at once.

But Twitch Plays Pokémon got much more than a couple hundred. By the time it finally completed the game, the group play phenomenon had gathered over one million participants, and over thirty-six million views (Chase 2014). Over a million participants caused the experience to be a sheer chaos. Many sections of the game demonstrated how incredibly difficult navigating a game with a million other people truly was. Even attempting to walk through some areas proved near impossible. The encounter with 'The Ledge', for example, took many tries. In the game, small ledges are present, where the player can hop over them but only in one direction, supposed to be representative of a small heightened drop down in the landscape. This meant that any pressing of the down arrow at the wrong moment made the group players reset their entire progress in the area.

To solve this problem, a subreddit for the participation in the phenomenon established an idea of hitting 'start' to bring up the menu. This would pause the character's progress and cause the down arrows to only be navigating a menu rather than resetting their progress. The pressing of start and movement in the menu caused even more chaos in what was already slightly chaotic, but participants started seeing certain patterns.

The most important of these patterns came after obtaining the Helix fossil. In *Pokémon Red*, this is a stone the player holds on to for a significant portion of

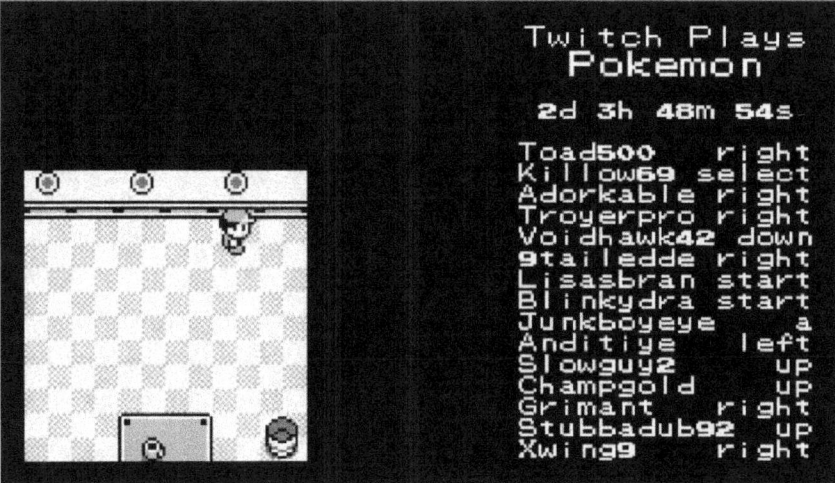

**Figure 10.1** Sample screenshot of *Pokémon Red* playthrough of Twitch Plays Pokémon (scorpionsrock55 2014).

the game, and later the stone is revived to be the Pokémon Omenyte. The player cannot get rid of this item, or use it or really do anything but look at it until the Pokémon is revived. When players started hitting 'start' as a way of calming the chaos, inadvertently, the other commands often led players to see the Helix fossil in their inventory. When the players were successful, they began to attribute this, jokingly, to the Helix fossil itself.

The greater mythology of Twitch Plays Pokémon began to grow. Mostly, the stories were created in chat, and spread and grown through online memes. The Helix fossil was considered a benevolent god, who was pitted against the evil Dome fossil. Each additional action in the emulated game led to a different series of images and narratives arising, depicting the mythology. Often, the language used in the mythology echoed more Christian-based phrasing. The myth of Twitch Plays Pokémon is as follows:

*Back in ancient times, there were two primary deities: the benevolent Helix, and the evil Dome. These deities were put away into fossilized shape, waiting for the day they may be brought back. Far later, Red, guided by the hive mind (the Twitch community), went in search of Pokémon and to be the best Pokémon trainer. The first Pokémon chosen was Charmander, lovingly named Abbey (originally ABBBBBBK), and later caught the Pokémon Pidgey, who would later earn the title of Bird Jesus. Little is known of Red's early days on the travel, but it is known they defeated the first gym leader.*

*Red then headed to Mount Moon. Deep in the cave, he was given a choice between the Helix and Dome fossils. He chose the Helix. When stumbling through menus,*

Red often selected the Helix fossil, making it appear as if it was being consulted for advice. It was also unable to be gotten rid of, which made it an immortal. At this point, the hive mind began to recognize the almighty power of Helix.

After making it through Mount Moon and arriving at Cerulean City, Red caught a Rattata who was nicknamed Jay Leno (originally JLVNWNNOOOO). The group beat the second gym leader, Misty. Quickly moving to the next gym, Red miraculously solved the puzzle on their first try, and Abby swiftly took out Lt. Surge, the third gym leader.

On the way to the next area, the hive mind and Red encountered a large and epic problem: the Ledge. The path, Route 9, was filled with ledges, and any wrong move would cause them to have to start over again. It took the hive mind almost an entire day to get through.

Red and the hive mind moved on to the Rock Tunnel. The move 'Dig' was taught to a second Rattata (not Jay Leno). On several occasions, the move was triggered out of battle sequences, which caused Red to automatically leave the tunnel. Because of this, the Rattata was nicknamed 'DigRat' by the community. The hive mind and Red finally finished the Rock Tunnel, emerging in Lavender Town, and quickly moving to Celadon City after. They made quick work of the fourth gym leader Erika.

At this point, the hive mind realized they needed a water Pokémon (for strategic purposes to make the following points of the game much easier). The hive mind decided to get the Pokémon Eevee, which could be changed into any one of several elemental Pokémon. This means they could get their needed water Pokémon. Unfortunately, they accidently got the wrong element, and ended up with a Flareon instead, which is also considered one of the weakest Eevee forms. When trying to put away Flareon in the Pokémon storage PC, the hive mind accidently released (meaning lost forever) both Abby and Jay Leno with no success. At this point, Flareon began to be considered a false prophet – once giving them hope before dashing it with giving them a worse situation. Every bad event at this point became blamed on Flareon and the unpicked Dome fossil, who stood against everything the Great Helix did.

The next great puzzle was in the Rocket Hideout, which was a large maze. Each time they attempted to make progress, DigRat would dig them out of the area and reset their progress. At this point, the developer shifted to a Democracy system for the first time, which led to the start9 riots (see later section) which essentially lobbied to return to the normal chaos. The compromise was the installation of a voting system for Democracy (where the input command would take the majority of inputs) and Anarchy (the original system of every input counting).

*As much as Democracy was not seen favourably, it was through Democracy mode that progress was finally made again. At this point, the hive mind came quickly back on track. A lengthy battle against the boss of the Rocket Hideaway, Giovanni, led to an epic showdown between the first Pidgey caught, now evolved, and Giovanni's final Pokémon. Finally winning with very little health left, earned the nickname Bird Jesus for his miraculous win.*

*The hive mind was on a winning streak and were successful in many of their endeavours: through the Pokémon Tower, the defeat of the fifth gym leader Sabrina (another miraculous win led by Bird Jesus), and the capture of the legendary bird Pokémon Zapdos. At this point, disaster struck. When attempting to get the new powerful Pokémon out of the storage PC, the hive mind accidentally released twelve Pokémon, including DigRat, in what was later dubbed 'Bloody Sunday'.*

*The hive mind rallied after the devastating blow, attempting to make progress as a way of soldiering on. At this point, they went to Cinnabar Island where the Great Lord Helix may be revived (see* Figure 10.2*). Now they had a team of six strong Pokémon. With that they beat the last two gym leaders. And after a long difficult fight against the Elite Four, the last four trainers to fight, the hive mind finally completed* Pokémon Red, *after sixteen days, seven hours, forty-five minutes and thirty seconds.*

### 10.1.1 TPP mythemes and structure

As can already be tangentially gleaned, the mythology of Twitch Plays Pokémon appears dyadic. Anything which helps the community progress was attributed to Helix, the fossil chosen, while anything which disrupted the progress was attributed to Dome, the fossil not chosen. The various Pokémon who did well were followers of Helix, and those who appeared to work against progress and the community were followers of Dome.

| Helix | Dome |
|---|---|
| Bird Jesus | Flareon |
| Abby | Giovanni |
| Red | PC |
| Anarchy | Democracy |

There are two important dichotomies to the structure of the Twitch Plays Pokémon mythology. The first is the Helix/Dome divide. Other characters and events are directly considered as under either the Helix or the Dome. When the Pidgeotto does well, it is considered under Helix. When a Flareon is produced instead of the Vaporeon the group wanted, it is seen as being under Dome.

The Helix/Dome divide is also expressed through another important mytheme: choice. The idea of choice is frequently found and expressed in different ways throughout the narrative. The primary difference between the Helix and Dome fossils is one was chosen in preference to the other. The moment is called 'The Great Choice', where the players chose the Helix over the Dome. The direct reasoning for the choice is not as detailed, as it was early in the playthrough and thus not as documented as moments further on. The Charmander Abby was chosen as the very first Pokémon at the beginning of the game. It was thus called 'The Chosen One', but it was released early in one of the first anguishes associated with attempting to gain a Pokémon out from the PC.

This essentially sets the structure as a strict dichotomy separating Helix and Dome, in which all other characters and events are allocated as belonging to one or the other. But the addition of the Anarchy/Democracy dichotomy reveals a different level of engagement. Anarchy and Democracy modes were associated, as all other aspects of the mythology, with Helix and Dome, respectively.

But the different game modes introduce a much less static element. Anarchy and Democracy are firmly attributed to their different fossil counterparts, but after their introduction, events and characters can move between. As mentioned earlier, the audience began to shift from Anarchy to Democracy when it was most beneficial for progress, such as when the group decided to attempt again to remove Zapdos from the PC following the events of Bloody Sunday. The Pokémon Venemoth is sometimes referred to as 'The Converted', as it came from Democracy, but was later 'converted' into Anarchy. Essentially, this means the Pokémon was gained when in Democracy mode, but later achieved greatness while in Anarchy mode.

This means the categories of the Helix and the Dome are not directly opposed with no way of movement between the two. Rather, the modes of Anarchy and Democracy show how characters can shift from one category to the other. What we see is something akin to Diagram 10.1.

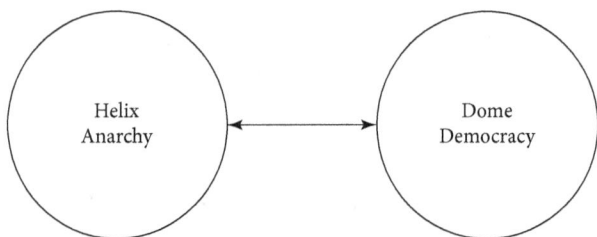

**Diagram 10.1** Structure of Twitch Plays Pokémon based on Helix/Dome.

Unlike any of the previous diagrams in the study, the former diagram does not have overlapping circles. In the previous diagrams, the overlapping of the circles demonstrated not only the ease of movement but also the presence of mediators. In the former diagram, there is no overlap. Despite the relative ease of movement between categories, there is no demonstration of mediators present in our study of Twitch Plays Pokémon so far. There is no mytheme which is in both categories simultaneously. Instead, the movement possible is designated by the arrows, double ended because one can always move back to the first position after movement.

Perhaps the most obvious group which moves between categories are the players/audience. The nature of Twitch Plays Pokémon, a type of play called 'crowd play', means the engagement with the audience is on the nature of a majority. This means the participation of an individual may not be expressed in the same manner as the collective whole. An individual may wish to enact on a particular action, but the game is at the whim of the larger group. While individuals may feel as if they wish to be aligned in a particular category, the mass moves as the mass moves. In direct comparison, the audience in the Slender Man's narrative was just placed in the Transformed position, and due to the Slender Man's control over the structure, were unable to shift positions as they wished.

Perhaps the best description for this is one used to describe the online, often political, movement Anonymous. One member said it was best to describe the way the group worked by thinking of a group of birds. 'One moment, everyone's flying very, very quiet. Suddenly, one bird flies in another direction and the mass fly into the same direction' (Anonymous Official 2014). The actual arrangement of Anonymous is much more complicated, sometimes dark, and too detailed to give a thorough examination of in contrast to the spontaneous formation of Twitch Plays Pokémon mythology, but the bird analogy is a useful one for our circumstances here. The single bird's movement which is individually lost in the larger movement shows how the single movement which shifts the group's thought can be difficult to trace. The flock analogy also demonstrates how individuals do not necessarily have to follow the way the group goes. An individual bird may choose not to follow the larger flock, but they will be on their own.

In Anarchy mode, each individual bird's wish is taken. An individual bird can still throw off the progress of the flock. In contrast, Democracy takes into consideration each bird's movement, but it follows the larger flock, and any bird in a different direction does not affect the larger movement.

In this way, the creation of the mythology is an expression of individuality while still being within the community group. The names and their relationship were communally conceived, while being individually expressed through memes. The images were spread on a variety of platforms. These expressed both individual aspects and events in the narratives, which are given their greater mythic importance through their expression in meme form.

Often these used Christian-based language in the telling of the mythology, and even more so the religious, often Christian-based, imagery sometimes used in the depiction of these characters and events. But the memes shared were not only on specific characters or events, nor were they always focused exclusively on Christian imagery. Figure 10.2, for instance, shows a form of depicting the full narrative as Egyptian lore. The artist titled the image 'A Most Sacred Tablet', again recalling more religious and iconographic thought. While these are on the narrative level, as in the appearance of images, and so forth, it reveals a connection to a cultural structure which is dyadic, especially one which separates good from evil.

**Figure 10.2** Egyptian tablet fan art of Twitch Plays Pokémon narrative (whoaconstrictor 2014).

The individual nature of the creation of the memes is still in line with the communal nature of the narrative itself. The communal narrative is depicted and given life in the individual narrative, and the individual is what shares and spreads the communal. The various depictions possible is where the agency of the individual shines, despite the individual's lack of agency within the structure as a whole. The structure is more concerned with the full collective of the community, while the individual expresses this structure in their imagery and telling of the story. The reliance on the individual creativity is part of the essence of meme-telling (Shifman 2014; Milner 2016), but as such does relate back to what we saw with the Slender Man. The freedom the mythos gave to individual creativity led to an ever-changing nature of the monster, which was often related to an understanding closer to apophatic theology (Chapter 2). Like the Twitch Plays Pokémon mythology, the leaning towards individual creativity lends itself to a leaning on religious literacy, either in understanding or the content of the narrative itself.

This is complicated by the nature of memes themselves, the nature in which these stories are directly told and shared. The point of memes is to be shared widely (Shifman 2014). When they are shared, they are often separated from their original authorial context. This means the individual creativity which went into the creation of the meme only remains with the image in spirit and in how it exists, but seldom actually attached to the image itself. So, while these individual image memes do help to express the individual creativity within the massive communal progression and experience of the playthrough, the actual individual's attachment to the image created is tenuous.

## 10.2 The Great Space Butterfly

The Great Space Butterfly is not nearly as expansive a narrative, nor with as many characters, as Twitch Plays Pokémon. Admittedly, the summary of the Twitch Plays Pokémon mythos earlier is concise necessarily, as this book is not about Twitch Plays Pokémon, and a fuller study would also reveal a fuller mythology, with all the various Pokémon as having their own role. In contrast, the story of the Great Space Butterfly is short and brief even in its fullest expanse.

*All of reality is only the product of the dream of the Great Space Butterfly. It roams the stars as it sips moon nectar and dreaming our lives. Not all is always well, as the Space Moth threatens the Space Butterfly's wonderful dream, threatening its peace with a looming sense of an oncoming battle. Or so sayeth his prophet, Jesse Cox.*

Jesse Cox is a gaming YouTuber, or, more specifically, a Let's Player. This means he records himself playing video games, along with his vocal commentary, and uploads this online for many to watch. And many do watch, as he has over 950,000 subscribers on his channel (as at the time of writing, Jesse Cox n.d.). The phenomenon of Let's Players is described briefly in Chapter 6, particularly with our implicit mythology analysis of Let's Players' experience of *Slender: The Arrival* in Chapter 7. But the popularity of Let's Plays and Let's Players was possibly understated. Some of the top-paid YouTubers are Let's Players, including Markiplier, Pewdiepie and VanossGaming (Lynch 2017). The gaming content on YouTube got to be so popular that a separate website, YouTube gaming, was launched to watch various gaming subscriptions as well as provide a streaming platform to rival that of Twitch (Dredge 2015).

The story of the Space Butterfly came on a boredom-induced episode of a playthrough of the game *Terraria* (2011) on Jesse Cox's YouTube channel. His playthrough was a collaborative video, joint with YouTuber TotalBiscuit. On the tenth part of his playthrough, Jesse's clear boredom with the game led him to begin to ramble, and the Space Butterfly's story was born. It started with him mimicking the voice of someone under the influence of marijuana and asking, 'What if this is all the dream of a space butterfly, man?' (Jesse Cox 2012). The original story started here by Jesse Cox was all of reality as being a dream of the Great Space Butterfly who drinks moon nectar as he dreams.

While the original narrative was started by a single person, his fan base added to the narrative as a collective. Jesse was soon considered the Prophet of the Great Space Butterfly. In contrast to TotalBiscuit's fanbase, which is known as the Cynical Army, Jesse's fanbase began to refer to themselves as The Space Butterfly Army, which was later shortened to just Space Butterflies. When exactly the Space Moth was introduced was not something I could specifically elucidate, as it came about through the interactions of the fanbase with itself and Jesse.

In this way, the story of the Great Space Butterfly is not as purely communal as the spontaneous creation of the Twitch Plays Pokémon narrative. It is spurred originally by an individual person, a narrative which the community then builds upon. Our two examples of the Great Space Butterfly and Twitch Plays Pokémon, therefore, give us two of the extreme ends in which the internet communally conceives of narratives. On one end, we have the spontaneous joint creation, in which the inciting incident is not very detailed, and the majority of the narrative is conceived of by the mass of the community at large. On the other side, we have a narrative mostly conceived of by one individual but is expanded on and given life through the community. Our primary case study of the Slender Man rests somewhere in between: originally conceived of by Something Awful forum user Victor Surge but grown and expanded upon through the continual production of narratives by the community.

The Slender Man, therefore, essentially began more like the Great Space Butterfly. A single user gave their own narrative of a monster who appears, at first, to be a tall man wearing a suit (Victor Surge 2009a). But the way the narrative spread and disseminated through the community echoed that of Twitch Plays Pokémon, emerging through individual creativity, and leaning on these individuals to expand the mythology's narrative.

### 10.2.1 Great Space Butterfly structure

As mentioned earlier, there are not as many characters or events in the story of the Great Space Butterfly. This is a narrative more referred to than developed. Our mythemes, therefore, are few. We have the Space Butterfly and all its connections, such as Jesse Cox and moon nectar. And we have, alternatively, the Space Moth which threatens to wake the Space Butterfly.

| Space Butterfly | Space Moth |
| --- | --- |
| Jesse Cox | Wakefulness |
| Sleep and moon nectar | |

Again, we see a dyadic structure, where the Space Butterfly is set in contrast to the Space Moth.

Our core distinction lies in the difference between the Space Butterfly and the Space Moth. Most of the other elements of the narrative rests in the same category as the Space Butterfly: moon nectar, Jesse Cox and the Space Butterflies as the collective. The Space Moth stands in contrast. The result is a one versus the other construct. Again, no mediation exists between the two as there is no mytheme which simultaneously exists in both categories.

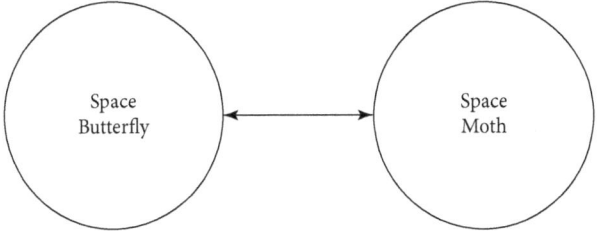

**Diagram 10.2** Structure of the Great Space Butterfly.

## 10.3 Joint structure

As the discussions earlier regarding both the mythology of Twitch Plays Pokémon and the story of the Great Space Butterfly, the structure we have found between the two are dyadic. The Helix/Dome divide is what established our primary categories, as different characters and events fell under one category or the other. We could simplify this further by seeing Helix as 'Benevolent' and Dome as 'Evil'. All things considered evil, primarily that which works against progress in the game, fall under the second category, while things 'benevolent' are those, including characters, which work to progress the game. Similar distinctions can be drawn for the Great Space Butterfly. The Space Butterfly is seen as benevolent, as it simply continues to dream our reality, but this peace is threatened by the Space Moth, which we consider as a form of 'Evil', working against the 'progress' of the Space Butterfly. Grouped together, we can drop the categorical distinctions of the 'Helix/Space Butterfly' as the first one (A) and 'Dome/Space Moth' as the second one (B) (Diagram 10.3).

Movement between the two categories is possible for the various characters and, more importantly, for the audience in Twitch Plays Pokémon. The movement is much less obvious in the Space Butterfly story. Looking at the mythemes in both narratives in a different way, however, may reveal a level of movement which is possible in both.

First, we should return to seeing those in A as working for progress, in relation to specifically Twitch Plays Pokémon, and B as those working against progress. These could be locations or even a location-turned-event such as the Ledge for instance, which was an incredibly difficult moment in the progress of Twitch Plays Pokémon and one which set back much time. The Ledge, then, is a location which works against progress, centring it in B. Bird Jesus's tremendous success in battles helps to propel progress forwards, and thus is in A. What works against

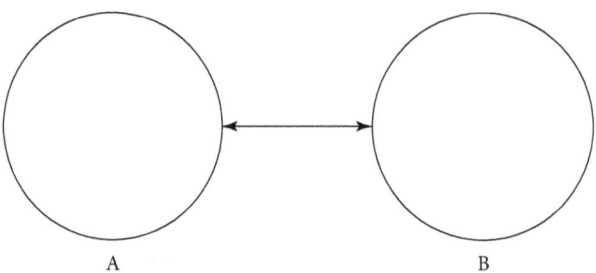

**Diagram 10.3** Joint communal narrative structure.

this distinction is the Anarchy/Democracy divide. When in Democracy mode, more progress is made, and yet it is considered under the Dome fossil. Anarchy makes progress tremendously difficult and yet is quite solidly considered alongside Helix and progress. These seem to be swapped from the perspective of progress.

To truly get a better understanding of this, we should consider more fully the time in which the Democracy concept, as pitted against Anarchy, was created for Twitch Plays Pokémon. Several days into the stream, the programmer shifted the program to take in all inputs and go with majority rather than with every individual input. This move upset players, even though the consideration of every input actually worked against the stream's progress as it had with the Ledge. However, quite a lot of the community reacted strongly against this, feeling it was an act which removed the original intention of the stream.

What followed became known as the 'start9' riots. Essentially, players would input the command 'start9'. The 'start' registered as bringing up the menu and the number after would constitute how many times the 'button' would be pressed. Therefore, most of the inputs would be to bring up the menu multiple times in a row. This essentially continued to halt progress as a protest against the new system. The programmer then decided, after only thirty minutes of the Democracy system being in play, to bring a slider bar between Anarchy and Democracy, and let the chat decide by needing 70 per cent to shift between the two.

Here, we still see concepts of Anarchy working against progress, especially with the start9 riots. But 'progress' is only one side of what we see. Those behind the start9 riots cared about their progress, but only when the terms were in line with the spirit of the stream. The community itself was brought together in the phenomena, the story arising out of chaos, and quite a lot of this was stripped with the beginning of Democracy. Progress is important, but only when connected to the community.

The 'benevolent' in category A in Diagram 10.3 earlier is not representative of progress so much as it is representative of the community itself. The Helix fossil is seen as helping the community, Bird Jesus as being a vessel through completion and Anarchy as being its spirit. In contrast, Democracy takes away this spirit, and thus is against the community, or at least is not a part of it. In the same way the Dome fossil works against the community's progress and their experience.

We can take the same consideration towards the Great Space Butterfly. The Space Butterfly is representative of Jesse Cox's community, so much so that they named themselves Space Butterflies after it. The community is one which came to be around Jesse himself, and thus he is also a part of this community. The Space Moth, however, rests outside of this – it is not the community.

The audience, then, is capable of movement between the two categories. When in A, the participant is a direct part of the community, but when in B they are not and, in some cases, actively working against it.

This dyadic model, then, is different than the one we found in Chapter 8. Chapter 8's structure, regarding the more humorous takes, followed almost every aspect of the broader Slender Man mythological structure, but with the middle mediatory category given less importance than in the other structures by it not being in its own category. Here, the mediatory position is almost unrecognizable as existing. The only possible mytheme to fit would be the audience or community itself, as they can move between the two. Although the audience does not hold the characteristics of each category, I am more comfortable not considering them mediatory elements as they do not actually embody a mediatory. Instead, they are an element which has the possibility of moving from one category to the other. As a mass they only hold the characteristics of one of these categories at a time, when within that category. As soon as they move categories, their characteristics also shift. Therefore, unlike a true mediator, they do not hold elements of both at once.

The movement is also not one directional as it is for the Slender Man mythology. Audience members, and even characters, can move back and forth quite easily. Most of the relationship is built on attachment to the community. Perhaps this is most seen in Twitch Plays Pokémon, where the audience, as a majority, moved from Anarchy to Democracy and back based on what they saw as best for progress. While this helped the community to finally beat the game, it also meant that, at times, they were working in a way which went against the spirit of the community.

This movement is also one which is based on the agency of the element itself (though sometimes the agency is given within the narrative, such as in the case for Twitch Plays Pokémon). The audience member can choose to remove themselves from Jesse Cox's community events and websites but can also return. The audience as a mass chooses to go to Category B for Democracy, and then to move back to A when beneficial. The second example is a bit more questionable, admittedly, as individual audience members have less agency than the audience as a mass but the possibility to push for one element and thus be in one category is still a possibility. Their individual inputs can influence actions and events.

This is in direct contrast to the way the structure works for the Slender Man. In his structure, the movement was utterly controlled by him, and the individual elements of the myth were moved without agency. The individual's agency was non-existent, and all control was given over to the Supernatural Other who controlled the structure from the outside. Here, there is no Supernatural Other on the outside of the structure. All elements are incorporated into the dyadic structure of the narrative, and the movement is left up to the individual audience member.

## 10.4 Conclusion

There may be several reasons why the structure here does not quite fit that of the Slender Man. Our first possibility is that the Slender Man structure found so far is incorrect, while the structure found here is the correct one. This possibility is not as likely. For one, there are several important aspects of the Slender Man structure not found here, the most important of which is the unidimensional controlled movement. The fact the Slender Man does not fit into the structure was once a concern, but now has become a staple I find important. It helps to define him as supernatural and eerie. It also demonstrates his ability to control the structure, an element important for his works. The sense of helplessness is crucial, especially when it is not directly represented in the narratives. The community which gave birth to him express this helplessness as what makes him so fearsome, and so to remove this element would do the mythology a disservice. Its unidirectional take is just as important as well. If the characters in the Slender Man narrative were able to move out of their position, much of the tension in the mythology would dissipate and there would be no need to resolve structural positioning issues. There would be hope where now there is only hopelessness. Seeing this element in the structure as possible is not seeing the narratives for what they are. In addition, the dyadic structure does not have any mediation. Mediation is incredibly important for the previous narratives studied in this book. The Transformed are entirely mediators, and so are the important element of proxies. A dyadic structure like that seen in this chapter, with no mediator and without the unidirectional movement, does not fit the Slender Man narratives we have grown to know.

The second possibility could be the structure found in this chapter, among our two examples of other communally created narratives, is incorrect, and they are, in fact, triadic. This is more of a possibility than the previous. The ability to test this properly, beyond what has already been done here, is more difficult without lengthening this study far beyond its limits. Our solution would be to test even more communally constructed digital narratives and continue to compare. This is what the present study here has done for the Slender Man, so would necessitate its own primary study. Even for the narratives presented here, there was not as much time spent on these narratives than would be preferable if we were to go down this line of work. This is more an avenue for future research endeavours to explore, as deciding definitively if this avenue was correct or not would take us too far from our purposes here.

The third, and perhaps most likely, possibility is that Twitch Plays Pokémon and the Great Space Butterfly are examples of myths from a different type of cultural group. Claude Lévi-Strauss had what I consider here a luxury, though perhaps it could be argued it was done incorrectly, of drawing cultural lines along linguistic boundaries (Lévi-Strauss 1969). The internet, as a massive group which spans a multitude of national boundaries, ethnic identities and native languages, makes it far more difficult to consider. This is, of course, if direct lines could be drawn at all. If we follow what early scholars called 'digital culture' as existing, then theoretically these different digital mythologies would have the same structure. However, if the structure found earlier is accurate, we have two different ones. The final chapter (Chapter 11) will consider these different cultural considerations in greater detail, along with the structures we found, and what this means ultimately for the Slender Man.

As it stands, it seems we have found a line, even if a rather blurry line, for which we can draw the boundary line of our community. The creepypasta community, the horror storytelling subcultural online group, seems to have a triadic structure of unidirectional movement (Chapter 9). This movement is controlled by some outside force which does not have a place in structure. The structure of the Slender Man is not, therefore, necessarily reliant on how it was formed, as a massive communal narrative. Rather, the structure is representative of the creepypasta community, with different structural elements such as the supernatural, the natural, the treatment of those both outside and yet still within society, and the trepidation in which the individual falls in all this. These concerns are not particularly held, perhaps, by all online subgroups. For some, the categories of the mind are determined to know which are in the community, and supported by the community, and which are outside of this.

The extreme difference, then, between the triadic structure from the previous chapters, and the strict binary dyadic structure found in this chapter, must be explainable somehow. Seth Kunin demonstrated how some of these vast shifts can occur over time, starting with the structure of the Hebrew Bible, to the New Testament, to the Book of Mormon. The first shift, from the Hebrew Bible to the New Testament, occurred from a dyadic structure which did not allow for a mediator, to a dyadic structure with overlap, or with a mediator. The mediation for the New Testament came in the form of the path to salvation, through Christ (Kunin 1998). Essentially, the movement went from the two circles without any overlap, as viewed in this chapter, and with overlap, like that found in the humour chapter (Chapter 8). The next shift came with the growth of the Book of Mormon, a triadic structure, which also echoed the structure of the US immigration system (Kunin 2003).

Obviously, there is much time which comes in the process of these changes for Seth Kunin's analysis. There were also important social shifts which occurred as well, with the growth of new radical movements and changes in geography – from the Middle East to the United States. We are essentially faced with two options: either each of these structures is present due to different people being involved, or, there was some kind of radical shift for the community to cause such a structural shift.

While we do not have the lengthy amount of time in Kunin's description as mentioned earlier, as we are only truly looking at around 2005 (if we are to take into consideration the beginning of the Rake instead of the Slender Man), and 2014, when many of the mass communal narratives featured here began. While this short amount of time is not long for larger social processes, it is a long time for popular culture, and especially for online culture. Migration online happens fast, and often in sudden schisms. It is impossible to track individual users and where they ended up. In that way, it is difficult to track the individual users who were on the Something Awful forum, and to discover if they made it to the specific subreddits or Twitch channels who are telling narratives now.

We could review one of our narratives in a previous chapter in a slightly different light. The video game we studied in Chapter 6 could, theoretically, be dyadic but with overlap and mediation. In this case, the category of the Untouched is completely removed from the equation. Instead of it being Transformed and Removed, it would possibly be better understood as Present and Removed. This could occur due to the Untouched category being not very well represented in this narrative. That is not to say, there is no mediation, however. The proxies still exist, and these are characters who are still halfway to death.

If this is a proper possibility, then the video game would present a halfway structure between the earlier creepypasta structure and the more contemporary mass communal narratives. This shift would be only vaguely related to time, and more based on differences between the online communities.

This full discussion leads us to an important question which has been gathering speed since the beginning of this book: What is the culture of the Slender Man? Are we incorrect to assume there can be different structures available? The following chapter seeks to answer these questions in greater detail, where we will discuss the concept of digital culture, and more specifically the Slender Man's culture.

# 11

# The Slender Man's culture

Our study began with specific questions regarding the Slender Man. For the Slender Man to linger on the internet for as long as it has, since 2009, it is interesting to indulge the curiosity of what, more structurally speaking, this narrative is doing online for its community. What is it truly saying as a collective mythos? What cultural group, if any, can claim the Slender Man as theirs?

In order to answer these questions, we analysed multiple different approaches to the Slender Man. We started with its own beginning on the Something Awful forum, looking across time on the forum thread. Near its end is when we first found our triadic formula, which consisted of mythemes from different parts and aspects of society. This structure held up through the experience of Marble Hornets, the web series, and the video game *Slender: The Arrival*. We also saw the same structure in other creepypasta narratives from around the same time period. The more romantic takes of the Slender Man also did not alter our perception. However, the humorous memes had a small transformation. We also saw a departure in structure in our previous chapter on other mass communal narratives online.

The previous chapter brought forward several of the questions which have yet to be answered from the beginning of the study – those regarding the cultural boundaries which surround this study. What is the Slender Man's culture? And where are the boundaries of Slender Man's structure? In this chapter, we are going to explore the concept of a digital culture, the structuralist concepts of culture and how these relate. We are going to explore the role of culture in regard to the Slender Man, and how the Slender Man mythos' structure relates to the concept of culture in our study.

## 11.1 Digital culture and structuralism

Claude Lévi-Strauss's analytical approach begins with an intuitive starting point. This starting point is not arbitrary for no reason, but rather because, according to the understanding of structuralism, the starting point itself is meaningless. The myth's structure is representative of the one present in the whole of the culture itself, and so the opening myth is not relevant. After finding the key myth, the practice of mythic analysis continues in an outward spiral. Once the spiralling reveals a shift in structure, a boundary point is marked, and the process continues from this new point. Each of these points reveals a cultural boundary. However, finding the cultural boundaries in our study is not as clear as it seems in this description.

The process of finding cultural boundaries based on shifts in structure does, at first, appear contradictory, however, to Lévi-Strauss's concept of the canonical formula, and the separate levels of structure he implicitly references (Lévi-Strauss 1969), more explicitly sketched out by neo-structuralists Seth Kunin (2004), Jonathan Miles-Watson (2009a; 2009b), and in this study (Chapter 1). The structure normally discovered, and the one which shifts at these boundary points, is that found on the $S^3$ or $S^2$ level. In this study, we have been primarily concerned with the $S^3$ level of structure found, with an infrequent dip into $S^2$.

For Lévi-Strauss, the $S^1$ is the most abstract level of structure, and is sometimes written out in what he calls the Canonical Formula (Lévi-Strauss 1963b). This is based on the more biological aspects of the theory underlying his method. For him, the structure is present in the universal unconscious, based on the biological workings of the human brain. The narrative level, and the $S^3$, is more concerned with the cultural and social differences, which paint over the $S^1$'s more formulaic and universal structure.

This $S^1$ level is, however, far too abstract for our purposes, not to mention that what form this $S^1$ level takes has been considered vastly different by various neo-structuralists who have taken to revisiting Lévi-Strauss's structuralist method. Neo-structuralists have completely restructured the concept of the Canonical Formula to fit their own perception of it (Mosko 1991; Kunin 1998; Miles-Watson 2009b). For Kunin, this level is considered contentless (Kunin 1996, 196). Kunin's view of this bottom level is different than Lévi-Strauss's Canonical Formula. The Formula allows for mythemes to be plugged into it, bringing it from the lower structural levels to a higher one, but supposedly demonstrating the universal nature of the concept. This is rather different than the blank slate or contentless concept of this bottom level, mostly due to the shifting in nature of Kunin moving away from the Lévi-Straussian formula to a more biological approach. Thus, Lévi-Strauss's concept of the $S^1$ level is less blank than it is for Kunin. Primarily, this stems from the fundamental difference in approach of the supposed universal nature of the structure, stemming from the difference between the brain and the mind.

This discussion is not out of place here, and especially in this chapter, for one primary reason. Lévi-Strauss's assertion of the universal quality of the brain, the less blank fundamental structural level, led him frequently to cross cultural and social boundaries. Most of the research in his lengthy series focused on different cultural groups in the Americas. His jumping from one mythic group to another mythic group was based on both geographic and linguistic connections. That being said, he frequently compares widely to other cultural groups and mythos far from both the geographic and linguistic areas of his primary study. For example, Japanese mythology is frequently drawn on for comparison in mythemes (Lévi-Strauss 1973a; Lévi-Strauss 1997). He justifies this by asserting a 'common heritage' between the American and Asiatic mythology and people (1973, 378).

The shifting from brain to mind is described more fully by Jonathan Miles-Watson (2009a), but I will sum up here what the admittedly complex concept is. A main criticism levelled against Lévi-Strauss's structuralism is the biological centring of the brain (Ingold 2000). Mind, in a more 'post' structuralist sense, relies more on the relationship between both humans and non-humans in the surrounding environment, as exemplified in the work of Bourdieu (1990). Bourdieu's *habitus*, however, actually carries hints at more connections to structuralism than post-structuralists may prefer to admit. His notion of structure combines the more theoretical concepts as well as everyday life and practices. Miles-Watson combines Bourdieu's *habitus* with Lévi-Strauss's concepts of structure to demonstrate how structure can be impacted by the environment the person is surrounded by (Miles-Watson 2009a). Shifting our concept away from Lévi-Strauss's brain, to a more contextual rendering of a mind, does not remove much from what structuralism is trying to achieve.

What all this means for our purposes is the boundaries we are to draw around the Slender Man mythos is not connected to linguistics or geography, but something which we should look at through more contextual means. On the internet, geography, even if we were to rely on this, is not easily drawn. So how, and where, do we draw our boundaries?

Considering our online environment is a nonphysical space, the boundaries are difficult to draw based on physical world boundaries. Culture itself though has been considered in nonphysical space before, as culture is primarily a mental construct (Mead 2000; Bourdieu 1990; Berger and Luckmann 1991). Culture has, for some time, been more aligned with lists of elements, from the early

Tylorian definition of culture as the list of elements such as 'beliefs, art, morals, law, custom and any other capabilities and habits' (Tylor 2010, 1).

Early studies of the internet and the online environment began to use the term 'Digital Culture', though often indiscriminately and without much in-depth thought. For example, Charlie Gere's book *Digital Culture* (2002) starts with a chapter titled 'the Beginnings of Digital Culture' but does nothing to actually trace the elements of this culture. Rather, it focuses more on the historical technological development of the computer and the internet (Gere 2002). Similarly, Bradley Wiggins and G. Bret Bowers's article on online memes describes how memes lead to cultural developments within the internet culture, though without any description of what internet culture is or should be defined as (Wiggins and Bowers 2015). When discussing the social implications and usage of memes, Nissenbaum and Shifman's (2017) work regarding memes and Bourdieu chose to rely on social capital instead of cultural capital, perhaps because demonstrating some form of social cohesion is much easier than attempting to define and find what this culture is. This issue is incredibly important when we begin to see the collection of types of environments which are possible in the online environment.

John Foley (2012) uses the term 'culture', but sees culture as working differently. He better understands culture as a form of network, as networks provide avenues for change. Culture, for Foley, thrives 'by remaining forever in play' (2012, 68). Networks, as a name, recall something more Latourian. A 'network', as understood by both Latour and Foley, is not understood as a *thing*, but as an expression meant to 'check how much energy, movement, and specificity our own reports are able to capture' (Latour 2005, 131). It makes sense that Latour's emphasis on network can be connected to both Foley and our purposes of an online environment because of the inspiration from technology (Castells 2000).

Milad Doueihi also uses the term 'digital culture', which he defines as that which is comprised of communication and information exchange modes which displace, redefine and reshape knowledge into new forms, formats and the methods for acquiring and transmitting this knowledge (Doueihi 2011, 12). This is an abstract definition which gives space for new and constantly changing forms of literacy, allowing the different forms of online communication to shift while not altering our understanding.

This is like Foley's concept of culture as constantly in play, rather than static. This also relates back to the more neo-structural concept of mind as expressed by Kunin and Miles-Watson. By seeing the cultural and social situation, the myth is placed in as being more nuanced. Seth Kunin, for example, introduced his concept of *jonglerie* to better depict how structuralism can incorporate shifts in culture, and thus in structure. *Jonglerie* allows for emphasizing and de-emphasizing aspects of structure, which allows for gradual transformation (Kunin 2001; Kunin 2009). This different emphasizing can be either conscious or unconscious, as individuals demonstrate their agency within their own cultural understanding or individual identities. Kunin's *jonglerie* shows how culture can be understood as not static, but in a constant state of becoming, to use Ingold's phrase (Ingold 2000). Lévi-Strauss acknowledged this more fluid concept of culture when he admitted the attempt to find all variations of a particular myth as almost 'meaningless, since we are dealing with a shifting reality, perpetually exposed to the attacks of a past that destroys it and a future that changes it' (Lévi-Strauss 1969, 3).

The digital environment's constantly changing nature leads to difficulty in pinning down any type of definition for a digital culture. One of the most useful understandings of culture in the digital world is Henry Jenkins's *participatory culture*. Participatory culture, according to Henry Jenkins, is defined by seven factors: (1) a relatively low barrier for civic engagement; (2) strong support for sharing one's creations with others; (3) informal levels of mentorship; (4) the members believe their various contributions matter; (5) they feel a social connection; (6) it shifts the focus from the individual to the community; (7) and it looks at technology with an ecological approach, and thinks about the interrelationship of communication technologies, cultural communities and its activities (Jenkins 2009, 5–6). Participatory culture is perhaps the most cohesive view of what could be called a comprehensive digital culture. However, a participatory culture is not specific to the digital world. A participatory culture, as described by Jenkins, is not necessarily wholly connected to the digital sphere, but rather a way to describe it.

Structuralism, in both theory and method, is, however, not always necessarily tied to a concept of culture in the first place. Terence S. Turner, for example, revisited some of the myths originally reviewed in Lévi-Strauss's *Raw and the Cooked* (1969) though with some of the shifts in structuralism led by neo-structuralists. His work, for example, focuses on the myth's relationship to its social contexts, including ethnographic meaning and exegesis (Turner 2017, 6–7). Turner ends up shifting Lévi-Strauss's original formulation away from an idea of culture. Instead, he leans more towards a concept of 'society', and a focus on different Transformations (ibid., 122).

Throughout the present study, the power of agency in the storyteller has been important. The mythology of the Slender Man is a communal narrative, but is one built on the individual creativities of the community members. This concept has pushed us to consider the concept of mind to be more aligned with the neo-structuralist view of being contextual rather than biological (Chapter 1). If culture is aligned with Bourdieu's *habitus*, rather than Freud or Jung's unconscious, it allows for the agency of storytellers to affect the structure in their own way, whether this be consciously or subconsciously. This allows for storytellers to express the mythology of the Slender Man in a truly folkloric way – from the folk themselves, and the folk's creativity. This also allows them to bring the narrative from an outside source to the home group.

If there is such a thing as digital culture, then it must be defined by the creativity of the individuals involved and their own influence on the way the culture is expressed. It is best to view the overarching digital culture as one more generally described as along the lines of Jenkins's participatory culture, but one which exists in a virtual world. By 'virtual' I do not necessarily mean fictional, nor does the term specifically necessitate an online dimension. Literature, for example, can craft virtual worlds, as do video games, which, despite the increasing number of online games, are not necessarily tied to an online environment. Virtual worlds are those which interact in real time, are shared, are built on rules and are embodied (Bartle 2004: 3–4). This more general overarching 'digital culture' is made up of different communities. These communities are united into the larger digital culture through their virtual geographic connections, and the similarities in their way of communicating and interacting. For example, the creepypasta community is different from the video game community, though there may be a few individuals who shift between these due to their virtual proximity. They may interact on similar websites, such as reddit which is incorporated of a variety of subreddits, or subforums based on interest. Users can jump between these subreddits, or even discover new communities simply by browsing the site. Even when communities have little to no overlap in their community members, their visibility speaks to the close virtual geography. Their ways of interacting or communicating is also similar, as they all resemble participatory culture of the digital culture they comprise.

I should stress here the importance of the previous paragraph beginning with 'if'. Following this survey of culture, we should review Roy Wagner's statement that culture, as anthropologists have learned to accept it, has been invented (Wagner 2016). Through the process of cultural relativism, anthropologists have constructed the idea of culture, particularly culture as a *thing*. Similarly, the way the term 'culture' is used in relation to the digital has begun to shift from a more generic use of the term to other considerations of social cohesion. Peter Drucker, for instance, has chosen to refer to communities online not as cultures or even communities but as an 'organization', reasoning that a community is something which is fated, while an organization implies a voluntary membership (1994, 33–80). I believe the notion of a 'digital culture' is neither relevant nor helpful, especially given our previous studies of structures as being different depending on the community. Understanding the full digital world as being the same culture, structurally speaking, would be inaccurate. The structure we are most concerned with would be based on the communities themselves.

Healy (1997) has described how a community is spontaneous and emerges in constantly changing circumstances. It is best we think more in terms of community rather than culture. The community aspect to the online environment is of primary concern for participants, and therefore for us as academics. The online environment at this current point is too diverging and wide reaching in order to consider as one cohesive culture, but rather a virtual geography in which multiple communities exist within. Therefore, our *cultural* boundaries should be *communal* boundaries. These boundaries are bound to be as porous as cultural boundaries, but also demonstrate how two different communities could conceive of the world, either consciously or unconsciously, in two widely different ways.

## 11.2 The Slender Man: Mythos and community

When we review the structure found throughout the study, we see two main points of structural divergence. These raised questions about the reasoning for their shift in structure, the boundary points of the communities of Slender Man more generally speaking, and the specific communities which contributed to the narrative in particular. Now that we have a better understanding of what type of boundary points we are looking for, the community the structure rests with can start to be deciphered.

The first divergence was in the more humorous approaches to the narrative (Chapter 8), where we saw two primary categories with an overlapping mediator. Our initial triadic formula highlights the importance and presence of the mediatory category, which we have called the Transformed. The humour narratives did not give as much presence to this mediatory category, except in a more implicit way. The jokes nodded to the presence of this middle category, and the anxiety which it accompanies, as well as the movement which is present between the more triadic categories. However, due to the less emphasized middle category, we depicted the structure of the humour narratives as more dyadic, with overlapped categories for the mediatory position (see Chapter 8).

We saw some justification for this through Kunin's *jonglerie* (Kunin 2001; Kunin 2009). The process of the shift is from the triadic to the dyadic in relation to the humour narratives we previously claimed as one of emphasis versus de-emphasis. However, we should not be so quick to connect to *jonglerie* for two reasons. The first being that Kunin's process of *jonglerie* does not change structure for quite some time (Kunin 2009), a length which does not exist between the inception of the Slender Man to the inception of these memes. Even if we are to step back and say the structure of the Slender Man's mythology existed in other narratives prior to the mythos' creation, the online environment which is the focus of our study has not existed for as long as the structural transformations Kunin looks at. Kunin's studies of Crypto-Jews (Kunin 2001; Kunin 2009) as well as the shift from the Hebrew Bible to the New Testament (Kunin 1998) and even to Mormonism (Kunin 1996) emphasizes the importance of how these shifts occur over time.

The second reason to not jump quite so quickly is due to the change seemingly connected to genre rather than community, which is not how structure works. Genre, like narrative form, does not alter the structure, but reflects it evenly. Therefore, we would have to view those doing this emphasizing and de-emphasizing as their own community. During that chapter, we needed to have a much fuller discussion of the boundary lines of culture or community, which we have now considered.

The second main structural departure point was in our study of other mass communal narratives, with our two main case studies of Twitch Plays Pokémon and the Great Space Butterfly (Chapter 10), where we saw two primary categories with no mediator possible. Here, the structure was not just dyadic, but did not even have a mediatory position. This is in great contrast to the triadic model, with mediators so heavily present. This huge departure cannot be due to *jonglerie*, as it is not a process of different levels of emphasis, but rather a different structure entirely. While questions regarding our different cultural or communal boundaries have been risen throughout the study, this current chapter has brought the question to a much stronger and necessary focus. As discussed in the chapter itself, the structure found in these narratives can be re-applied to the Slender Man under an assumption of our previous triadic model being incorrect. Nor does it initially appear as if this strong dyadic structure found for these narratives is necessarily incorrect. The triadic model can no way fit these narratives, as there is no mediator, so the presence of neither the dyadic overlap model found in the humorous narratives (Chapter 8) nor the triadic models fit.

If we remove the concept of an all-inclusive 'digital culture', and instead shift to ideas of multiple communities, then we can see where these communal boundaries may lie. The online sphere allows for individuals to garner a community around identity. This means an individual may find where they think and belong. Communities are not only based on interest, but language, way of communicating, humour, inside jokes, gestures and so forth. As Trevor Blank writes about the online environment, it has 'folk groups, customs, lingo and dialects, neighbourhoods, crimes, relationships, games, discussion groups, displays of emotion, banking, commerce, and various other forms of communication and education' (Blank 2009, 11). The question then becomes what is the community we are concerned with here, and where does it end?

Our primary starting place for the Slender Man is in the creepypasta community. 'Creepypasta' is a term which comes from early online forms of communication, when sharing narratives required the user to copy the words and paste them into the messaging format to share. Narratives shared online were called copypastas, after the copy/paste formula. The horror version began to be called creepypastas. But creepypasta is more than just a horror narrative found online. The term has come to define a community, one which has a way of sharing narratives as separate from authorial connection. These narratives are meant to blur the lines between reality and fiction. Their format is more akin to the folklore, myth and urban legend than set narratives like Stephen King.

This is important to understand, as horror narratives online have begun to change in their approach. One of the most useful centres for horror writing communities to gather is a subreddit, on the forum site reddit, called No Sleep. These narratives share some elements with the types of approaches taken with creepypasta but diverge also in important ways. No Sleep is not creepypasta. It does share similarities, such as the attempt to blur lines between reality and fiction; the rules of the subreddit state 'Everything is true here, even if it isn't' (r/nosleep n.d.), a statement which is supposed to encourage in-character communication. Each narrative is expected to be written in the first-person, as if the narrating character is the user on the site and telling a true story. The importance of the role of 'in-character communication' in relation to some elements of creepypasta, especially Slender Man, is talked about more in depth in Chapter 4.

In-character communication is not the only thing defining creepypasta. Perhaps most important to the community is the connection of author, or more importantly the lack thereof. Creepypasta creates narratives like folklore or urban legend – narratives shared simply as stories from a community group.

These are simply shared, often with no knowledge of where the original came from.

Jan Brunvard describes the urban legend as a subsection of folklore, ones that are believed to some extent, or at least believable (1981, 3). While no one in the community presented here would fully believe in the Slender Man's existence, nor in the 'truth' of many of the other creepypasta narratives such as the Curious Case of the Smiling Dog or Ben Drowned, these narratives are carried with an air of believability. Often this is brought down to the disconnect the narratives have with any sense of the author. When the place of author, or historical origin, is not easily found, it becomes much easier to present the narrative as rumour supposedly true. This is heavily present in the Slender Man narratives. As the story became more popular, and the origin more easily traceable, the community developed what is called the Tulpa Theory – or the idea that, while the Slender Man was created as a fictional story on the Something Awful forums, the power of the thoughts of the internet thinking about him led to a physical manifestation (Chapter 2). Again, this theory is not 'believed' real in the way many religious studies scholars talk about their participants' 'beliefs', but it is a playful theory in order to retain the ability to engage with the grey area between reality and fiction. Essentially, creepypasta's importance is in the *possibility* of belief, often more in an act of play.

In contrast, No Sleep is a place for horror storytelling online where authorial connection is important. Due to the in-character communication rules, the subreddit created other subreddits which allow for more direct conversation about the narratives as narratives, rather than truth. One of the most important for our consideration here is r/nosleepOOC, or Out of Character. Several threads on the OOC subreddit are ones which point out or complain about narratives which are taken from the subreddit and repeated elsewhere without credit being given to the author. One user directly pointed out to me that No Sleep is not creepypasta. In fact, many of the participants on r/nosleep I chatted with are looking to make a name for themselves. One, for instance, expressed how she had recently received the opportunity to write a horror movie based on her abilities.

One of the most striking examples of this strong difference is in relation to the Slender Man Movie, which was released in 2018. When the idea of a Slender Man movie was first broached closer to 2009, the community was not pleased with the idea. Underlying this objection was how a movie would present something official – an industry canon which would undermine the communal aspect of the narrative. In contrast, the community on No Sleep have members, such as the user earlier, who have been hired to write horror movies.

The role of creepypasta as it used to be is gradually fading. There are still loci online which claim themselves as being centres for creepypasta narratives, but more and more these share from No Sleep, or are being accompanied by the author. CreepsMcPasta, for instance, is a YouTuber who reads creepypastas on his channel, and accompanies his videos with information as to where he got his narrative (CreepsMcPasta 2014; 2018; as examples).

So the community which gave birth to the Slender Man is a different community, either from the perspective of a collective of individuals or a different outlook, to the current community which shares and tells horror narratives. In one of our divergent structures, on mass communal narratives, these narratives were created and shared much closer to the time of writing than the Slender Man. Both case studies in that chapter, for instance, were begun to be shared around 2014, versus 2009 of the Slender Man's birth. Perhaps this is more reflective of how the communities are composed and think in the more contemporary online environment. Or, they can be more indicative of a different community entirely, where the world view and way of thinking is different.

Even though Chapter 10 looked at other mass communal narratives, which is also like the Slender Man, their different formulations reveal a bit more about this shift in narrative telling online. The narratives are not told via individual narratives which are gathered and shared without authorial connection. The narrative of Twitch Plays Pokémon is perhaps the closest possible to this type of narrative formation and sharing, not from choice but necessity. The communication and mythology formation happened so fast, due to the quick nature of the Twitch chat, that it would be overly difficult to attribute any part of the narrative formation to any one audience member. In contrast, the story of the Great Space Butterfly is also not quite fully a mass communal narrative. The narrative began as one told by a single person, Jesse Cox, which was then taken up by the community to expand. These expansions were minor though.

The difference found in this structure could also be due to the difference in the communities themselves. Despite the sharing of various elements or narratives from the online environment to video games and vice versa, such as memes and game topics (Chapter 6), these could very well be different communities. Unfortunately, the topic of horror video games did not come up during my time with the No Sleep community. However, I did manage to broach the topic with members of video game communities. When asked if they were interested in creepypasta, very few responded in the positive, if at all. Most only were focused on horror narratives as presented in video games, preferring the interactivity of the format. In the conclusion of the previous chapter, we posited a possibility for the video game structure to be dyadic with mediation. This was considered due to the lack of one of the primary categories not being well represented in the narrative. Thus, it could be argued the video game structure could be the representation of a different community, or a possible in-between stage.

The difference between creepypasta and No Sleep is more than just a superficial difference in approach. The connection to the author is a large part of the more underlying approach to both the narrative and the community. The very first user on the Something Awful forum to post the Slender Man, Victor Surge, never stepped in to correct when users took the concept in a new direction, or even to claim some kind of ownership or authorial resonance (Slender Nation Podcast 2011). By allowing the audience to take part and interact in a full sense, to partake and conceive away from a strict authorial narrative, the structure brings in the audience itself. The audience is a mytheme to be placed within, and often gets placed in the fearful mediator category as those who have already been affected by the Slender Man. The structure of the narratives is thus coming from the community as a whole, rather than from one who is supposed to represent the community. The shift to connect to authorial ownership is not just a superficial move for the community, but one which represents a greater shift in communal understanding and definition. The creepypasta community is gradually becoming overtaken.

## 11.3 Conclusion

This admittedly theoretical and reflexive chapter has attempted to paint some sort of understanding of cultural or communal boundaries for the structure of the Slender Man mythos which we have discovered in this study. What we have determined is how it is possibly best to discount an idea of digital culture being cohesive, especially due to the wide array of community options and relationships possible online. We decided a focus on community was better than a focus on culture, as the digital environment seems more related to community elements than cultural ones.

Instead, we should view our structural 'culture' here as more of a community, with communal boundaries. These boundaries are porous, especially online, as audience members are capable of being members of multiple communities, slightly different than the more fated version of communities based on geographic location, linguistic group or ethnicity. There is, however, a sense of community which is created in these interest groups which reflect the type of community often expected from the more traditional versions. During conversations at Jesse Cox's England-based convention, CoxCon, one participant described it as being easy to talk to strangers at the convention due to the shared interest, going so far as to state that she knew these people 'shared the same values'. This may appear a strong assumption to make based solely on interest, but often the continual visitation of these social groups also requires a connection of more ideological bases, and, growingly, political interests.

The difficulty for our present study is how the community under question, the creepypasta community, has changed over time. While the fieldwork I conducted is useful in understanding the current position of this community, it is impossible to truly do much fieldwork for those who were participating back in 2009. There are some sites which still cling to old ways of doing creepypasta, for example Secure, Contain, Protect (SCP) Foundation. The Slender Nation website, a forum site for the centre of the Slender Man narratives, has very little interaction. During over a year of online presence on the forum, only one other member ever posted. Even the lines between No Sleep and more traditional creepypasta still sometimes get blurred (Mikey Knutson 2017). But this is not representative of either all the loci for the community, nor the most popular.

The speed of the communal shift is one which is an unfortunate consequence when doing research with any element of popular culture. Popular culture moves fast, and by the time one finds an interesting study, does the preliminary research necessary and fills out any grant research proposals, the project may already be outside of popularity before the actual research has begun. Our study began with an understanding that this was a combined anthropological study along with a historic one. The Slender Man is not a new concept online, and a decade is quite a lot of time by both popular culture and online community standards.

However, what we have determined in this chapter is how the differences in structure which we found throughout the study are more likely due to a difference in community, and therefore of structure. What we have found for the creepypasta community, structurally speaking, is a categorical understanding of a triadic model, due to the increased emphasis and anxiety of the mediators.

After this full discussion, we can bring this back to the questions we first asked in our introduction: What does the Slender Man narrative say, what it fully means in the deeper narrative? And what community group can really claim that ownership to the Slender Man? These are two pertinent questions which have taken us through a lengthy study.

Let us first review our initial question over what the narrative is saying more structurally speaking. This question first came about in the review of seeing the spread of the mythology and the length of time it spent in the online sphere. Structuralism seemed the best suited to answer this question, as it digs down into the organization of the narrative and what it reflects more socially speaking. Through this process, we have discovered what this narrative is saying. The story is organized triadically and describes the process of helpless transitions.

The three categories also reveal a certain level of understanding between the digital society's view of mental health issues, as well as its relation to itself to the non-digital world. The middle category of the Transformed is frequently connected to those with mental health issues (Chapters 4, 5, 9). This is important considering this middle category is considered to have touched death, being a true mediator between the living 'normal' society and those who have been Removed, frequently through death. The Transformed are socially dead. The connection to those with mental health demonstrates an understanding of the place of mental health in society – as socially dead and marginalized. They are pushed to the boundary.

In some ways, our views of how the structure has changed in different communities and at different time frames can reveal a different level of how this triadic structure echoes the way the digital world sees itself. Back in 2009 when the Slender Man narrative started, and especially in 2005 when the Rake was first being established (Chapter 9), a community online was a fairly new concept. The internet had yet to reach the stages of development. To put into perspective, YouTube was first launched in 2005, and in the same year Facebook was still limited to university email addresses (and perhaps one day my choices in these examples will also reflect the time frame of my writing). The rise of the online celebrity had not reached levels it has reached now. The environment was massively different in its understanding of itself. In many ways, the concept of the virtual environment as being capable of providing real relationships was still met with some scepticism. This is reflected in some of the early studies of the online environment we looked at briefly in Chapter 1, perhaps most summed up by Fialkova and Yelenevskaya's 2001 study which said that virtual communication and environments 'can only give an illusion of friendship, involvement, and belonging' (2001, 87). Perhaps the study's time frame in 2001 can give us a bit of an understanding of how one can believe this line of thinking.

This was also reflected in the language often used online to distinguish between the friendships made online and those offline. IRL, a common chat phrase meaning 'in real life', essentially describes the virtual environment as therefore not real. This means any real relationship or connection made online lies somewhere in between what is real and what is not real – a strange mediatory category in which their full online experience exists.

Returning to our main two questions, our second question was regarding what culture or community can claim the Slender Man originated with them. Again, structuralism is well suited. According to Lévi-Strauss, the $S^3$ and $S^2$ level structures are going to be based on social and cultural influences, and these structures shift from culture to culture. By using structuralism, we are easily able to attempt to draw these boundaries.

Through this analysis we have found that the creepypasta community uses the triadic structure. The middle category is the larger mediator, extended out due to its importance in the narrative. Though all the different uses of the Slender Man (except for, perhaps, the video game as discussed previously) echo this, and, most importantly, so do the other creepypasta narratives as discussed in Chapter 9.

We have, therefore, answered our two primary questions. The creepypasta community holds the Slender Man, which may have been expected. Despite its spread into other areas of the online environment, the structure of the narrative shifts upon entering these other communities.

# 12

# Conclusion

Our project started when we recognized how long the lingering figure of the Slender Man has lasted in the imagination of the internet. A decade is a long time in internet years, with the speed of communication, and even the locations through which this communication occurs, as constantly changing and moving. In 2009, Facebook was still restricted only to users who had a university email account, meaning the everyday user still used Myspace as their primary social media location, and the word 'selfie', in reference to self-portraits, was still a new term. The online digital landscape shifts quickly, but through this time of quick changes and communication alterations and additions, the Slender Man still haunts the background of photos.

This led us to two primary questions. The first asks what this narrative is truly saying when we look deeper than the simple narrative of a tall thin man in a suit haunting people and making children disappear. Our second question probes the cultural background of the Slender Man: What is the Slender Man's culture?

In order to answer these questions, we turned to structuralism. Structuralism is the method most suited to the two specific questions of our study. Structuralism allows us to dig deeper into the narrative in order to see how it orders the world, and what it says about the people who tell these narratives. The method doubles as a way of showing cultural lines and distinctions, which is the best way to test our second question regarding the Slender Man's culture. This cultural question is the best way to also test the concept of an overarching 'digital culture'.

Let us start first, however, with our first question: What is it that this narrative is truly saying? We found the deeper structure of the Slender Man mythos is a triadic structure (see Diagram 12.1), stepping out from the Lévi-Straussian concept of binaries. Our triadic structure seemed necessary, however, as the mediatory position, which we labelled as Transformed, is such a stressed and elongated position that characters, and even sometimes locations, find themselves in. Rather than the mediator resting in between the two primary

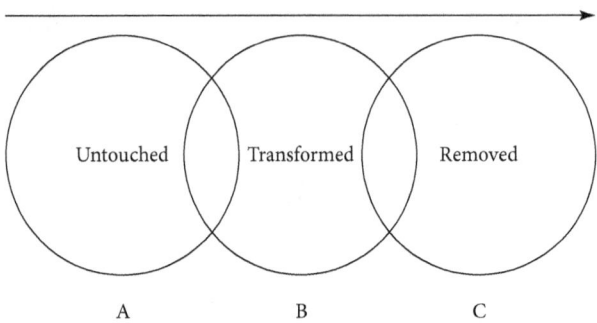

**Diagram 12.1** Triadic structure with category labels.

binary categories, the third, more elongated category for the mediator serves two purposes: the first is to connect it more closely to what Seth Kunin found to be present in the society of the United States (Kunin 2003); the second is to demonstrate the nature of the category as one possible to end in. In Chapter 4, we equated the mediator with a ritual, where a participant can be both categories simultaneously, but a ritual in which one can be trapped within. Given the full nature of this category, it seemed best to separate what would be a crossover to a third category (Diagram 12.1).

The first category is representative of normal society. The Untouched is the average person who goes through life without knowledge of the existence of the Supernatural Other; the Slender Man, or, in some creepypasta narratives as we discovered in Chapter 9, some other Supernatural Others. Movement out of this category is based on an acquisition of knowledge. The Untouched are essentially defined by ignorance.

The Transformed, on the other hand, have garnered knowledge of the Slender Man, but typically do not feel as if they have gathered all the knowledge necessary. They typically are constantly in search of more knowledge. In the story of the Rake, the narrative is a compilation of different experiences, narratively gathered by a woman who is in search of more information of the Rake after her own encounter (Chapter 9). The encounter with the Supernatural Other, while moving away from a category of no knowledge of this other existence, only causes more questions to arise regarding the experience of the world.

The last category is that of the Removed. These are the people who have been completely removed from the social world of the Untouched. These characters are sometimes Removed through disappearance, and sometimes through extreme violence. Surprisingly, the actual method of Removal is often not important. The importance is on the fact that they have been Removed at all.

The stress for the structure, however, is on the elongated mediatory position of the Transformed. These are true mediators between the Untouched and the Removed. Marginalized from society, they have been touched by the death of the Removed resulting in a social death. They are still touched by the ignorance of the Untouched, as they are still in some desperate search of truth and knowledge. The social marginalization and the feeling of being already partly Removed pushes them to feel out of place and alone. Often, these characters separate themselves voluntarily based on their search, such as Jadusable in Ben Drowned (Chapter 9). They are also typically associated with those who are mentally ill, due to their explanations of the Supernatural Other's existence (Chapter 4; Chapter 5; Chapter 9).

We found this triadic structure through the Something Awful forum posts (Chapters 3 and 4), in the Marble Hornets web videos (Chapter 5), in the romantic fanfiction (Chapter 7) and in the other creepypasta narratives (Chapter 9). This demonstrates, structurally speaking, a similar cultural thought process among these various narratives, their virtual geographies and the communities who tell and share them. But this brings us to important questions regarding the areas not mentioned in the former list. While the video game structure seemed at first study as also holding the triadic structure (Chapter 6), when we gave it fresh eyes after finding the dyadic structure of other mass communal narratives, we found it could, under a different consideration, actually have more of a dyadic structure which has overlap (Chapter 10). The mediatory position would then still be present, but all three categories of the triadic structure are not represented in the narrative. This would also be consistent with the humour narratives and the structure found there, where the narratives appear to be more dyadic with mediation (Chapter 8). Essentially, the primary difference between the dyadic and the triadic models we found, most notably in the humour and the possible video game structure, was the nature of the interaction and possibilities of the mediator. In these more dyadic models, the mediator is a transitory state, a temporary location if a location at all, before moving again. However, in the triadic formula, it is the opposite of a transitory state. The state of those found in the mediatory position have a possibility of permanence. These two different narratives may provide some insight to the way transition of structure happens between the triadic nature in the other chapters and the strict dichotomy with no mediation found in the other mass communal narratives (Chapter 10).

This brings us to our second question: What is the Slender Man's culture? As discussed in the previous chapter, the framework of a cohesive and overarching digital culture seems to not exist (Chapter 11). We can see how complicated an idea of this can be with the structures sketched out in our previous chapters. How can a cultural group like those in Chapter 10, with Twitch Plays Pokémon, be considered in the same cultural group as those who structure the world like the triadic nature found in the previous chapters? Instead of 'digital culture' as an overarching joint culture, it is best to consider these various groups like communities, where members can move, shift and flow. If we imagine the virtual geography as a physical geography, we can also imagine these various communities as being nearby both temporally and geographically. Essentially, the creepypasta community, with their triadic structure, is historically different and nearby the other communities discussed. This would fit the idea of structural change and flow in Lévi-Strauss's *Mythologiques* series (Lévi-Strauss 1969; 1973b; 1978; 1981).

Essentially this means we are not actually looking for the Slender Man's culture as such, but the Slender Man's *community*. The structure of the Slender Man's narratives also fits with the structure found for the creepypasta community. This would place the Slender Man's primary community as the creepypasta community. At first, it appears we have not really discovered anything new or revelatory. The Slender Man has always been associated with creepypasta, so connecting the Slender Man to the creepypasta community does not appear, at first, to be anything of a surprise.

The creepypasta community can be defined by more than their actions of writing horror narratives online. Creepypasta is defined by its communal interactions, typically in-character communication. Whether this in-character communication is undertaken or not, the communication both in the narratives and around the narratives is marked by its assumption of truth. Like the rule of No Sleep, 'Everything is true here even if it isn't', the creepypasta interaction takes on an air of belief, even if belief is not present. The community is also marked by their interest in the separation of the author. The goal of the creepypasta community is to share narratives without authorial connection. The authorship is, instead, attributed to the community itself.

This leads to a bigger question though. These two initial explorations were sparked because of how different the Slender Man is, especially in how it was spread, compared to other creepypasta characters and narratives. The Slender Man's influence has spread to other areas online in a way no other creepypasta narrative really has. His name has become incredibly known even outside of creepypasta. So if we are to see it as, essentially, no different than these other narratives, both in community and structure, than we have failed to answer the more implicit question of how these narratives have spread more than their other creepypasta counterparts.

The answer, I believe, rests in the agency of storytellers and the malleability of the narrative. When first looking at the Slender Man mythology, seeing the theoretical workings of the mythos, we saw how the mythology struggled with its own identity at first, especially in relation to the individuality of creative expression. The answer the community rested on was how each individual representation of the Slender Man stood as authoritative. This led to an understanding of the Slender Man in line with both apophatic theology and Lovecraft's cosmic fear – the human mind is unable to properly comprehend the true inhumanity of the Slender Man (Chapter 2).

This means the individual storyteller has full authorial power over their own version. They can take the bare bones of the Slender Man narrative and alter it to fit their own cultural structural understanding. Thus, we see small shifts in the structure when we look only for the narrative level first. For example, the humour narratives showed a slightly different structure while still having a representation of the Slender Man as an individual creature and myth. This means individual storytellers were able to bring the narrative to their own community group and have it fit their own structure.

We can once again return to Kunin's concept of *jonglerie*, the idea of which is how people can emphasize or de-emphasize different elements of a narrative which can potentially impact the structure (Kunin 2001; Kunin 2009; see also Chapter 8). Essentially, individual storytellers can juggle their personal identity with their communal identity and the identity of the myth itself. When we think of community groups as being near to each other, as if actually placed on a virtual geographic landscape, then the flow of narrative from group to group is made possible through its ability to be altered structurally, either consciously or unconsciously, by their storytellers.

Compared to some of the other creepypasta narratives, and even the ones we studied in this study, the narrative level of the Slender Man and the way the narrative spread allowed for much more direct individual interpretation and agency in the telling. The mythos is built on the multitude of individual narratives which contributed to the larger story, allowing for a power to the individual narrative. The Rake, by contrast, was a controlled mass. The elements were compiled over time by 4chan, which provided a blueprint for the stories and the monster itself. The Curious Case of the Smiling Dog is, in all reality, simply a picture. The full narrative was only sketched out by an individual, but most of the creepypasta is solely based on the image itself, which does not alter from user to user. Ben Drowned, too, is more of one narrative, a set series of YouTube videos and a set narrative which goes along with them. Despite being disconnected from the author when shared, in true creepypasta fashion, the narrative does not actually alter with different authorial takes.

The nature of this study is admittedly rather strange. The tracing of a narrative in a community or cultural group, which has yet to be truly defined, can end up with lots of jumping from place to place, although the jumping was virtual rather than physical. We moved from community to community, attempting to find traces of rumour and story, either current or historical, which we could grab hold of. To some extent, this was necessary for such a study of the online environment. There is less material or historical anthropological explorations of this virtual world as there are on some more physical world counterparts. And despite the fact these environments are inhabited by human beings regardless of virtual location, the online environment is a new medium which has altered the way communication may happen. The word 'community' and the idea of a 'digital culture' have been used both academically and by participants themselves, though what this means, looks like or functions as, is much less demonstrated or explored.

A much larger result from this study, which goes far beyond the Slender Man himself, is more working knowledge of the online environment. Firmly seeing a lack of overarching digital culture, and more focus on individual communities, greatly impacts the future of anthropology online. In all forms of practice, the actual knowledge of how community groups are comprised, and how they relate to other communities online, is a very difficult definitive information to know. Instead, by revealing a shared sense of world views, and depicting the flow of these world views between groups, we see the possibilities of how the flow of communities can be understood online.

Bringing Lévi-Strauss into the digital world called for an occasional change. Some of these alterations are not new to this study, for example the relation of ethnographic material with a structuralist study (Hugh-Jones 1979; Kunin 2009; Miles-Watson 2012; Turner 2017). In addition, I followed the example of Miles-Watson (2009a) who followed Bourdieu's concept of *habitus* as a view of structuralism, which allowed for some agency in the way of structural movement and change (also Kunin 2004).

I have built upon the foundation set from previous neo-structuralists in order to build upon the inspiration and theoretical background of Lévi-Strauss. With this, I built upon Lévi-Strauss's concept of implicit mythology, especially in relation to a structuralist analysis of video games (Chapter 6; see also Asimos 2019). If a myth is made up of all its variants (Lévi-Strauss 1963b), then every different individual engagement with a video game should be considered on an equal level. The concept of implicit mythology can help us here. Originally conceived as a simply ritualized version of the textual myth (Lévi-Strauss 1978), I have adapted both Lévi-Strauss's more ritualized notion of the concept action, but pairing this concept with Jonathan Miles-Watson's conception of implicit myth as personal experience of myth (Miles-Watson 2015). This allows for a more individualized experience of the myth to be considered on an equal level. This is important when the structuralist method is brought to video games, which are, by their nature, interactive.

I believe this conception of implicit mythology, especially when related to video games, can help to extend the study of religion and popular culture when video games are primary case studies. The stressing of the variety of narratives which are occurring simultaneously when playing a game (the narrative of the game, the narrative of the action of gameplay, and the personal narrative of the player) is important, as one aspect of the game should not be privileged over the others; the combined effect is what causes a video game to be what it is. The concept of implicit mythology gives a definitional approach to these other narratives, which can help to orient the researcher to their existence and their importance.

Bringing Lévi-Strauss into the digital world has two primary outcomes. The first is to demonstrate a usefulness of the method in the contemporary world. By showing how structuralism can help to reveal the possibilities of how communities are situated online helps to demonstrate the usefulness of the method in the contemporary and virtual sphere. The second outcome in the use of the method also helped us to see the community groups the way they do online.

Despite the fact that we reached some kind of solution with our two primary questions, the present study has opened up several avenues for future research. The first is a bit more obvious, as it would be a testing ground for the analysis found here. The narratives used in the case studies of the other creepypasta narratives (Chapter 10) and other mass communal narratives (Chapter 11) were not given as detailed a study as the Slender Man mythology. Clearly, it was impossible to do so, given the scope of this study. It would be beneficial to have the structure discovered here tested with further analysis and study.

Lévi-Strauss's *Mythologiques* series started with one myth and ended up expanding to incorporate the full analysis of a large canon of myths from multiple communities in the Americas, spanning multiple groups such as the Bororo and Ge. But to do such a complicated work he needed four volumes, and most of them much larger than this book. Each work builds from the first, expanding and extrapolating from previous analysis. Essentially, this means my three expansions proposed earlier are unable to fit into this study, but that this study provides the foundations for next to build from. In order to look further into the narratives in both Chapters 9 and 10, as well as to perhaps garner even more case studies than the few presented here, the paranormal narratives and the contemporary horror narratives, we would have to expand into new volumes of work, and would necessarily be referring back to what has been achieved here.

Through the meanderings of different narrative formats, we have chased the Slender Man: through images, text and web videos; through horror, romance and humour, and even through other narratives from other areas of the virtual sphere. Through this, we have seen the Slender Man's true nature, and the way he controls the structure he represents. We see the agency he grants his storytellers, while stripping the agency from those in his narratives themselves. We have seen how this structure impacts audience members, who can sometimes find themselves horribly part of the structure. We have seen how individuals have played with structure and horror, and how they have manipulated it to fit their own communal understandings, shifting him to be a figure of humour or a figure of romance. We have seen his similarities, or, more accurately, a lack of similarity, with an online hive mind's playing of *Pokémon Red*, and of a Great Space Butterfly who dreams of the world. And we have seen how he works alongside other horror creatures, like a creepy smiling dog, a haunted video game cartridge, and an animalesque creature who speaks the names of his victims.

Ultimately, we see what the Slender Man is doing for the community he originated from. We see how he gave them an avenue of agency and individual creativity. He provided a way for individuals to play with their own religious literacy and cultural structural understandings, whether he is horrific or humorous. Perhaps this agency given to individual creators is the most important aspect of his life, as this is what has allowed his image to spread online like the haunted figure he is, lingering in the back of photographs as we may also sometimes feel his presence lingering behind us as we sit in front of our computer screens.

Like a true Tulpa, he has created a life of his own outside of the narratives he lives within, building from those who know about him and think about him. If we are to also incorporate the idea of myth proposed by Bruce Lincoln (1999) that academic work itself could be myth, than this study could be added to the larger corpus of narratives which help to build his mythos, and the large thought exercise which makes up this book has also contributed to the thoughts which build him as a true Tulpa.

# Bibliography

Aarseth, Espen. 2004. 'Genre Trouble: Narrativism and the Art of Simulation'. In *First Person: New Media as Story, Performance, and Game*, edited by Noah Wardrip-Fruin and Pat Harrington, 45–55. Cambridge: MIT Press.

Achievement Hunter. 2017. *Let's Watch Resident Evil 7 (Playlist)*. https://www.youtube.com/playlist?list=PLTur7oukosPFBaRT_4mXUMkqhbC7lAedd.

Achievement Hunter. n.d. 'Achievement Hunter Home Page'. YouTube. https://www.youtube.com/user/AchievementHunter.

Aiken, Michael. 2014. 'Anarchy vs. Democracy: The Politics of "Twitch Plays Pokémon"'. *Diplomatic Courier*, 4 March 2014. https://www.diplomaticourier.com/2014/03/04/anarchy-vs-democracy-the-politics-of-twitch-plays-pokemon/.

Aleph Null. 2009a. 'Create Paranormal Images'. Forum Reply. *Something Awful*. https://forums.somethingawful.com/showthread.php?threadid=3150591&userid=0&perpage=40&pagenumber=12.

Aleph Null. 2009b. 'Create Paranormal Images'. Forum Reply. *Something Awful*. https://forums.somethingawful.com/showthread.php?threadid=3150591&userid=0&perpage=40&pagenumber=21.

Alex Hall. 2010a. *Day Four.wmv*. YouTube Video.

Alex Hall. 2010b. *BEN.wmv*. YouTube Video.

Alex Hall. 2010c. *DROWNED.wmv*. YouTube Video.

Alex Hall. 2010d. *Jadusable.wmv*. YouTube Video.

Andreski, Stanislav. 1972. *Social Sciences as Sorcery*. London: Deutsch.

An observer. 2009. 'Create Paranormal Images'. *Something Awful Forums*. https://forums.somethingawful.com/showthread.php?threadid=3150591&userid=0&perpage=40&pagenumber=11.

Anonymous Official. 2014. *Anonymous Documentary – How Anonymous Hackers Changed the World Full Documentary*. YouTube Video. https://www.youtube.com/watch?v=FAECyLvSCHg&t=2147s&list=WL&index=7.

Apte, Mahadev L. 1985. *Humor and Laughter: An Anthropological Approach*. Ithaca, NY: Cornell University Press.

Aresta, Mónica, Luis Pedro, Carlos Santos, and António Moreira. 2015. 'Portraying the Self in Online Contexts: Context-Driven and User-Driven Online Identity Profiles'. *Contemporary Social Science* 10 (1): 70–85. https://doi.org/10.1080/21582041.2014.980840.

Asimos, Vivian. 2019. 'Video Games as Contemporary Mythology'. *Implicit Religion* 21 (1): 92–109.

Babcock, Barbara A. 1978. 'Introduction'. In *The Reversible World: Symbolic Inversion in Art and Society: [Papers]*, edited by Barbara A. Babcock and American Anthropological Association, 13–36. Symbol, Myth, and Ritual Series. Ithaca: Cornell University Press.

Bachelard, Gaston. 1964. *The Poetics of Space*. Translated by Maria Jolas. New York: Orion Press.

Backwardz Compatible. n.d. 'Backwardz Compatible Series Page'. Rooster Teeth. https://roosterteeth.com/series/backwardz-compatible.

Bailey, Edward. 1998. *Implicit Religion: An Introduction*. London: Middlesex University Press.

Bainbridge, William Sims. 2013. *eGods: Faith versus Fantasy in Computer Gaming*. Oxford: Oxford University Press.

Bargh, John A., A. McKenna, and Grainne M. Fitzsimons. 2002. 'Can You See the Real Me? Activation and Expression of the "True Self" on the Internet'. *Journal of Social Issues* 58 (1): 33–48.

Bartle, Richard A. 2004. *Designing Virtual Worlds*. Indianapolis, IN: New Riders Pub.

Bascom, William. 1984. 'The Forms of Folklore: Prose Narratives'. In *Sacred Narrative: Readings in the Theory of Myth*, edited by Alan Dundes, 5–29. Berkeley: University of California Press.

Ben-Amos, Dan. 1983. 'The Idea of Folklore: An Essay'. In *Fields of Offerings: Studies in Honor of Raphael Patai*, edited by Victor D. Sanua, 57–63. London: Herzl Press.

Berger, Peter L., and Thomas Luckmann. 1991. *The Social Construction of Reality: A Treatise in the Sociology of Knowledge*. Harmondsworth: Penguin.

Bertrand. 2015. '*Fifty Shades of Grey* Started Out as *Twilight* FanFiction'. *UK Business Insider*. http://uk.businessinsider.com/fifty-shades-of-grey-started-out-as-twilight-fan-fiction-2015-2.

Besant, Annie and C.W. Leadbetter. 1925. *Thought-Forms*. London: Theosophical Publishing House Ltd.

Bethel, Brian. 2013. 'Brian Bethel Recounts His Possible Paranormal Encounter with "BEKs"'. *Abilene Reporter-News*, 13 April 2013. https://web.archive.org/web/20151208221117/http://www.reporternews.com/news/columnists/brian-bethel/brian-bethel-recounts-his-possible-paranormal-encounter-with-beks-ep-384772497-348207271.html.

Blank, Trevor J. 2009. 'Introduction: Toward a Conceptual Framework for the Study of Folklore and the Internet'. In *Folklore and the Internet: Vernacular Expression in a Digital World*, 1–20. Logon, Utah: Utah University Press.

Blank, Trevor J., ed. 2012. *Folk Culture in the Digital Age: The Emergent Dynamics of Human Interaction*. Logan, Utah: Utah State University Press.

Bloch, Maurice. 1991. 'Language, Anthropology and Cognitive Science'. *Man* 26 (2): 183. https://doi.org/10.2307/2803828.

Blue Isle Studios, and Parsec Productions. 2015. *Slender: The Arrival*. Xbox One.

Bohn, Willard. 1991. *Apollinaire and the Faceless Man: The Creation and Evolution of a Modern Motif*. Rutherford, NJ; London ; Cranbury, NJ: Fairleigh Dickinson University Press ; Associated University Presses.

BooDoug187. 2009. 'Create Paranormal Images'. Forum Reply. *Something Awful*. https://forums.somethingawful.com/showthread.php?threadid=3150591&userid=0&perpage=40&pagenumber=9.

Bourdieu, Pierre. 1990. *The Logic of Practice*. Translated by Richard Nice. Reprinted. Cambridge: Polity Press.

brett824. 2009. *Marble Hornets Entry #6 Missing Audio Found!* YouTube Video. https://www.youtube.com/watch?v=acBnEHT-fBo.

Brownman. n.d. 'Brownman Twitch Page'. Twitch.tv. https://www.twitch.tv/brownman.

Brunvand, Jan Harold. 1981. *The Vanishing Hitchhiker: American Urban Legends and Their Meanings*, 1st edn. New York: Norton.

Burgess, Jean. 2008. 'All Your Chocolate Rain Are Belong to Us? Viral Video, YouTube and the Dynamics of Participatory Culture'. In *Video Vortex Reader: Responses to YouTube*, edited by Geert Lovink and Sabine Niederer, 2nd edn, 101–9. INC Reader 4. Amsterdam: Inst. of Network Cultures.

Butler, Judith. 1990. *Gender Trouble: Feminism and the Subversion of Identity*. Thinking Gender. New York: Routledge.

Caillois, Roger. 1962. *Man, Play, and Games*. Translated by Meyer Barash. Glencoe: Thames and Hudson.

Capcom. 2017. *Resident Evil 7*. PlayStation 4.

Carroll, Noël. 1990. *The Philosophy of Horror, Or, Paradoxes of the Heart*. New York: Routledge.

Castells, Manuel. 2000. 'Materials for an Exploratory Theory of the Network society1'. *The British Journal of Sociology* 51 (1): 5–24. https://doi.org/10.1111/j.1468-4446.2000.00005.x.

ce gars. 2009. 'Create Paranormal Images'. Forum Reply. *Something Awful*. https://forums.somethingawful.com/showthread.php?threadid=3150591&userid=0&perpage=40&pagenumber=14.

Certeau, Michel de. 2013. *The Practice of Everyday Life. 1: . . . 2*. print. Berkeley, CA: University of California Press.

Chance, Jane, ed. 2004. *Tolkien and the Invention of Myth: A Reader*. Lexington: University Press of Kentucky.

Chaos Hippy. 2009. 'Create Paranormal Images'. Forum Reply. *Something Awful*. https://forums.somethingawful.com/showthread.php?threadid=3150591&userid=0&perpage=40&pagenumber=11.

Chase. 2014. 'TPP Victory! The Thundershock Heard around the World'. Twitch.tv (blog). 1 March 2014. https://blog.twitch.tv/tpp-victory-the-thundershock-heard-around-the-world-3128a5b1cdf5.

Chess, Shira and Eric Newsom. 2015. *Folklore, Horror Stories, and the Slender Man: The Development of an Internet Mythology*. Palgrave Pivot. New York: Palgrave Pivot.

Chooboo. 2013. 'Be at Peace'. Fanfiction.net. https://www.fanfiction.net/s/9377319/1/Be-At-Peace.

Clockspider. 2009. 'Create Paranormal Images'. Forum Reply. *Something Awful Forums*. https://forums.somethingawful.com/showthread.php?threadid=3150591&userid=0&perpage=40&pagenumber=5.

cloudy. 2009. 'Create Paranormal Images'. Forum Reply. *Something Awful*. https://forums.somethingawful.com/showthread.php?threadid=3150591&userid=0&perpage=40&pagenumber=10.

Cohen, Jeffrey J. 1996. 'Monster Culture (Seven Theses)'. In *Monster Theory: Reading Culture*, edited by Jeffrey J. Cohen, 1–20. Minneapolis, MN: University of Minnesota Press.

Corneliussen, Hilde and Jill Walker Rettberg, eds. 2008. *Digital Culture, Play, and Identity: A World of Warcraft Reader*. Cambridge, MA: MIT Press.

Cover, R. 2006. 'Audience Inter/active: Interactive Media, Narrative Control and Reconceiving Audience History'. *New Media & Society* 8 (1): 139–58. https://doi.org/10.1177/1461444806059922.

Cox, Jesse. 2017. *Scary Game Squad – Resident Evil 7 (Playlist)*. https://www.youtube.com/playlist?list=PLFx-KViPXIkH45GiQNM_Nu8-Yphc-gP9c.

CreepsMcPasta. 2014. *'Penpal' Creepypasta*. YouTube Video. https://www.youtube.com/watch?v=DIhLDKrePPY.

CreepsMcPasta. 2018. *I'm Selling the Meaning of Life to the Highest Bidder" Creepypasta*. YouTube Video. https://www.youtube.com/watch?v=PcQqWx0_qrI.

Creepypasta Indexer. 2013a. 'The Curious Case of Smile.jpg'. Creepypasta.org. 10 April 2013. http://www.creepypasta.org/creepypasta/the-curious-case-of-smile-jpg.

Creepypasta Indexer. 2013b. 'The Rake'. Creepypasta.org. 11 April 2013. http://www.creepypasta.org/creepypasta/the-rake.

Creepypasta Wiki. n.d. 'The Rake'. Creepypasta Wiki. http://creepypasta.wikia.com/wiki/The_Rake.

Crome, Andrew. 2015. 'Religion and the Pathologization of Fandom: Religion, Reason, and Controversy in My Little Pony Fandom'. *Journal of Religion and Popular Culture* 27 (2): 130–47.

Cusack, Carole. 2013. 'Play, Narrative, and the Creation of Religion: Extending the Theoretical Base of invented Religions'. *Culture and Religion: An Interdisciplinary Journal* 14 (4): 364–77.

Cusack, Carole M. and Pavol Kosnác, eds. 2017. *Fiction, Invention, and Hyper-Reality: From Popular Culture to Religion*. Inform Series on Minority Religions and Spiritual Movements. New York: Routledge.

Dark_Spectre2013. 2012. 'Cutie Mark Crusaders Slender Man Hunters!' FanFiction Story. https://www.fimfiction.net/story/42733/cutie-mark-crusaders-slender-man-hunters.

David-Néel, Alexandra. 1936. *With Mystics and Magicians in Tibet*. London: Penguin.

Davidsen, Markus Altena. 2012. 'The Spiritual Milieu Based on J.R.R Tolkien's Literary Mythology'. In *Handbook of Hyper-Real Religions*, edited by Adam Possamai, 185–204. Leiden: Brill.

Davies, Christie. 1999. 'Jokes about the Death of Diana, Princess of Wales'. In *The Mourning for Diana*, edited by Tony Walter, 253–68. Oxford: Berg.

Dawkins, Richard. 2006. *The Selfish Gene*. 30th anniversary edn. Oxford; New York: Oxford University Press.

Dégh, Linda. 2001. *Legend and Belief: Dialectics of a Folklore Genre*. Bloomington: Indiana University Press.

Dorson, Richard M. 1976. *Folklore and Fakelore: Essays toward a Discipline of Folk Studies*. Cambridge, MA: Harvard University Press.

Doueihi, Milad. 2011. *Digital Cultures*. American edn. Cambridge, Mass: Harvard University Press.

Douglas, Mary. 1968. 'The Social Control of Cognition: Some Factors in Joke Perception'. *Man, New Series* 3 (3): 361–76.

Douglas, Mary. 1999. 'The Meaning of Myth'. In *Implicit Meanings: Selected Essays in Anthropology*, 2nd edn, 131–45. London; New York: Routledge.

Douglas, Mary. 2001. *Purity and Danger: An Analysis of the Concepts of Pollution and Taboo*. London: Routledge.

Dredge, Stuart. 2015. 'Google Launches YouTube Gaming to Challenge Amazon-Owned Twitch'. *The Guardian*, 26 August 2015. https://www.theguardian.com/technology/2015/aug/26/youtube-gaming-live-website-apps.

Drucker, Peter F. 1994. 'The Age of Social Transformation'. *The Atlantic Monthly*, 1994.

Duffett, Mark. 2003. 'False Faith or False Comparisons? A Critique of the Religious Interpretation of Elvis Fan Culture'. *Popular Music and Society* 26 (4): 513–22.

Duffett, Mark. 2013. *Understanding Fandom: An Introduction to the Study of Media Fan Culture*. New York: Routledge.

Dumézil, Georges. 1977. *Gods of the Ancient Northmen*. Berkeley: University of California Press.

Dundes, Alan. 1966. 'Metafolklore and Oral Literary Criticism'. *The Monist* 50 (4): 505–16.

Dundes, Alan. 1980. *Interpreting Folklore*. Bloomington: Indiana University Press.

Dundes, Alan. 1985. 'Nationalistic Inferiority Complexes and the Fabrication of Fakelore: A Reconsideration of Ossian, the Kinder- Und Hausmärchen, the Kalevala, and Paul Bunyan'. *Journal of Folklore Research* 22 (1): 5–18.

Dundes, Alan. 1987. 'At Ease, Disease—AIDS Jokes as Sick Humor'. *American Behavioural Scientist* 30 (3): 72–81. https://doi.org/10.1177/000276487030003006.

Ellis, Bill. 2001. 'A Model for Collecting and Interpreting World Trade Centre Disaster Jokes'. *New Directions in Folklore* 5.

Emigh, John. 1996. *Masked Performance: The Play of Self and Other in Ritual and Theatre*. Philadelphia: University of Pennsylvania Press.

Erikson, Erik. 1972. 'Play and Actuality'. In *Play and Development: A Symposium*, edited by Maria W. Piers, Jean Piaget, Erikson Institute, and Loyola University, Chicago, 1st edn. New York: Norton.

Eskelinen, Markku. 2001. 'The Gaming Situation'. *Game Studies* 1 (1).

Evans-Wentz, Walter Y., ed. 1960. *The Tibetan Book of the Dead or: The after-Death Experiences on the Bardo Plane, according to Lama Kazi Dawa-Samdups English Rendering*. 2. publ. Delhi: Oxford University Press.

EverymanHYBRID. n.d. 'EverymanHYBRID [all Videos]'. YouTube. https://www.youtube.com/user/EverymanHYBRID/videos.

FalcoFanBoy. 2013. 'Plot Analysis (spoilers Thread)'. *Gamefaqs*. https://gamefaqs.gamespot.com/boards/705665-slender-the-arrival/65827244.

Fedorak, Shirley. 2009. *Pop Culture: The Culture of Everyday Life*. Toronto; Buffalo: University of Toronto Press.

Fernback, Jan. 2003. 'Legends on the Net: An Examination of Computer-Mediated Communication as a Locus of Oral Culture'. *New Media & Society* 5 (1): 29–44.

Fialkova, Larisa and Maria Yelenevskaya. 2001. 'Ghosts in the Cyber World: An Analysis of Folklore Sites on the Internet'. *Fabula* 42: 64–89.

Fineman, Mia. 2003. 'Photography, Vernacular'. In *The Encyclopaedia of American Folk Art*, edited by Gerard C. Wertkin and Lee Kogan. New York: Routledge.

Foley, John Miles. 2012. *Oral Tradition and the Internet: Pathways of the Mind*. Urbana: University of Illinois Press.

Fox, William S. 1980. 'Folklore and Fakelore: Some Sociological Considerations'. *Journal of the Folklore Institute* 17 (2/3): 244–61.

Frank, Russell. 2009. 'The Forward as Folklore: Studying E-Mailed Humor'. In *Folklore and the Internet: Vernacular Expression in a Digital World*, 98–122. Logon, Utah: Utah University Press.

Frasca, Gonzalo. 2003. 'Ludologists Love Stories, Too: Notes from a Debate That Never Took Place'. http://www.ludology.org/articles/Frasca_LevelUp2003.pdf.

Frazer, James George. 1994. *The Golden Bough: A Study in Magic and Religion*. World's Classics. Oxford; New York: Oxford University Press.

Friedman, Ted. 1999. 'Civilization and Its Discontents: Simulation, Subjectivity, and Space'. In *On a Silver Platter: CD-ROMs and the Promises of a New Technology*, edited by Greg Smith, 132–50. New York: New York University Press.

FromSoftware. 2016. *Dark Souls 3*. Xbox One.

Galinier, Jacques. 2004. 'A Levi-Straussian Controversy Revisited: The Implicit Mythology of Rituals in a Mesoamerican Context'. *Journal of the Southwest* 46 (4): 661–77.

Game Freak. 1996. *Pokémon Red*. GameBoy.

Geertz, Clifford. 1973. *The Interpretation of Cultures: Selected Essays*. New York: Basic Books.

genesplicer. 2009. 'Create Paranormal Images'. Forum Reply. *Something Awful*. https://forums.somethingawful.com/showthread.php?threadid=3150591&userid=0&perpage=40&pagenumber=39.

Genette, Gérard. 1982. *Figures of Literary Discourse*. Translated by Alan Sheridan. Oxford: Blackwell.

Geraci, Robert M. 2014. *Virtually Sacred: Myth and Meaning in World of Warcraft and Second Life*. Oxford: Oxford University Press.

Gere, Charlie. 2002. *Digital Culture*. London: Reaktion Books.
Gerogerigege. 2009. 'Create Paranormal Images'. Forum Post. *Something Awful*. https://forums.somethingawful.com/showthread.php?threadid=3150591&userid=0&perpage=40&pagenumber=1.
Gray, Jonathan, Cornel Sandvoss, and C. Lee Harrington. 2007. 'Introduction: Why Study Fans?' In *Fandom: Identities and Communities in a Mediated World*, edited by Jonathan Gray, Cornel Sandvoss, and Harrington, 1–16. New York: New York University Press.
Green, Ryan. 2016. 'On Let's Plays'. *That Dragon, Cancer* (blog). 24 March 2016. http://www.thatdragoncancer.com/thatdragoncancer/2016/3/24/on-lets-plays.
GunRecon. 2012. 'The Rake Is Where It's At'. Thread. *Slender Nation Forum*. http://slendernation.forumotion.com/t2928-the-rake-is-where-it-s-at?highlight=the+rake.
GyverMac. 2009a. 'Create Paranormal Images'. Forum Reply. *Something Awful*. https://forums.somethingawful.com/showthread.php?threadid=3150591&userid=0&perpage=40&pagenumber=8.
GyverMac. 2009b. 'Create Paranormal Images'. Forum Reply. *Something Awful Forums*. https://forums.somethingawful.com/showthread.php?threadid=3150591&userid=0&perpage=40&pagenumber=10.
Halena, Megan. 2011. 'Identity, Power, and Ritual "Rape Play" in the S/M Community'. MA Thesis, Boca Raton, FL: Florida Atlantic University.
Hamayon, Roberte. 2016. *Why We Play: An Anthropological Study*. Translated by Damien Simon. Chicago: Hau Books.
Hammers, Corie. 2012. 'A Radical Opening: An Exploration of Lesbian / Queer BDSM Public Sexual Cultures'. In *Sexualities, Past Reflections, Future Directions*, edited by Sally Hines and Yvette Taylor, 246–65. Genders and Sexualities in the Social Sciences. Houndmills, Basingstoke, Hampshire; New York: Palgrave Macmillan.
Hansen, Gregory. 2009. 'Public Folklore in Cyberspace'. In *Folklore and the Internet: Vernacular Expression in a Digital World*, edited by Trevor J. Blank, 194–212. Logon, Utah: Utah State University Press.
Happy Pasta Wikia. n.d. 'Jeff the Hugger'. http://happypasta.wikia.com/wiki/Jeff_the_Hugger.
Harpham, Geoffrey Galt. 1982. *On the Grotesque*. Princeton, NJ: Princeton University Press.
Harvestwind. 2001. 'The Black Eyed Kids of Portland, Oregon'. Listserve reply. *Alt.folklore.ghost-Stories*. https://groups.google.com/forum/#!msg/alt.folklore.ghost-stories/sYKKEkeUrGs/ZkBPCbHgh-cJ.
hauntings. 2008. 'The Rake'. *Live Journal*. http://hauntings.livejournal.com/613232.html.
Healy, Dave. 1997. 'Cyberspace and Place: The Internet as Middle Landscape on the Electronic Frontier'. In *Internet Culture*, edited by David Porter, 55–68. New York: Routledge.
Hernandez, Patricia. 2013. 'Some Don't Like BioShock's Forced Baptism. Enough to Ask for a Refund'. *Kotaku*, 16 April 2013. https://kotaku.com/some-dont-like-bioshocks-forced-baptism-enough-to-as-473178476.

Hernandez, Patricia. 2014. 'Rejoice, for "Twitch Plays Pokémon" Has Revived the Helix Fossil'. Kotaku (blog). 24 February 2014. https://kotaku.com/rejoice-for-twitch-plays-pokemon-has-revived-the-hel-1529832673.

Hiley, Margaret. 2004. 'Stolen Language, Cosmic Models: Myth and Mythology in Tolkien'. *MFS Modern Fiction Studies* 50 (4): 838–60. https://doi.org/10.1353/mfs.2005.0003.

Hog Inspector. 2009. 'Create Paranormal Images'. Forum Reply. *Something Awful Forums*. https://forums.somethingawful.com/showthread.php?threadid=3150591&userid=0&perpage=40&pagenumber=8.

Houseman, Michael. 1998. *Naven or the Other Self: A Relational Approach to Ritual Action*. Leiden: Brill.

Howard, Robert Glenn. 2008. 'Electronic Hybridity: The Persistent Processes of the Vernacular Web'. *Journal of American Folklore* 121 (480): 192–218. https://doi.org/10.1353/jaf.0.0012.

Howard, Robert Glenn. 2015. 'Introduction: Why Digital Hybridity Is the New Normal (Hey! Check This Stuff Out)'. *Journal of American Folklore* 128 (509): 247–59.

Hugh-Jones, Stephen. 1979. *The Palm and the Pleiades: Initiation and Cosmology in Northwest Amazonia*. Cambridge: Cambridge University Press.

Huizinga, J. 1980. *Homo Ludens: A Study of the Play-Element in Culture*. London: Routledge.

Hutcheon, Linda. 1985. *A Theory of Parody: The Teachings of Twentieth-Century Art Forms*. New York: Methuen.

Hymes, Dell. 1985. 'Language, Memory, and Selective Performance: Cultee's "Salmon's Myth" as Twice Told to Boas'. *The Journal of American Folklore* 98 (390): 391. https://doi.org/10.2307/540365.

Ingold, Tim. 2000. *The Perception of the Environment: Essays on Livelihood, Dwelling & Skill*. London; New York: Routledge.

Irisi. 2009. 'Creating Paranormal Images'. Forum Reply. *Something Awful Forums*. https://forums.somethingawful.com/showthread.php?threadid=3150591&userid=0&perpage=40&pagenumber=8.

Jacobs, Joseph. 1893. 'The Folk'. *Folklore* 4 (2): 233–38. https://doi.org/10.1080/0015587X.1893.9720155.

Jadusable. 2010. 'The Truth.txt'. http://jadusable.wikia.com/wiki/TheTruth.rtf.

James, Jonathan. 2018. 'Exclusive First Look at New Slender Man Photographs from Original Creator Eric "Victor Surge" Knudsen'. *Daily Dead*. 8 September 2018. https://dailydead.com/exclusive-first-look-at-new-slender-man-photographs-from-original-creator-eric-victor-surge-knudsen/.

Jenkins, Henry. 1992. *Textual Poachers: Television Fans & Participatory Culture*. Studies in Culture and Communication. New York: Routledge.

Jenkins, Henry. 2004. 'Game Design as Narrative Architecture'. In *First Person: New Media as Story, Performance, and Game*, edited by Noah Wardrip-Fruin and Pat Harrington, 118–30. Cambridge, MA: MIT Press.

Jenkins, Henry. 2006. *Convergence Culture: Where Old and New Media Collide*. New York: New York University Press.

Jenkins, Henry. 2009. *Confronting the Challenges of Participatory Culture: Media Education for the 21st Century*. The John D. and Catherine T. MacArthur Foundation Reports on Digital Media and Learning. Cambridge, MA: The MIT Press.

Jesse Cox. n.d. 'Jesse Cox Home Page'. YouTube. https://www.youtube.com/user/OMFGcata.

Jesse Cox. 2012. *Terraria – The Next World Generation – Part 10 – Jesse Is Bad at Expressing His Feelings*. YouTube Video. https://www.youtube.com/watch?v=h3RlF_vUTkg&t=2s.

Jesse Cox. 2015a. *THAT'S WASTED CHILI // Scary Game Squad – Slender: The Arrival*. YouTube Video. https://www.youtube.com/watch?v=mGRpobfnQ8k&t.

Jesse Cox. 2015b. *IMMA SHANK YOU SLENDERMAN!!! // Scary Game Squad – Slender: The Arrival*. YouTube Video. https://www.youtube.com/watch?v=RO8bmwwKiuU&t.

Jesse Cox. 2015c. *The Idiot Train \\ Scary Game Squad – Slender: The Arrival*. YouTube Video. https://www.youtube.com/watch?v=Y1aAZkUpzYk&t.

Jesse Cox. 2015d. *NOT THIS WAY!!!! \\ Scary Game Squad – Slender: The Arrival*. YouTube Video. https://www.youtube.com/watch?v=TI3Zb6ztaow&t.

Jesse Cox. 2015e. *YOU WERE OUR LEADER!!!! \\ Scary Game Squad – Slender: The Arrival*. YouTube Video. https://www.youtube.com/watch?v=-C4Bhz6JL88&t.

Jesse Cox. 2015f. *RUN RUN RUN!!!! \\ Scary Game Squad – Slender: The Arrival*. YouTube Video. https://www.youtube.com/watch?v=hklm94kT1tU&t.

Jesse Cox. 2015g. *THE END \\ Scary Game Squad – Slender: The Arrival*. YouTube Video. https://www.youtube.com/watch?v=sE59G9Yhf8w&t.

Jesse Cox. 2015h. 'The Scary Game Squad – Slender: The Arrival (Playlist)'. YouTube. 26 January 2015. https://www.youtube.com/playlist?list=PLFx-KViPXIkGCKlEIiynvzuQPX-Z87EDR.

'Just Another Fool'. 2009. Blog. Just Another Fool. 2009–2010. https://jafool.wordpress.com/.

KatWithHands. 2009. 'Create Paranormal Images'. *Something Awful Forums*. https://forums.somethingawful.com/showthread.php?threadid=3150591&userid=0&perpage=40&pagenumber=8.

Kibby, Marjorie D. 2005. 'Email Forwardables: Folklore in the Age of the Internet'. *New Media & Society* 7 (6): 770–90. https://doi.org/10.1177/1461444805058161.

Kidd, Dustin. 2007. 'Harry Potter and the Functions of Popular Culture'. *The Journal of Popular Culture* 40 (1): 69–89. https://doi.org/10.1111/j.1540-5931.2007.00354.x.

Kimori94. 2016. 'The Bride of Slender Man'. Fanfiction.net. 2012–2016. https://www.fanfiction.net/s/8795772/1/The-Bride-of-Slender-Man.

Kingdomheartslover123. 2015. '50 Shades of Slender'. Fanfiction.net. 2012–2015. https://www.fanfiction.net/s/8548249/1/50-Shades-of-Slender.

King, Stephen. 1987. *Danse Macabre*. New York: Berkley Books.

Kinsella, Michael. 2011. *Legend-Tripping Online: Supernatural Folklore and the Search for Ong's Hat*. Jackson, MS: University Press of Mississippi.

Kirkland, Ewan. 2005. 'Restless Dreams in Silent Hill: Approaches to Video Game Analysis'. *Journal of Media Practice* 6 (3): 167–78. https://doi.org/10.1386/jmpr.6.3.167/1.

Kissel, Ben, Marcus Parks and Henry Zebrowski. n.d. *Ep. 323: Men in Black Part I: You Fed the Tulpa*. Last Podcast on the Left. Accessed 30 June 2018. https://soundcloud.com/lastpodcastontheleft/episode-323-the-men-in-black.

Knobel, Michele and Colin Lankshear. 2007. 'Online Memes, Affinities, and Cultural Production'. In *A New Literacies Sampler*, edited by Michele Knobel and Colin Lankshear. New Literacies and Digital Epistemologies, vol. 29. New York: P. Lang.

Know Your Meme. 2009. 'All Your Base Are Belong to Us'. Know Your Meme. 2009–2018. http://knowyourmeme.com/memes/all-your-base-are-belong-to-us.

Know Your Meme. 2012. 'The Rake'. Know Your Meme. 2012–2017. http://knowyourmeme.com/memes/the-rake.

Know Your Meme. 2018. 'Slender Man'. Know Your Meme. 2010–2018. http://knowyourmeme.com/memes/slender-man.

Kuipers, Giselinde. 2002. 'Media Culture and Internet Disaster Jokes: Bin Laden and the Attack on the World Trade Centre'. *European Journal of Cultural Studies* 5 (6): 450–70.

Kuipers, Giselinde. 2005. '"Where Was King Kong When We Needed Him?" Public Discourse, Digital Disaster Jokes, and the Functions of Laughter after 9/11'. *The Journal of American Culture* 28 (1): 70–84.

Kunin, Seth. 1996. 'Death/Rebirth Mytheme in the Book of Mormon'. In *Mormon Identities in Transition*, edited by Douglas Davies, 192–203. London: Cassell.

Kunin, Seth. 2003. 'The Allegory of the Olive Tree: A Case Study for (neo) Structuralist Analysis'. *Religion* 33 (2): 105–25.

Kunin, Seth. 2004. *We Think What We Eat: Neo-Structuralist Analysis of Israelite Food Rules and Other Cultural and Textual Practices*. London: T&T Clark International.

Kunin, Seth. 2012. 'Structuralism and Implicit Myth'. *Suomen Anthropologi: Journal of the Finnish Anthropological Society* 37 (4): 11–29.

Kunin, Seth D. 2001. 'Juggling Identities among the Crypto-Jews of the American Southwest'. *Religion* 31 (1): 41–61. https://doi.org/10.1006/reli.2000.0313.

Kunin, Seth Daniel. 1998. *God's Place in the World: Sacred Space and Sacred Place in Judaism*. Cassell Religious Studies. London; New York: Cassell.

Kunin, Seth Daniel. 2003. *Religion: The Modern Theories*. Edinburgh: Edinburgh University Press.

Kunin, Seth Daniel. 2009. *Juggling Identities: Identity and Authenticity among the Crypto-Jews*. New York: Columbia University Press.

laglycerine. 2013. 'It's Not Real'. Fanfiction.net. https://www.fanfiction.net/s/9946917/1/It-s-Not-Real.

Lang, Andrew. 1893. 'The Method of Folklore'. In *Custom and Myth*, 10–28. Longmans, Green and Company.

Latour, Bruno. 2005. *Reassembling the Social: An Introduction to Actor-Network-Theory*. Clarendon Lectures in Management Studies. Oxford; New York: Oxford University Press.

Laycock, Joseph. 2010. 'Myth Sells: Mattel's Commission of The Masters of the Universe Bible'. *The Journal of Religion and Popular Culture* 22 (2): 4–4. https://doi.org/10.3138/jrpc.22.2.004.

Leach, Edmund. 1969. *Genesis as Myth: And Other Essays*. London: Jonathan Cape.

Leach, Edmund. 1972. 'Anthropological Aspects of Language: Animal Categories and Verbal Abuse'. In *Mythology; Selected Readings*, edited by Pierre Maranda, 39–67. Penguin Modern Sociology Readings. Harmondsworth, Eng., Baltimore: Penguin Books.

Leach, Edmund, and Alan D. Aycock. 1983. *Structuralist Interpretations of Biblical Myth*. Cambridge: Royal Anthropological Institute of Great Britain and Ireland.

LeechCode5. 2009. 'Create Paranormal Images'. Forum Reply. *Something Awful*. https://forums.somethingawful.com/showthread.php?threadid=3150591&userid=0&perpage=40&pagenumber=4.

Leenhardt, Maurice. 1979. *Do Kamo: Person and Myth in the Melanesian World*. Translated by Basia Miller Gulati. Chicago: University of Chicago Press.

Let's Play. 2014. *Let's Watch – Slender: The Arrival*. YouTube Video. https://www.youtube.com/watch?v=iwFW3gKzeBc&t.

Let's Play. n.d. 'Let's Play Home Page'. YouTube. https://www.youtube.com/user/LetsPlay.

Lévi-Strauss, Claude. 1963a. 'The Effectiveness of Symbols'. In *Structural Anthropology*. Translated by C. Jacobson and B.G. Schoepf, 232. New York: Basic Books.

Lévi-Strauss, Claude. 1963b. 'The Structural Study of Myth'. In *Structural Anthropology*. Translated by C. Jacobson and B.G. Schoepf, 206–31. New York: Basic Books.

Lévi-Strauss, Claude. 1966. *The Savage Mind: (La Pensée Sauvage)*. London: Weidenfeld & Nicolson.

Lévi-Strauss, Claude. 1969. *The Raw and the Cooked*. Translated by John Weightman and Doreen Weightman. Introduction to a Science of Mythology, vol. 1. Chicago: University of Chicago Press.

Lévi-Strauss, Claude. 1973a. *From Honey to Ashes*. Introduction to a Science of Mythology, vol. 2. London: Cape.

Lévi-Strauss, Claude. 1973b. 'The Story of Asdiwal'. In *Structural Anthropology Vol. 2*. Translated by Monique Layton, 146–97. New York: Penguin Books.

Lévi-Strauss, Claude. 1978. *The Origin of Table Manners*. Introduction to a Science of Mythology, vol. 3. London: J. Cape.

Lévi-Strauss, Claude. 1981. *The Naked Man*. Translated by John Weightman and Doreen Weightman, vol. 4. Introduction to a Science of Mythology. London: Jonathan Cape Limited.

Lévi-Strauss, Claude. 1982. *The Way of the Masks*. Translated by Sylvia Modelski. Seattle: University of Washington Press.

Lévi-Strauss, Claude. 1983. 'How Myths Die'. In *Structural Anthropology*, edited by University of Chicago Press, vol. 2, 256–68. Chicago, IL: University of Chicago Press.

Lévi-Strauss, Claude. 1997. *Look, Listen, Read.* 1st American edn. New York: BasicBooks.
Lincoln, Bruce. 1999. *Theorizing Myth: Narrative, Ideology, and Scholarship.* Chicago: Chicago University Press.
Lincoln, Kenneth. 1993. *Indi'n Humor: Bicultural Play in Native America.* New York: Oxford University Press.
Louth, Andrew. 2012. 'Apophatic Theology and Cataphatic Theology'. In *The Cambridge Companion to Christian Mysticism*, edited by Amy Hollywood and Patricia Beckman, 137–46. New York: Cambridge University Press.
Lovecraft, H.P. 1973. *Supernatural Horror in Literature.* New York: Dover Publications.
Luhrmann, T.M. 1989. *Persuasions of the Witch's Craft: Ritual Magic and Witchcraft in Present-Day England.* Oxford, UK: B. Blackwell.
Lynch, John. 2017. 'Meet the YouTube Millionaires: These Are the 10 Highest-Paid YouTube Stars of 2017', *Business Insider* 8 December 2017. http://uk.businessinsider.com/highest-paid-youtube-stars-2017-12/#no-3-dude-perfect-14-million-8.
Madar, Heather. 2015. 'Dracula, The Turks, and the Rhetoric of Impaling in Fifteenth- and Sixteenth-Century Germany'. In *Death, Torture and the Broken Body in European Art, 1300–1650*, edited by John R. Decker and Mitzi Kirkland-Ives, 165–90. Visual Culture in Early Modernity. Farnham, Surrey, England ; Burlington, VT: Ashgate.
Malinowski, Bronislaw. 1948. 'Myth in Primitive Psychology'. In *Magic, Science and Religion and Other Essays*, 72–124. Glencoe, IL: The Free Press.
Marble Hornets. 2009. 'Marble Hornets [videos]'. 2009–2014. https://www.youtube.com/user/MarbleHornets/videos.
Markiplier. 2013a. *Slender: The Arrival | Part 1 | SLENDER HAS ARRIVED.* YouTube Video. https://www.youtube.com/watch?v=RsIcF3-MTsk&t=16s.
Markiplier. 2013b. *Slender: The Arrival | Part 2 | BIGGEST SCREAMS EVER.* YouTube Video. https://www.youtube.com/watch?v=nlEm09J6t1Y.
Markiplier. 2013c. *Slender: The Arrival | Part 3 | TERRIFYING SUCCESS.* YouTube Video. https://www.youtube.com/watch?v=HhHmMUKUIcs&t.
Markiplier. 2013d. *Slender: The Arrival | Part 4 | THE FLASHBACK.* YouTube Video. https://www.youtube.com/watch?v=_q5nw5dgLEE&t.
Markiplier. 2013e. *Slender: The Arrival | Part 5 | THE BITTER END.* YouTube Video. https://www.youtube.com/watch?v=7pNLQApDoYc&t.
Markiplier. 2014. *ALL BY MYSELF | Alien Isolation – Part 1.* YouTube Video. https://www.youtube.com/watch?v=AGR764RSZG8&t.
Markiplier. n.d. 'Markiplier Home Page'. YouTube. https://www.youtube.com/user/markiplierGAME.
McNeill, Lynne S. 2009. 'The End of the Internet: A Folk Response to the Provision of Infinite Choice'. In *Folklore and the Internet: Vernacular Expression in a Digital World*, 80–97. Logon, Utah: Utah University Press.

Mead, George Herbert. 2000. *Mind, Self, and Society: From the Standpoint of a Social Behaviourist*. Edited by Charles W. Morris. Works of George Herbert Mead, George Herbert Mead, vol. 1. Chicago: University of Chicago Press.

Mechling, Jay. 2004. 'Picturing Hunting'. *Western Folklore* 63 (1/2): 51–78.

Merleau-Ponty, Maurice. 1974. *Phenomenology, Language and Sociology: Selected Essays of Maurice Merleau-Ponty*. Edited by John O'Neill. London: Heinemann Educational.

Mikey Knutson. 2017. 'Story Stealing Question'. Reply. *r/nosleepOOC*. https://www.reddit.com/r/NoSleepOOC/comments/7bp5t4/story_stealing_question/.

Mikles, N.L. and J.P. Laycock. 2015. 'Tracking the Tulpa: Exploring the "Tibetan" Origins of a Contemporary Paranormal Idea'. *Nova Religio: The Journal of Alternative and Emergent Religions* 19 (1): 87–97. https://doi.org/10.1525/nr.2015.19.1.87.

Miles-Watson, Jonathan. 2009a. 'Structuralism: A Key Methodology for the New Millennium?' *Man in India* 89 (1–2): 67–80.

Miles-Watson, Jonathan. 2009b. *Welsh Mythology: A Neo-Structuralist Analysis*. Amherst: Cambria Press.

Miles-Watson, Jonathan. 2015. 'The Cathedral on the Ridge and the Implicit Mythology of the Shimla Hills'. *Suomen Antropologi: Journal of the Finnish Anthropological Society* 37 (4): 30–46.

Milner, Ryan M. 2016. *The World Made Meme: Public Conversations and Participatory Media*. The Information Society Series. Cambridge, MA: The MIT Press.

Milspaw, Yvonne J. and Wesley K. Evans. 2010. 'Variations on Vampires: Live Action Role Playing, Fantasy and the Revival of Traditional Beliefs'. *Western Folklore* 69 (2): 211–50.

Mosko, Mark. 1991. 'The Canonic Formula of Myth and Nonmyth'. *American Ethnologist* 18 (1): 126–51.

Mosko, Mark S. 1985. *Quadripartite Structures: Categories, Relations, and Homologies in Bush Mekeo Culture*. Cambridge [Cambridgeshire]; New York: Cambridge University Press.

Moto42. 2009. 'Create Paranormal Images'. *Something Awful*. https://forums.somethingawful.com/showthread.php?threadid=3150591&userid=0&perpage=40&pagenumber=23.

Mr. 47. 2009. 'Create Paranormal Images'. Forum Reply. *Something Awful*. https://forums.somethingawful.com/showthread.php?threadid=3150591&userid=0&perpage=40&pagenumber=7.

Munz, Peter. 1973. *When the Golden Bough Breaks: Structuralism or Typology?* London, Boston: Routledge & K. Paul.

Murray, Janet. 2005. *The Last Word on Ludology v Narratology in Game Studies*' Talk delivered at DiGRA: Vancouver, Canada.

Musharbash, Yasmine and Geir Henning Presterudstuen, eds. 2014. *Monster Anthropology in Australasia and Beyond*, 1st edn. New York, NY: Palgrave Macmillan.

Napier, A. David. 1986. *Masks, Transformation, and Paradox*. Berkeley: University of California Press.

Nardi, Bonnie. 2010. *My Life as a Night Elf Priest: An Anthropological Account of World of Warcraft*. Ann Arbor: University of Michigan Press.

Nashie 0. 2009. 'Create Paranormal Images'. *Something Awful*. https://forums.somethingawful.com/showthread.php?threadid=3150591&userid=0&perpage=40&pagenumber=14.

Needham, Rodney. 1979. *Symbolic Classification*. The Goodyear Perspectives in Anthropology Series. Santa Monica, CA: Goodyear Pub. Co.

Neil Cicierega. 2010. *Splendorman*. YouTube Video. https://www.youtube.com/watch?v=4MXYC_jX2Wc.

Nicol Bolas. 2009. 'Create Paranormal Images'. Forum Reply. *Something Awful*. https://forums.somethingawful.com/showthread.php?threadid=3150591&userid=0&perpage=40&pagenumber=21.

Nintendo. 1991. *The Legend of Zelda: A Link to the Past*. Super Nintendo Entertainment System.

Nintendo. 1998. *The Legend of Zelda: Ocarina of Time*. Nintendo 64.

Nintendo. 2000. *The Legend of Zelda: Majora's Mask*. Nintendo 64.

Nintendo. 2017. *Legend of Zelda: Breath of the Wild*. Wii U.

Nissenbaum, Asaf and Limor Shifman. 2017. 'Internet Memes as Contested Cultural Capital: The Case of 4chan's /b/ Board'. *New Media & Society* 19 (4): 483–501. https://doi.org/10.1177/1461444815609313.

Ohanesian, Liz. 2012. 'Lauren Faust on Her Favorite Childhood Toy and Pitching Animated Shows for Girls'. *LA Weekly*, 21 May 2012. http://www.laweekly.com/content/printView/2373537.

OpaliteMoon. 2012. 'The Slender Man Who Tied Me to a Tree'. Fanfiction.net. https://www.fanfiction.net/s/8483514/1/The-Slender-Man-who-tied-me-to-a-tree-slenderman.

Oring, Elliot. 1987. 'Jokes and the Discourse on Disaster: The Challenger Shuttle Explosion and Its Joke Cycle'. *Journal of American Folklore* 100 (397): 276–86.

Ortner, Sherry B. 1999. *Life and Death on Mt. Everest: Sherpas and Himalayan Mountaineering*. Princeton, NJ: Princeton University Press.

Otto, Rudolf. 1923. *The Idea of the Holy : An Inquiry into the Non-Rational Factor in the Idea of the Divine and Its Relation to the Rational*. London: Oxford University Press.

Pálsson, Gísli. 1994. 'Enskilment at Sea'. *Man, New Series* 29 (4): 901–27.

Parsec Productions. 2012. *Slender: The Eight Pages*. PC.

Pearce, Celia. 2011. *Communities of Play: Emergent Cultures in Multiplayer Games and Virtual Worlds*. Cambridge, MA; London: MIT Press.

Peck, Andrew. 2015. 'Tall, Dark, and Loathsome: The Emergence of a Legend Cycle in the Digital Age'. *Journal of American Folklore* 128 (509): 333–48.

PewDiePie. n.d. 'PewDiePie Home Page'. YouTube. https://www.youtube.com/user/PewDiePie.

Plattor, Candace. 2014. '12-Year-Olds Stabbing 12-Year-Olds: Are We Paying Attention Yet?' Candace Plattor. 4 June 2014. http://candaceplattor.com/blog/12-year-olds-stabbing-12-year-olds-are-we-paying-attention-yet/.

Possamai, Adam, ed. 2012. *Handbook of Hyper-Real Religions*. Brill Handbooks on Contemporary Religion, vol. 5. Leiden; Boston: Brill.

PriorMarcus. 2009. 'Creating Paranormal Images'. Forum Reply. *Something Awful*. https://forums.somethingawful.com/showthread.php?threadid=3150591&userid=0&perpage=40&pagenumber=15.

Porteous, Alexander. 2002. *The Forest in Folklore and Mythology*. Mineola, NY: Dover Publications.

Raj, Selva J. and Corinne Dempsey. 2010. 'Introduction: Ritual Levity in South Asian Traditions'. In *Sacred Play: Ritual Levity and Humor in South Asian Religions*, edited by Selva J. Raj and Corinne Dempsey, 1–20. Albany: State University of New York.

reddit. n.d. 'You Will Hear The Rake'. https://www.reddit.com/r/the_rake/.

Redfern, Nicholas. 2011. *The Real Men in Black: Evidence, Famous Cases, and True Stories of These Mysterious Men and Their Connection to UFO Phenomena*. Pompton Plains, NJ: New Page Books.

Redfield, Robert. 1960. *The Little Community: Peasant Society and Culture*. Chicago: University of Chicago Press.

Re-Logic. 2011. *Terraria*. Video Game.

Reyson, Stephen. 2006. 'Secular versus Religious Fans: Are They Different? An Empirical Examination'. *Journal of Religion and Popular Culture* 12: 1–17.

rinski. 2009. 'Create Paranormal Images'. Forum Reply. *Something Awful*. https://forums.somethingawful.com/showthread.php?threadid=3150591&userid=0&perpage=40&pagenumber=39.

Robertson, Venetia Laura Delano. 2014. 'Of Ponies and Men: *My Little Pony: Friendship Is Magic* and the Brony Fandom'. *International Journal of Cultural Studies* 17 (1): 21–37. https://doi.org/10.1177/1367877912464368.

Robertson, David G. 2016. *UFOs, Conspiracy Theories and the New Age: Millennial Conspiracism*. Bloomsbury Advances in Religious Studies. London; New York: Bloomsbury Academic.

Salen, Katie and Eric Zimmerman. 2004. *Rules of Play: Game Design Fundamentals*. Cambridge, MA: MIT Press.

Sandvoss, Cornel. 2005 *Fans: The Mirror of Consumption*. Cambridge: Polity.

scorpionsrock55. 2014. *Twitch Plays Pokémon Part 2 Red Part 2*. YouTube Video. https://www.youtube.com/watch?v=33EccHnUyls&t=17575s.

Segal, Robert A. 1996. 'Does Myth Have a Future?' In *Myth and Method*, edited by Laurie L. Patton and Wendy Doniger, 82–106. Studies in Religion and Culture. Charlottesville; London: University Press of Virginia.

Sewell, William H. 1992. 'A Theory of Structure: Duality, Agency, and Transformation'. *American Journal of Sociology* 98 (1): 1–29.

Shai-Hulud. 2009. 'Create Paranormal Images'. Forum Reply. *Something Awful*. https://forums.somethingawful.com/showthread.php?threadid=3150591&userid=0&perpage=40&pagenumber=7.

Shifman, Limor. 2012. 'An Anatomy of a YouTube Meme'. *New Media & Society* 14 (2): 187–203. https://doi.org/10.1177/1461444811412160.

Shifman, Limor. 2013. 'Memes in a Digital World: Reconciling with a Conceptual Troublemaker'. *Journal of Computer-Mediated Communication* 18 (3): 362–77. https://doi.org/10.1111/jcc4.12013.

Shifman, Limor. 2014. *Memes in Digital Culture*. MIT Press Essential Knowledge. Cambridge, MA: The MIT Press.

'Slender Man'. n.d. Know Your Meme. Accessed 30 October 2017. http://knowyourmeme.com/memes/slender-man.

Slender Nation Podcast. 2011. *VICTOR @#$%ING SURGE*. Podcast Episode.

snucks. 2009. 'Creating Paranormal Images'. Forum Reply. *Something Awful*. https://forums.somethingawful.com/showthread.php?threadid=3150591&userid=0&perpage=40&pagenumber=20.

Steinman, Gary. 2016. 'Bethesda & Game Reviews'. *Bethesda* (blog). 25 October 2016. https://bethesda.net/en/article/42QH1pTNpKSYIcgKK2C4wW/bethesda-and-game-reviews.

Storey, John. 2018. *Cultural Theory and Popular Culture: An Introduction*, 8th edn. London; New York: Routledge.

Taussig, Michael T. 1993. *Mimesis and Alterity: A Particular History of the Senses*. New York: Routledge.

Taylor, T.L. 2006. *Play Between Worlds: Exploring Online Game Culture*. Cambridge, MA: The MIT Press.

telltale games. 2013. *Wolf Among Us*. Xbox One.

The Angry Scholar. 2014. 'Slender Man in the News'. *Slender Nation Forum*. http://slendernation.forumotion.com/t4062-slender-man-in-the-news?highlight=slender+man+in+the+news.

The Game Theorists. 2013. *Game Theory: Is Link Dead in Majora's Mask?* YouTube Video. https://www.youtube.com/watch?v=7S1SVkysIRw.

TheRiffie. 2009. 'Create Paranormal Images'. Forum Reply. *Something Awful*. https://forums.somethingawful.com/showthread.php?threadid=3150591&userid=0&perpage=40&pagenumber=10.

Thompson, Stith. 1955. *Motif-Index of Folk Literature: A Classification of Narrative Elements in Folktales, Ballads, Myths, Fables, Medieval Romances, Exempla, Fabliaux, Jest-Books, and Local Legends*. Revised and Enlarged Edition. Bloomington: Indiana University Press. http://www.ualberta.ca/~urban/Projects/English/Motif_Index.htm.

Thoreau-Up. 2009. 'Create Paranormal Images'. Forum Reply. *Something Awful*. https://forums.somethingawful.com/showthread.php?threadid=3150591&userid=0&perpage=40&pagenumber=6.

TrenchMaul. 2009. 'Create Paranormal Images'. Forum Reply. *Something Awful*. https://forums.somethingawful.com/showthread.php?threadid=3150591&userid=0&perpage=40&pagenumber=5.

*Trender Man: I Will Kill You If You Wear Those Crocs Again.* 2012. https://memegenerator.net/instance/26381690/trenderman-i-will-kill-you-if-you-wear-those-crocs-again.

Turner, Terence S. 2017. *The Fire of the Jaguar.* Chicago, IL: Hau Books.

Tylor, Edward Burnett. 2010. *Primitive Culture: Researches into the Development of Mythology, Philosophy, Religion, Art, and Custom.* Cambridge Library Collection Anthropology. Cambridge: Cambridge University Press.

Underhill, Paco. 2005. *The Call of the Mall: A Walking Tour through the Crossroads of Our Shopping Culture.* New York: Simon & Schuster Paperbacks.

Valve. 2007. *Portal.* PC.

Verloc. 2009. 'Create Paranormal Images'. *Something Awful Forums.* https://forums.somethingawful.com/showthread.php?threadid=3150591&userid=0&perpage=40&pagenumber=30.

Victor Surge. 2009a. 'Create Paranormal Images'. Forum Reply. *Something Awful.* https://forums.somethingawful.com/showthread.php?threadid=3150591&userid=0&perpage=40&pagenumber=3.

Victor Surge. 2009b. 'Create Paranormal Images'. Forum Reply. *Something Awful.* https://forums.somethingawful.com/showthread.php?threadid=3150591&userid=0&perpage=40&pagenumber=4.

Victor Surge. 2009c. 'Create Paranormal Images'. Forum Reply. *SomethingAwful.* http://forums.somethingawful.com/showthread.php?threadid=3150591&userid=0&perpage=40&pagenumber=5.

Victor Surge. 2009d. 'Create Paranormal Images'. Forum Reply. *Something Awful.* https://forums.somethingawful.com/showthread.php?threadid=3150591&userid=0&perpage=40&pagenumber=5.

Vielmetti, Bruce and Meg Kissinger. 2015. 'Family History of Mental Illness Revealed in Slender Man Case'. *Journal Sentinel,* 17 June 2015. http://archive.jsonline.com/news/crime/critical-hearing-in-slender-man-case-to-begin-today-b99520903z1-307851871.html.

VR Native American. 2009. 'Create Paranormal Images'. Forum Reply. *Something Awful.* https://forums.somethingawful.com/showthread.php?threadid=3150591&userid=0&perpage=40&pagenumber=10.

Wagner, Rachel. 2014. 'The Importance of Playing in Earnest'. In *Playing with Religion in Digital Games,* edited by Heidi Campbell and Gregory Price Grieve, 192–213. Bloomington: Indiana University Press.

Wagner, Roy. 2016. *The Invention of Culture,* 2nd edn. Chicago; London: The University of Chicago Press.

Watercutter, Angela. 2012. 'Romney's "Binders Full of Women" Gaffe Sparks Instant Internet Meme'. *Wired.* 17 October 2012. https://www.wired.com/2012/10/romney-binders-full-of-women-meme/.

Watt, B. and F.V. Brown. 1975. 'Letter: Sensitivity Testing of Anaerobes on Solid Media'. *The Journal of Antimicrobial Chemotherapy* 1 (4): 440–42.

whoaconstrictor. 2014. 'A Most Sacred Tablet (fan Art)'. *Reddit*. https://www.reddit.com/r/twitchplayspokemon/comments/1yhopy/a_most_sacred_tablet_fan_art/.

Wiggins, Bradley E. and G. Bret Bowers. 2015. 'Memes as Genre: A Structuralist Analysis of the Memescape'. *New Media & Society* 17 (11): 1–21.

Willis, Ika. 2016. 'Amateur Mythographies: Fan Fiction and the Myth of Myth'. *Transformative Works and Cultures* 21 (March). https://doi.org/10.3983/twc.2016.0692.

Wright, Will. 1975. *Six Guns and Society: A Structural Study of the Western*. Berkeley: University of California Press.

Zipes, Jack. 1988. *The Brothers Grimm: From Enchanted Forests to the Modern World*. New York: Routledge.

# Index

abandon   8, 85, 87, 88, 93–5, 110, 112, 115, 132, 135, 139, 140
absurd   125, 133, 135
Achievement Hunter   118–24, 126
affirmations   37
agency   21, 23, 25, 56, 70, 72–4, 80, 95, 96, 103, 108, 117, 130, 133, 135, 158, 159, 161–3, 170, 173, 175, 177, 187, 192, 193, 201, 202, 217, 218, 220
Aleph Null   7, 45, 63, 65–7, 69, 76, 77, 174
alter   4, 6, 17, 20, 22, 25, 45, 77, 89, 94, 99, 126, 144, 145, 147, 148, 157, 159–62, 165, 172, 197, 200, 204, 213, 217, 218
analyse   7–9, 19, 20, 23–5, 27, 44, 45, 47, 62, 63, 65, 66, 71, 76, 78, 79, 91, 103, 105, 107, 113, 130, 131, 133, 137, 138, 140, 143, 147, 148, 163, 168, 176, 188, 195, 197, 198, 211, 218–20
anomalies   48, 78
anthropology   1, 2, 4, 6, 9, 12, 20, 22, 23, 26, 40, 42, 65, 80, 98, 154, 202, 209, 218
anxiety   55–7, 62, 71–3, 77, 79, 91, 122, 158, 203, 209
apophatic theology   35, 187, 217
audience   8, 15, 16, 29, 31, 32, 34, 38, 42, 44, 48–51, 65, 69–74, 78, 86, 87, 89, 101, 103, 105, 107, 118, 122, 125, 129, 130, 135, 139, 152, 158–60, 162, 166, 167, 173, 184, 185, 190, 192, 193, 207, 208, 220
authentic   18, 34–6, 39–41, 43
author   5, 6, 17, 26, 30, 32, 34–6, 38, 42, 45, 60, 65, 69–71, 73, 74, 130, 131, 155, 177, 187, 205–8, 216–18
authority   30, 35, 55, 70, 73, 154, 155, 217
awe   36

Babcock, Barbara   152
Backwardz Compatible   104
baptism   106

Bascom, William   12
BDSM   133
behaviour   17, 54, 80, 87, 90, 152
belief   1–6, 12, 13, 18, 35, 38, 40, 51, 55, 57, 61, 62, 70, 81, 85, 86, 122, 158, 160, 200, 201, 203, 206, 210, 216, 217, 219
Ben-Amos, Dan   73
Ben Drowned   9, 164, 170–7, 206, 215, 217
bias   17, 18
binary   74, 76, 78, 79, 125, 194, 213, 214
Black-Eyed Kids   40
Blank, Trevor   17, 18, 59, 205
body   39, 48, 51, 52, 75, 90, 111, 115, 134, 168, 173
boundary   2–4, 6, 19, 26, 42–4, 96, 129, 130, 145, 161–4, 179, 194, 197–9, 203–5, 208, 210, 211
Bourdieu, Pierre   23, 199, 200, 202, 218
bricoleur   16, 34, 42, 43, 130, 150, 154
Brunvard, Jan   165, 206

Caillois, Roger   42, 105
Carroll, Noël   174
catalyst   7, 34, 99
category   2, 3, 12, 21, 22, 50, 52–4, 56, 58, 59, 61–3, 65–9, 71–82, 90–101, 112–15, 117, 124–7, 131, 135–9, 141, 143, 144, 152, 154, 157–60, 162, 167, 170, 172–5, 177, 184, 185, 189–92, 194, 195, 203, 204, 208–11, 214, 215
censor   60, 65, 70, 72, 73
character   4, 24, 35, 46, 54–8, 69, 70, 72, 74, 78, 79, 81, 86, 87, 90–4, 96, 99, 101, 106, 111–15, 117, 120, 122–6, 131, 133, 134, 136, 138–41, 149, 153, 160, 164, 170, 171, 173, 175, 179, 205, 206
child   1, 11–13, 30, 35, 38, 39, 42, 46, 48, 49, 51–4, 58, 59, 62, 67–9, 72–5, 77, 79, 97, 99, 111, 114, 115, 117, 118, 131, 133, 134, 138, 141, 142, 154, 156, 174, 213
Chooboo   137, 138

comedy   29, 148, 153, 155
comfort   46, 135, 136, 192
communicate   5, 10, 14, 16–18, 20, 26, 34, 41, 51, 59–61, 70, 81, 86, 87, 147, 165, 166, 179, 200–202, 205–7, 210, 213, 216, 218
community   2, 4–10, 12, 13, 15, 18, 19, 22–7, 30, 32–5, 41, 43, 44, 46, 49, 51, 69–73, 78, 81, 82, 87, 100, 105–7, 115, 127, 129, 130, 133, 145, 147, 148, 155, 161–4, 177, 179–83, 186–97, 201–11, 215–20
compare   3, 9, 15, 24, 26, 39, 49, 53, 61, 119, 123, 130, 140, 163, 167, 185, 194, 199, 216, 217
connect   7–9, 13–19, 21–3, 26, 34, 36–9, 41, 43–5, 48, 53, 60, 62, 71, 75, 77, 82, 85, 87, 94, 97, 108, 110, 111, 115, 116, 118, 119, 121, 126, 130, 135, 136, 139, 140, 144, 147, 148, 150, 155, 158, 159, 162, 164, 168, 169, 179, 186, 189, 191, 199–202, 204–10, 214, 216
context   12, 20, 21, 25, 51, 55, 79, 86, 87, 103, 107, 108, 124, 127, 143, 150, 151, 154, 187, 199, 201, 202
copypasta   25, 26, 205
cosmic fear   35, 36, 68, 71, 217
Cox, Jesse   104, 105, 123, 125, 187–9, 207
CoxCon   209
CreepsMcPasta   207
creepy   37, 112, 171, 220
creepypasta   9, 18, 24–6, 32, 44, 49, 51, 61, 70, 71, 73, 86, 100, 131, 136, 153, 161–9, 171–4, 176, 177, 179, 194, 195, 197, 202, 205–9, 211, 214–19
culture   1–7, 9, 10, 13–17, 19–26, 29, 33, 34, 40, 41, 43, 44, 82, 97, 100, 104, 105, 107, 143–5, 148, 150, 152, 154, 157, 159, 161–3, 174, 177, 179, 186, 194–205, 208, 209, 211, 213, 215–20
cyber-legend   164

danger   69, 111–13, 122, 125, 174
dark   66, 103, 112, 121–6, 138, 156, 157, 171, 185
David-Néel, Alexandra   37
Davies, Christie   158, 159
Davis, Michael   123, 124

Dawkins, Richard   18
death   5, 14, 46, 48, 54, 55, 57–9, 74, 75, 78, 90, 93–6, 98, 99, 112–14, 117, 122, 126, 135–7, 140–3, 166, 167, 172–5, 195, 210, 215
de Certeau, Michel   16, 34, 42, 43, 130
definition   1, 12, 13, 15, 18, 19, 26, 32, 35, 40, 44, 68, 82, 95, 108, 114, 147, 149, 150, 193, 200–202, 205, 208, 214, 216, 218, 219
Dégh, Linda   17, 18
deities   81, 181
demon   39
diachronic   91, 92
diagram   53, 54, 56, 62, 69, 71, 74–6, 97, 100, 118, 126, 134, 136, 142, 160, 184, 185, 189–91, 213, 214
dichotomy   13, 40, 41, 47, 74, 90, 125, 183, 184, 215
digital   2, 6, 7, 9–12, 14, 16, 22, 24, 26, 31, 32, 41, 43, 44, 48, 50, 51, 73, 74, 103, 139, 194, 196, 197, 200–203, 205, 208, 210, 213, 215, 216, 218, 219
digital campfire   31, 50, 51
disappearance   1, 17, 30, 53–60, 62, 67, 72, 75, 88, 96, 118, 134, 142, 175, 213, 214
divinity   35, 78
Douglas, Mary   80, 98, 152, 174
Dracula   52
Dumézil, Georges   76
Dundes, Alan   40, 41, 147
dyadic   65, 76–8, 92, 159, 162, 183, 186, 189, 190, 192–5, 204, 208, 215

email-chains   18, 72, 164–7, 210, 213
embodiment   16, 29, 31, 38, 44, 96, 117, 152, 192, 202
emic/etic   3, 15
Emigh, John   96
emotion   8, 15, 17, 18, 34, 36, 42, 43, 59, 62, 76, 108, 111, 112, 118, 122, 123, 140–5, 205
Enderman family   148, 153, 155
*enskilment*   23
entertainment   105, 118, 119, 124, 125
erotica   8, 129, 134, 137, 141, 143, 144, 155, 162
ethnic   163, 194, 208

ethnography 18, 22, 25, 201, 218
EverymanHYBRID 168
explicit myth 47, 107–11, 113–15, 120–4, 126

facelessness 69, 71, 73–5, 79, 87, 90, 91
fairies 1, 38, 39
faith 77, 106
fakelore 39–41, 60, 85
fandom 15, 16, 106, 120, 137, 156, 171, 186, 188
fanfiction 8, 16, 129–31, 137, 140, 148, 154–6, 158, 215
Faust, Lauren 155, 156
fear 1, 4, 29, 35–9, 66, 69, 71, 73, 80–2, 100, 116, 117, 120, 122, 124, 125, 133–7, 140–4, 157, 158, 160, 168, 170, 171, 173, 177, 193, 208
fiction 3, 4, 12, 29, 31, 41, 43, 44, 131, 137, 155, 159, 202, 205, 206
fieldwork 9, 25, 209
Foley, John 200
folk 1, 18, 39–41, 43, 59, 202, 205
folklore 1, 2, 12, 14, 16–18, 26, 34, 38–41, 59, 60, 73, 85, 86, 106, 113, 147, 152, 202, 205, 206
Frazer, James 12, 13
functionalism 13, 14, 23, 25

Galinier, Jacques 107, 119, 148
Geertz, Clifford 42
genesplicer 7, 45, 63, 65, 67, 69, 71, 72, 77, 174
Gerogerigege 30, 45
ghosts 45, 69
Great Space Butterfly 9, 105, 179, 187–91, 194, 204, 207, 220
Grimm 113

habitus 23, 199, 202, 218
hallucination 114–17
happypasta 9, 153
health 88, 90–3, 95, 98, 99, 132, 133, 167, 172, 183, 210
helplessness 193, 210
hierarchy 52, 54, 74, 75, 107
history 9–14, 19, 29, 30, 32, 33, 36, 41, 109, 113, 117, 130, 133, 145, 149, 164, 165, 200, 206, 209, 216, 218

horror 3, 5, 6, 8, 9, 11, 26, 29, 31, 32, 35–7, 42, 46, 50, 56, 61, 68, 70, 79, 81, 94, 100, 104, 109, 118, 120–4, 127, 129, 131, 133, 141, 144, 145, 147, 148, 150, 158, 159, 161, 163, 171, 175, 177, 194, 205–7, 216, 220
Huizinga, Johan 41, 42, 105
human 6, 8, 11, 15, 17, 18, 20, 23, 35, 38, 39, 52, 54, 59, 66–8, 70, 71, 74, 75, 77, 78, 90, 96, 97, 111, 133, 136, 140, 142, 144, 164, 166, 173, 198, 199, 217, 218
humour 8, 29, 32, 120, 121, 123–7, 145, 147, 148, 150, 151, 153–5, 157–63, 166, 177, 192, 195, 197, 203–5, 215, 217, 220
hyper-real religions 3, 14, 15

idea 3, 4, 12, 13, 16, 21, 23, 26, 35–8, 42, 45, 58, 66, 68, 69, 71, 75, 76, 90, 105, 108, 112, 114, 123, 142, 143, 152, 158, 159, 163, 168, 177, 180, 184, 201, 202, 205, 206, 208, 216–18, 220
identity 35, 54, 74, 89–91, 96, 110, 115, 150, 159, 161, 194, 201, 205, 217
ideology 13, 17, 209
image 1, 5, 6, 8, 16, 18, 26, 30–5, 38, 41, 45–52, 57, 65–8, 71, 74, 85, 86, 101, 105, 106, 115, 116, 134, 147–51, 154, 158, 164–9, 173, 176, 181, 186, 187, 217, 220
imagination 17, 55, 59, 137, 213, 216
implicit myth 8, 47, 103, 106–11, 113, 114, 118, 119, 121–6, 148, 188, 218, 219
Ingold, Tim 201
inhuman 39, 48, 50, 52, 58, 75, 173, 217
internet 4, 7, 17, 18, 26, 27, 29, 31, 32, 40, 41, 43, 44, 59, 103, 104, 118, 127, 129, 149, 150, 165, 166, 174, 179, 180, 188, 194, 197, 199, 200, 206, 210, 213

Jadusable 172, 174–6, 215
Jenkins, Henry 86, 130, 201, 202
joke 9, 10, 105, 120, 121, 147–54, 157–61, 181, 203, 205
*jonglerie* 23, 159, 161, 201, 204, 217

Khalil, Jirard 123, 124
kidnapping 59, 60, 67, 75
Kinsella, Michael 17
Kuipers, Giselinde 159

Kunin, Seth  6, 13, 20, 23, 76, 77, 79, 107, 119, 148, 159, 161, 194, 195, 198, 200, 201, 204, 214, 217

landscape  94, 121, 123, 180, 213, 217
language  20, 22, 58, 107, 156, 163, 181, 186, 194, 205, 210
Latour, Bruno  200
laughter  3, 49, 53, 67, 147, 148, 153, 163, 172
Laycock, Joseph  156
Leach, Edmund  6, 13, 174
legend  12, 14, 17, 26, 40, 60, 74, 113, 183, 205, 206
Let's Play  8, 31, 104, 105, 110, 118–23, 125, 126, 145, 188
Lévi-Strauss  1, 2, 6–8, 11–14, 16, 19–24, 26, 34, 44, 47, 48, 54, 65, 71, 74, 76, 78, 103, 107, 108, 113, 118, 119, 130, 143–5, 148, 150, 152, 154, 163, 194, 197–9, 201, 211, 213, 216, 218, 219
linguistics  14, 20, 26, 44, 163, 194, 199, 208
location  1, 4, 6, 13, 16, 18, 31, 53, 58, 77, 88, 89, 94, 95, 98, 101, 104, 109, 111–13, 115, 126, 129, 139, 140, 142, 147, 158, 190, 208, 213, 215, 218
loneliness  172
lore  3, 15, 37, 39, 120, 124, 186
Lovecraft, HP  35, 36, 68, 71, 217
ludological  105, 106

machinima  105
magic  42, 66, 75, 155, 156, 171
*Majora's Mask*  164, 170–2
Malinowski, Bronislaw  13
manifest  4, 35, 37, 38, 74, 95, 96, 153, 206
manipulation  31, 41, 51, 53, 65, 74, 91, 139, 220
Markiplier  104, 118, 121–3, 125, 126, 188
mediation  54, 56, 59, 62, 63, 72–82, 91, 94, 97, 98, 100, 152, 157–60, 162, 170, 172, 173, 175, 177, 185, 189, 192, 193, 195, 203, 204, 208–11, 213–15
meme  8, 16, 18, 19, 26, 27, 29, 32–4, 42, 43, 71, 103–5, 127, 130, 147–51, 153–5, 158–62, 168, 179, 181, 186, 187, 197, 200, 204, 207

meta-mythology  147
methodology  2, 6–8, 12, 13, 19–22, 24–6, 39, 52, 82, 162, 198, 200, 201, 213, 214, 219
Miles-Watson, Jonathan  19, 20, 23, 107, 108, 119, 148, 149, 198–200, 218, 219
monster  2, 7, 27, 29, 35, 36, 41, 43, 52, 71, 75, 80–2, 98, 117, 129, 136, 138, 142, 144, 145, 147, 151, 157, 158, 160, 163, 164, 167–9, 173, 174, 187, 189, 217
mystery  1, 31, 36, 54, 65, 89, 93, 115
mytheme  20, 21, 24, 65, 71, 74, 75, 82, 87, 89, 92, 121, 123, 124, 135, 140–4, 159, 161, 173, 175, 176, 183–5, 189, 190, 192, 197–9, 208
mythographer  12, 20, 103, 107, 129
mythology  1–9, 11–17, 19–27, 29–31, 33–6, 40, 41, 43–8, 51, 54, 60, 65, 70, 71, 73, 74, 76–9, 82, 87, 95, 99, 101, 103, 106–11, 113–15, 118–27, 129–31, 137, 139, 143–5, 147–51, 153–5, 159, 161–3, 168, 177, 179, 181, 183–90, 192–4, 197–205, 207, 208, 210, 213, 216–20

narrative  1, 3–9, 11–16, 18–27, 30–2, 34–6, 39–52, 54–63, 65–79, 81–3, 85–7, 89–97, 99–101, 103–10, 112–15, 117, 118, 121, 122, 124, 126, 127, 129–45, 147–9, 151, 153–68, 170–7, 179–81, 184–90, 192–8, 201–11, 213–20
narratological  105, 106
Needham, Rodney  76
neo-structuralism  6, 7, 19–23, 25, 26, 107, 143, 161, 198, 200–202, 218
Nintendo  164, 170, 171
nosleep  61, 133, 205, 206

*Ocarina of Time*  170, 171
online  1, 3–11, 14, 16–18, 24–7, 29, 31–3, 35, 36, 40–3, 46, 58–61, 65, 69, 71, 83, 86, 103–5, 118, 119, 121, 127, 129–31, 133, 137, 145, 147, 149, 159, 161, 163, 165, 166, 168, 172, 177, 179–81, 185, 188, 194–7, 199, 200, 202–11, 213, 216, 218–20
oral  14, 26, 34, 43, 107, 152
Otto, Rudolf  36

paedophilia  38, 39
Pálsson, Gísli  23
paranormal  30–2, 36, 45, 46, 60, 164, 168, 220
parody  8, 148, 151–5, 157, 158
performance  2, 8, 17, 48–52, 70, 79, 82, 107, 110, 118, 119, 125, 152, 161
photos  27, 29–31, 36, 37, 43, 45, 46, 48–53, 65, 134, 135, 139, 163, 213, 220
place  1, 2, 4, 7, 15, 17, 29, 43, 52–5, 59, 61, 65, 66, 70, 75, 82, 83, 88, 94–6, 98, 99, 105, 112–16, 134–6, 139–41, 143, 144, 150, 158, 166, 169, 171, 172, 175, 194, 199, 201, 205, 206, 210, 215, 216, 218
play  3, 4, 8, 31–3, 36, 38, 41–5, 51, 60, 81, 82, 85, 96, 98, 103–15, 117–26, 130, 132, 133, 139, 140, 145, 147, 154–9, 170–2, 175, 177, 180, 181, 184, 185, 188, 191, 200, 206, 219, 220
podcast  26, 31, 71, 208
Pokémon  9, 32, 180, 181, 183, 220
post-structuralists  199
powerlessness  71, 73, 74, 112, 135
prohibit  49, 50, 62, 125, 135, 138, 139, 167
proxy  8, 90–9, 101, 109–13, 115, 122, 126, 131, 135, 136, 147, 193, 195

Rake, The  9, 164, 167–70, 172–7, 195, 210, 214, 217
Ramsey, Geoff  119–21
rape  132, 133
reality  13–15, 17, 22, 23, 30, 38, 40, 41, 43, 44, 60, 61, 70, 81, 85, 86, 88, 100, 137, 139–42, 187, 188, 190, 201, 202, 205, 206, 210, 211, 217
reason  19, 20, 25, 26, 37, 45, 50, 82, 106, 115, 126, 131, 135, 137, 144, 155, 164, 170, 184, 193, 197, 199, 203, 204
reddit  16, 61, 168, 202, 205
religion  1–4, 7, 14, 15, 36, 41–3, 68, 81, 106, 148, 186, 187, 206, 219, 220
rinski  29, 30, 32, 34, 37, 43
ritual  2, 12, 21, 41, 42, 47, 78, 96, 107, 108, 119, 148, 214, 219
romance  8, 14, 127, 129–31, 133, 135–7, 144, 145, 155, 162, 197, 215, 220

sacred  186
safety  88, 94, 95, 111–17, 126, 140, 175
Sandvoss, Cornel  15
sanity  66, 99, 172, 174
scare  29, 37, 54, 57, 120, 122, 124, 126, 131, 156
Scary Game Squad  104, 118, 121, 123–5
Segal, Robert  13, 14
senses  49, 50, 62, 63, 75, 87, 125, 134, 135, 138, 139
silence  24, 46, 49, 50, 72, 73, 134, 167, 176
Slender Man  1, 3–9, 12, 15, 19, 20, 22, 24–7, 29–32, 34–46, 48–63, 65–8, 70–5, 77, 79–83, 85–99, 101, 103, 104, 109–27, 129–45, 147–70, 172–7, 179, 180, 185, 187–9, 192–7, 199, 201–11, 213–20
Slendy  157
snucks  35, 38, 39
society  2, 13, 22, 23, 25, 32, 34, 40, 43, 44, 55, 56, 58, 59, 61–3, 67, 73–80, 82, 90–6, 98–101, 110, 112, 113, 115, 116, 135, 136, 140, 143, 145, 147, 149, 150, 152, 157–9, 161, 164–7, 170, 172–5, 177, 180, 194, 195, 197–202, 209–11, 213–15
Something Awful  1, 4, 6–9, 24, 29–32, 34, 36–8, 44–6, 48, 51, 54, 57, 58, 60, 63, 65–7, 69, 70, 75, 77, 82, 83, 85–7, 91–4, 96–101, 103, 114, 115, 117, 118, 125, 127, 139, 141, 143, 144, 149, 160, 163, 167, 168, 174, 175, 189, 195, 197, 206, 208, 215
space  9, 25, 43, 105, 118, 129, 143, 176, 179, 187–92, 194, 199, 200, 204, 207, 220
Space Moth  187–90, 192
spirit  138, 172, 187, 191, 192
Splendor Man  148, 152, 153, 155, 158, 160
story  1, 5, 11–16, 19–21, 26, 29–32, 34, 36–43, 45, 46, 49, 51, 54, 57, 60, 65, 69–71, 73, 78, 79, 82, 86, 87, 89, 101, 103, 106, 107, 113–15, 117, 120, 126, 127, 129, 131, 137, 140, 141, 143, 145, 147, 153, 157, 158, 160–6, 168, 171, 175–7, 179, 181, 187–91, 201, 205–7, 210, 214, 217, 218

storytelling   3, 4, 9, 11, 16–18, 21, 23, 25–7, 31–4, 36, 38, 41–3, 50, 51, 58, 60, 61, 70–3, 81, 82, 86, 101, 104, 107, 119, 127, 130, 132, 137, 143, 148, 150, 159, 163, 164, 166, 167, 177, 179, 194, 202, 206, 217, 220
structuralism   2, 6–8, 12–14, 19–26, 44, 46–8, 56, 65, 66, 76, 77, 79–82, 96–101, 103, 106, 107, 119, 129, 133, 135, 136, 143–5, 148–50, 152–4, 159–63, 175, 179, 193–5, 197–9, 201, 203, 204, 208, 210, 211, 213, 216–20
structure   8, 9, 13, 14, 19–25, 34, 44, 45, 47, 56, 62, 65, 69, 75–8, 82, 83, 91, 92, 95, 97–100, 107, 113–15, 117, 121, 123, 124, 126, 127, 133, 135, 136, 143–5, 147, 150, 152–4, 157–64, 170, 173–7, 179, 180, 183–7, 189, 190, 192–9, 201–4, 207–11, 213–17, 219, 220
suicide   79, 115, 117, 166, 169, 170, 174, 175
supernatural   13, 35, 38, 39, 46, 51–4, 56–62, 68, 70, 72, 74, 75, 78, 81, 96, 114, 116, 132–4, 136, 139, 141, 142, 173–5, 177, 193, 194, 214, 215
symbol   13, 52, 71, 96, 113, 137, 152, 156

taboo   174
tale   1, 8, 11, 31, 34, 39, 136
Taussig, Michael   42
technology   16, 17, 107, 125, 167, 173, 174, 200, 201
television   14, 16, 111, 130, 155
theme   18, 24, 45, 69, 86, 126, 173
Theosophy   37, 70
Thoreau-Up   38
TotalBiscuit   188
tradition   2, 3, 6, 18, 22, 25, 38–40, 53, 60, 76, 130, 155, 209
transform   21, 23, 32, 35, 66, 67, 69, 70, 75–7, 79–82, 87, 91–100, 111–17, 124–7, 132, 135, 136, 139–43, 152, 154, 157, 158, 160, 161, 166, 169, 171, 172, 174, 175, 177, 185, 193, 195, 197, 201, 203, 204, 210, 213–15
transmedia   16, 31, 32, 86
trauma   69, 114–16, 132, 133, 158, 159, 174

Trender Man   148–53, 155, 158, 160
triadic   65, 69, 76–80, 82, 91, 97, 99, 115, 135, 136, 143, 157, 159, 162, 175–7, 193–5, 197, 203, 204, 209–11, 213–16
Tulpa   4, 7, 37–9, 70, 74, 179, 206, 220
Twitch Plays Pokémon   9, 32–4, 179–81, 183–7, 189–92, 194, 204, 207, 216
Tylor, Edward Burnett   12, 13

UFO   39
unfamiliar   29, 50, 51, 58, 59, 61, 69, 94, 95, 139, 140, 158, 173
unhealth   90–4, 98, 99, 140, 157, 167, 172, 173
unnatural   30, 45, 57, 60, 168

victim   30, 31, 52–4, 58, 75, 139, 169, 170, 174, 220
Victor Surge   7, 30, 31, 45–52, 54, 59, 61, 62, 65, 67, 70, 74, 85, 125, 134, 139, 152, 158, 167, 182, 189, 208
video games   5, 8, 14, 16, 29, 31, 101, 103–9, 115, 118–22, 127, 138, 139, 144, 147, 157, 158, 160, 163, 164, 170, 172, 173, 175, 188, 202, 207, 218, 219
violent   1, 30, 48, 49, 51–5, 57–9, 69, 72, 75, 88, 90–5, 132–4, 137, 142, 150, 170, 214
virtual   1, 2, 17, 18, 26, 43, 59, 60, 86, 101, 126, 129, 145, 147, 164, 167, 202, 203, 210, 215–20
visual   8, 11, 23, 74, 82, 85, 87–90, 93, 94, 108, 148, 149, 152, 164, 179
voice   34, 40, 55, 57, 68, 70, 72, 73, 95, 104, 132, 133, 136–8, 141, 142, 144, 167–70, 173, 176, 188

Wagner, Roy   202
websites   5, 16, 29, 31, 32, 51, 60, 70, 77, 131, 149, 168, 180, 188, 192, 202, 209
wilderness   112, 113, 123, 131, 139
witness   54–8, 67, 68, 72, 87, 158

YouTube   8, 16, 83, 85, 86, 88, 104, 105, 118, 120, 121, 123, 152–4, 172, 188, 207, 210, 217

www.ingramcontent.com/pod-product-compliance
Lightning Source LLC
Chambersburg PA
CBHW072141290426
44111CB00012B/1946